28/6/07

Hindu Children in Britain

Hindu Children in Britain

Robert Jackson and Eleanor Nesbitt

tb

Trentham Books

First published in 1993 by Trentham Books Limited

Trentham Books Limited
Westview House
734 London Road
Oakhill
Stoke-on-Trent
Staffordshire
England ST4 5NP

British Library Cataloguing Publication Data
Jackson, Robert
  Hindu Children in Britain
  I. Title II. Nesbitt, Eleanor M.
  370.19

ISBN: 0 948080 73 6

Cover Picture
Young Gujarati girls carrying traditional pots of water in procession from the old Shree Krishna Temple to the Bhumi Pujan ('worship of the earth') performed prior to building on the new site.

Photography: Robert Jackson

Designed and typeset by Trentham Print Design Limited
and printed in Great Britain by BPCC Wheatons Ltd, Exeter

Contents

Preface

No book has previously been published on the lives of Hindu children in Britain. As outsiders, with many years of contact with Hindu communities behind us, our attempt to remedy this situation has been a happy learning process. We have felt privileged by the welcome extended to us. We have realised that 'religious' activity in its many and varied forms is a significant aspect of life for children and their families and that the Hindu tradition in Britain is alive and well. But like any living organism Hindu tradition is changing and reshaping in a number of ways. Our findings will be of interest not only to professionals in education, the social sciences and South Asian studies but also to Hindus and to all who are interested in race and inter-faith relations, in religion and childhood.

The time taken to plan the research, to undertake fieldwork, to analyse data and to write the book has been considerable. In our case, as educationists, the task was complicated by the fact that we were also writing materials for children (Jackson 1989a and b; Jackson and Nesbitt 1990) and working on educational broadcasts using the same data.

This book is a series of ethnographic snapshots which interpret aspects of Hindu life in Coventry at particular times. The camera catches moments in the lives of people, but it does not make time stand still. Life has gone on in the Hindu families and communities that we studied and they have continued to develop and change. The eight to thirteen year old young people featured in our study are now in their late teens and early twenties, and some are already in higher education. The Shree Krishna Temple referred to in this book, a converted primary school which served Gujarati Hindus since 1972 (Jackson 1981a), has now been superseded by the splendid purpose-built Shree Krishna Temple which opened in 1992. More British Hindu children have been born and some older members of the communities have died.

These include Mr Lallubhai Lad, former President of the Shree Krishna Temple and headmaster of the Gujarati school in Coventry, who died in 1992. The help, encouragement and support which Mr Lad gave us during the research period typified the warm response we had from members of Hindu communities, especially the families whose children were the subjects of our case studies. As well as welcoming us into their homes in Coventry, relatives of our case study children have befriended us overseas at various times during the study period. Robert Jackson was welcomed to India in 1987 and to Canada in 1991 and 1992 by members of Coventry Hindu families and Eleanor Nesbitt enjoyed similar hospitality in India in 1988. Family life for many Coventry Hindus is truly transcontinental!

The studies on which this book is based were conducted under the auspices of the Religious Education and Community Project which encompasses a series of linked studies on children and young people from different religious traditions. The Project is based in the Department of Arts Education at the University of Warwick under the direction of Robert Jackson. Part of RECP's work is to design and produce curriculum material for schools based on its ethnographic studies. Enquiries about this are always welcome.

Acknowledgements

We are grateful to the following bodies for supporting our research financially: the University of Warwick Research and Innovations fund, for supporting our study on formal Hindu nurture, and the Leverhulme Trust for supporting our studies on Hindu Nurture in Coventry and on Punjabi Hindu Nurture. The Religious Education and Community Project subsequently undertook a three year study (1990-1993) of Christian, Jewish, Muslim and Sikh children funded by the Economic and Social Research Council (ref no R000232489) which enabled us to develop methodological and theoretical aspects of our work further.

Many Hindus gave generously of their time, their hospitality and their own knowledge, experience and friendship. It would be impossible to list them all (especially since, in the text, pseudonyms have been adopted for all the children who became the subjects of case studies). We would like to thank the dedicated teachers and organisers of supplementary classes in Birmingham, Bolton, Bradford, Coventry, Leicester and London who agreed to our interviewing them and observing their classes. Our thanks are also due to the officers of various organisations including, in Coventry, the Gujarati Education Society and the committees of the Hindu Temple and the Shree Krishna Temple and, nationally, the National Council of Hindu Temples and the International Society for Krishna Consciousness. Others are acknowledged in the text.

We are grateful to Coventry Education Authority and Warwickshire Education Authority for giving permission for children to be interviewed in school. Our thanks also go to the busy headteachers and teachers who facilitated our research.

We would like to thank the following individuals for their advice or for comments on various parts of the manuscript: Rohit Barot, Bob Burgess,

Harry Goulbourne, Dermot Killingley, Gillian Klein, Kim Knott, Ram Krishan, Penny Logan, Fernand Ouellet and Steven Vertovec. We are grateful to persons mentioned in the text for generously giving their time and expertise to provide us with translations of material. We are grateful to the secretaries in the Department of Arts Education at the University of Warwick for many hours of painstaking assistance. For remaining errors of omission and commission the authors are responsible.

Our greatest debt is to the children and their families who gave so unstintingly of their time and of themselves. To them this book is dedicated.

Robert Jackson and Eleanor Nesbitt
University of Warwick
Guru Purnima 1993

CHAPTER 1

Setting the Scene: Hindus in Britain

☐ Introduction

Britain has substantial ethnic minority communities. Within them are practised most of the world's major religions, one of which is the Hindu tradition, the ancient religion of India.

Current scholarly estimates suggest that there are about 360,000 Hindus in Britain (Knott 1991), a figure now higher than that estimated for Britain's Jewish population or for Baptist Christians in Britain. The Hindu organisation, Vishwa Hindu Parishad, gives a much higher estimate of one million. Analysis of the responses on ethnicity in the 1991 census return may enable scholars to make a better estimate than has been possible hitherto.

Where are these Hindu communities from? What is their character? How have their conceptions of their religious tradition and their religious practice changed in the cultural environment of the United Kingdom? What future is there in Britain for their religious tradition? These questions have been addressed in a relatively small number of publications (eg Bowen 1981, 1988; Burghart 1987; Jackson 1976; Kanitkar and Jackson 1982; Knott 1986a; Vertovec 1992c). Little attention has been given, however, to British born children from Hindu families, though Penny Logan has done important work with Gujarati children in London (1988a, 1988b). How is the tradition transmitted to them? What is their experience and understanding of their tradition? How, and under what influences, does the tradition as received by

1

children appear to be changing? These are the broad questions concerned with aspects of the reproduction of Hindu tradition with which this book is concerned. It is not a book about Hindu children in general, but is based mainly on ethnographic studies of eight to thirteen year old children from Hindu communities in Coventry, though we also draw on an earlier study of community-run supplementary schools in different parts of the country.[1] In the main the book reflects the experience of particular children from one age group in one city in the second half of the 1980s. As such it is an ethnographic snapshot, or perhaps a small album of photographs. We hope that the detail obtained by focusing narrowly is a compensation for not being able to generalise from our material.

☐ The Terms 'Hindu' and 'Hinduism'

To talk about certain children as Hindu suggests a distinct, recognisable category on which the child, the family's social network and members of the wider society are all agreed. But the terms 'Hindu' and 'Hinduism' are problematic and children's understanding and usages of the words 'religion' and 'Hindu' can differ from those of the researcher. In order that Hindu children's perceptions of their identity and their understanding of the word 'Hindu' may be better appreciated the history of the words Hindu and Hinduism, as well as the criteria and strategy for identifying children as Hindu, need to be examined.

The word 'Hindu' was originally a geographical term used by outsiders from farther West. It is the Persian form of the Sanskrit word *Sindhu* for the Indus river. Via Persian and subsequently Greek and other European languages a cluster of related words such as 'India' developed. In indigenous tradition, however, the land was known as Bharat and the diverse customs of its people had no one name to distinguish them from the religious traditions which arose outside India. As late as the nineteenth century the term 'Hindu Christian' was used by British writers to mean simply, 'Indian Christian'. More recently the term Hindu has come to designate not 'Indian' in general but rather the innumerable ceremonial practices and beliefs grounded in the Indian subcontinent which are not better described as Jain, Buddhist, Sikh or tribal.

Consideration also needs to be given to the term 'Hinduism'. Wilfred Cantwell Smith in his critique of the concept of religion calls Hinduism 'a particularly false conceptualisation' (Smith 1978:63). The term 'Hinduism', though adopted and used since the early nineteenth century by insiders as well as outsiders, is essentially a Western construct. It was the introduction of the concept of Hinduism, and the presence of Westerners talking, writing and asking about Hinduism which led Hindus to try to define true and false

2

Hinduism, which they did (and still do) in different ways. Thus, for example, Bankim Chandra Chatterjee (1838-94) distinguished between the 'false and corrupt Hinduism' which Europeans denounced and 'true Hinduism' which, in his case, involved devotion to God and a humanistic ethic (King 1978). For Swami Vivekananda (1863-1902), on the other hand, true Hinduism was the monistic philosophy of Advaita Vedanta, which Bankim had rejected as part of false Hinduism. Many more examples could be cited. For our purposes 'Hinduism' is an umbrella term for a great number of practices and beliefs each of which belongs to some of the millions of people who for historical reasons are called Hindus.

Despite countless differences of region and language, these practices and beliefs bear a family likeness. There may be no one founder and no over-arching credal statement but there are modes of worship and ways of thinking which appear like a recurrent motif. There is, for example, the division of society into structurally distinct hereditary communities, differentiated not only by occupation but by their degree of ritual purity in relation to one another. Each of these is known as a caste, another foreign word (derived from the Portuguese *casta*, 'breed') used as an equivalent to words such as *jati* in Indian vernacular languages. There is the use of light, sound, incense, water, flowers and food in welcoming the divine as a guest. There is the acceptance that every action has a necessary reaction (*karma*, the law of cause and effect) and that for every individual there is an appropriate behavioural code (*dharma*) depending upon a person's caste, gender, seniority and relationship by blood or marriage to others. Other features are not found among most groups of Hindus, whether the teachings and practices of a particular guru-led movement such as Pushtimarg or a local or regional festival whose mythology and associated ritual may be unknown elsewhere. Nevertheless, what is unknown to many Hindus is part of 'Hinduism' if it is familiar to some Hindus. In summary, the term 'Hinduism' is a Western invention of the early nineteenth century, a construction which interpreted and classified Indian religion as having an early 'golden age' and key texts. The term was adopted and used in different ways by 'insiders', and is used cautiously by scholars today as an 'umbrella' term.

To translate the words 'Hindu religion' a contemporary Hindu may say '*sanatana dharma*'. *Sanatana* means ancient and unchanging. *Dharma*, the term for social and religious duty, is most frequently equated with 'religion'. Clearly, however, the sense is very different from that of the word 'religion' with its roots in Roman civilisation and its layers of association drawn from the evolution of Christianity. What a Hindu eats and wears are expressions of *dharma* whereas Westerners would tend to consider these as 'culture' rather than 'religion'. Since not only children growing up in Britain but earlier

3

generations of Indians have been influenced by Western categories of thought, however, it is risky to make too hard and fast a distinction between what is understood by *'dharma'* on the one hand and 'religion' on the other.

☐ Boundaries of Hindu Identity

This brief discussion suggests that there could be difficulties in using the term 'Hindu' in formulating questions to ask children. Academics with a Western scholarly background tend to perceive 'Hinduism' as a loosely knit, highly variegated tradition, yet having certain general tendencies, of the type outlined above. Their use of the term 'Hindu' tends to be governed by their perception of the relationship between particular cases and general tendencies in the tradition. 'Insiders' may or may not use the term with the same sense. This depends on their provenance, their involvement with Hindu organisations, their 'sectarian' orientation, the type and extent of their interactions with 'non Hindus'. They may use it more inclusively or more exclusively, they may use the term differently according to the context in which they are asked about it, or they may not use it at all. In deciding on the limits of our study, we found ourselves using both insiders' perceptions of being Hindu and, in certain cases, our own.

The majority of Hindus in Britain originate from Gujarat and most of them are in no doubt of their Hindu identity. However in some Gujarati families, members — all of the same caste — will differ in religious orientation, some defining themselves as Jain, others as Hindu. The Jain religion developed in the context of Hindu tradition in the sixth century BCE. The close relationship between Jains and Hindus is illustrated by the fact that a priest serving at the Jain temple in Leicester formerly officiated in a Hindu temple. Many Hindus would subsume Jains into Hinduism. Similarly, at the level of popular devotion, no firm boundary can be drawn between Sikhism and Hinduism in the state of Punjab from which nearly all Coventry's other Hindus migrated. Sikhism grew in a Hindu environment and many Hindus regard Sikhism as simply part of the Hindu tradition, although most Sikhs are in no doubt about having a distinct and separate identity. However, in some cases, different members of the same family will describe their allegiance as Sikh or Hindu according to whether their major devotional focus or emphasis is on the *Guru Granth Sahib* (the Sikh sacred book) or on *puja* (worship involving offerings) to deities. Included in this study are some children from the Valmiki and Ravidasi communities, both of which are religious movements in which caste and sect are coterminous (Nesbitt 1990a and b; 1991). Although their relatives, who shared in the same acts of corporate worship, define themselves as Sikh these children are included since by their own and their parents' definition they are Hindu.

4

☐ Hindus in Britain

How did Britain acquire its Hindu communities? Apart from a few Hindu migrants whose families settled in Britain before 1914, the bulk of the Hindu population migrated after the second world war (Burghart 1987). Some were students who intended to practise their professions in Britain (Kanitkar 1972). The first significant movement was by male Hindus who responded to the labour shortage in Britain's industrial cities in the 1950s with the objective of gaining employment in order to supplement the family income back in India. By a process of 'chain migration', early migrants were joined by male relatives or fellow villagers, the established residents providing accommodation and helping to find work for the new arrivals (Desai 1963; Tambs-Lyche 1980a). By the mid to late 1960s, in the wake of increasingly restrictive immigration legislation, the situation had changed, with an increasing number of wives and children migrating to join their husbands, establishing a more permanent form of settlement while continuing to preserve economic and other ties with families in India. The majority of these migrants were from Gujarat and the Punjab, two Indian states with a tradition of population movement. The second wave of migration began in the late 1960s, not directly from India but from eastern and central African states to which Indians had moved — often as indentured labourers — in the nineteenth century, although large numbers of Gujaratis also migrated to African countries after the Second World War. Africanisation policies in countries such as Kenya and Tanzania accounted for the desire to move. Tens of thousands of Ugandan Asians had no choice in the matter and were expelled from the country in 1972. Of those African Asians who came to Britain, around sixty per cent were Hindus, mainly Gujarati by language and culture. One of the prominent differences between this and the earlier wave of migration was that where passports permitted it whole families entered the United Kingdom together.

It is extremely difficult to assess with accuracy the size of the British Hindu population, though recent estimates indicate that there are now around 1,271,000 people of South Asian ethnic origin living in the United Kingdom (Knott 1991). According to the same source, about 360,000 of these are Hindus, with around seventy per cent of them Gujarati, fifteen per cent Punjabi, and fifteen per cent from a variety of other Indian linguistic and cultural backgrounds (e.g. Maharashtrian, Bengali, Tamil), many of whom came as students or doctors. Over half of the Gujarati population has a migration history which includes residence in an East or central African state (e.g. Kenya, Uganda, Tanzania, Malawi) (Knott 1986d). Coventry has a population of about 7,000 Hindus, of whom about 5,000 are Gujarati in background.[2] The rest are mainly of Punjabi origin. The Hindu population of London differs from other British cities in being more representative of the

5

Hindu world. In Coventry it is easy to forget the significance of south Indian Hindu tradition and the considerable diaspora communities in Fiji, Mauritius and Trinidad, for example — all represented more strongly in London than in any other British city.

☐ Religious Practice

There are several factors which determine the nature of the religious life of Hindus in Britain. Because Hindu traditions are so amorphous, with a wide variety of practice and belief, one would expect diversity of religious activity among British Hindus. The principal factor in determining this variety is provenance. Gujaratis and Punjabis, for example, speak different languages, have notable variations in life cycle rites and their cycles of festivals, plus many other social and cultural differences, food preferences being just one. These distinctions, based broadly on geography and language, can be very misleading, however, for within each category are further significant differences of precise geographical origin, migration experience (whether from an African country, for example), economic base, language and dialect, caste, kinship and domestic structures as well as religious practice (often related to membership or otherwise of a *sampradaya* or religious movement). Different 'levels' of provenance can become important reference points informing particular social identities and networks (Vertovec 1992b).

British Gujaratis, for example, have family origins in different regions of Gujarat state, from the mainland area which includes Surat, and from Saurashtra and Cutch (Kachh) further west.

The language of Cutch differs markedly from that of Saurashtra and there is evidence that speakers of the former have used their language to distinguish themselves from other Gujarati groups (Barot 1981:124). The differences between 'Indian' Gujaratis and 'African' Gujaratis are also significant (see below), though it should be noted that just as the 'Indian' Gujarati population is not homogeneous, so the 'African' population included descendants of nineteenth century migrants (mainly from Saurashtra and Cutch) and post Second World War migrants, (principally, though by no means exclusively, from Churottar and Surat).

In tracing the pattern of settlement of Gujaratis and Punjabis it has often been the case that Gujaratis moved to areas of cities that already had a Gujarati presence, while Punjabis tended to set up homes near other Punjabis, whether Hindu or Sikh by religion (e.g. Sims 1981:128-130).

A second factor which has influenced the development of Hindu practice in Britain is the difference between the first and second waves of migration. The most important aspect of these is that while the first 'Indian' movement consisted initially of men of wage-earning years, the second 'African' group comprised a population of normal age structure. Among the latter were many respected elders whose knowledge and influence has done much to preserve aspects of the religious life and caste structure of the Gujarati population. These include male 'community leaders' but, as we will see from the Coventry study outlined below and from Logan (1988b) and McDonald (1987), the presence of women in families has been highly significant in the perpetuation of domestic religious practices. The 'African' wave of Hindu migrants consisted almost entirely of Gujaratis. Punjabi Hindu migrants have in most cases come to Britain direct from north India, although their family roots were often west of the border with Pakistan which dates from 1947.

Reference to caste introduces a further factor which plays a part in determining the variety of religious life amongst British Hindus. A caste (*jati*) is a hereditary social group which is normally endogamous and into which each person is born. Castes are ranked hierarchically on a scale of ritual purity and pollution (Dumont 1970) with Brahmin castes at the top and with groups involved in ritually polluting activities at the bottom. A variety of Gujarati and Punjabi castes is present in Britain, and caste identity has great importance in relation to marriage, status, social networks, institutions such as caste associations. The caste 'system' in its full ritual and hierarchical sense cannot operate in a non-Indian cultural setting, however.

A *samaj* is a caste association, originally formed by Gujarati migrants in African countries, which caters in various ways for certain aspects of the religious and social life of caste members. In the city of Coventry there are about ten of these Gujarati caste associations. There are many temples whose style of worship attracts people from across caste boundaries. Likewise there are *bhajan mandals* (devotional singing groups) and *satsangs* (religious gatherings) which attract people from a range of castes. Nevertheless there are other organisations and activities that belong to individual castes. Further, the details of domestic religious practice and life-cycle rites tend to vary from caste to caste. Among Punjabis there are castes with a distinctive corporate religion which it is problematic to classify as Hindu or Sikh (Nesbitt 1990a and b; 1991).

The existence of distinct 'religious movements' provides another variable in the pattern of Hindu life. Membership of a *sampradaya* (literally a 'handing on') is a long established feature of the Hindu tradition. These are generally centred around founders with whom are associated particular doctrinal and ethical teachings which are maintained by each founder's spiritual heirs. Although the majority of British Hindus are not *sampradaya* members, several such movements flourish in the United Kingdom; some, like the distinctively Gujarati Pushtimarg and Swaminarayan movements, being associated with (though not exclusive to) certain Gujarati castes. Others transcend caste and regional barriers and, in the case of the Arya Samaj, oppose caste distinctions. The International Society for Krishna Consciousness (ISK-CON), more popularly known as the Hare Krishna movement, has attracted some British Hindus (Carey 1987). Although it has its traditional origins in medieval Bengal, this movement developed in its modern form in the USA from the late 1960s. Movements such as this one are sometimes classified as 'neo-Hindu'.

There are also 'minority' Hindu communities with their own styles of religious practice, including Bengalis and Tamils, and Hindus with part of their ancestry in the Caribbean, Mauritius and Fiji. There are also groups which blur the distinction between what are commonly perceived to be separate religious traditions, especially 'Hinduism' and 'Sikhism' (Nesbitt 1990a and b; 1991) and 'Hinduism' and 'Jainism' (Michaelson 1984).

In addition there are branches of Indian religious associations which promote a particular interpretation of 'Hinduism' and associations bringing together particular local bodies in order for them to be able to work in concert. The Vishwa Hindu Parishad, an Indian based institution aiming to promote a broad definition of 'Hinduism' transcending regional, doctrinal and ritual differences, is an example of the former while the National Council of Hindu Temples (UK), which engages in activities ranging from fund raising to youth activities and which publishes the quarterly *Hindu Today*, fits the latter description.

Finally one should note influences of different kinds which come from the surrounding cultural environment of Britain. These can result from negative experiences of racism and marginalisation and from positive inter-cultural encounters. Influences include the media, the workplace, the education system and religious institutions.

☐ The Hindu Scene in Coventry

Coventry's Hindus are, with few exceptions, Gujarati and Punjabi. Initially they settled in the cheapest houses in the North of the city. The wards of Foleshill and St. Michael's still have the highest proportion of residents of South Asian origin. Here are to be found most of the non-Christian places of worship, including Hindu *mandirs*, and here are the shops which provide foodstuffs, clothing, jewellery and other items for the Gujarati and Punjabi communities (Winchester 1975). Many Hindu families have moved to the south of the city, to the greener area of Cheylesmore and the more upmarket Styvechale. Both men and women seek outside paid employment. Many run shops and sub-post offices (Robinson and Flintoff 1982). Many work in public transport, medicine, engineering and the teaching professions. The range of employment is widening.

Attendance at a public temple is not a reliable gauge of a Hindu's religious involvement, but the recent increase in Hindu places of worship indicates a certain vitality. Since 1968 the Shree Krishna Temple has served the Gujarati community as a centre for individual and corporate worship (Jackson 1981a). For almost as long, the smaller Punjabi Hindu community has been served by the Hindu Temple (*Ram Mandir*). The members of the Shree Krishna Temple left their old premises for a new purpose-built temple in July 1992 (Jackson and Nesbitt 1990 charts the development of the new building). Since the two castes which constitute the Punjabi Valmiki and Ravidasi communities have always felt stigmatised by higher caste Hindus, they established separate temples during the 1970s (Nesbitt 1990a and b; 1991).

In 1986 a Punjabi set up the Bawa Balak Nath Mandir. He had a growing reputation for being able, while in a trance, to diagnose the cause of people's ailments and so draws hundreds of followers. This temple houses *murtis* of Balaknath and Bhartrhari.[3] In 1988 the Shri Shri Radha Krishna Community Centre was established by the followers of the International Society for Krishna Consciousness. In January 1989 a group of Punjabi Hindus opened the Sanatan Dharm Hindu Temple. The Brahmakumaris (a 'neo-Hindu' movement) now have a centre where they instruct enquirers in meditation.[4] Several hundred Punjabis gather for the weekly Radhasoami *satsang* in a school hall.[5] Meanwhile the Pushtimargis, the devotees of Sathya Sai Baba and members of the Arya Samaj continue to gather for worship in private houses.[6]

According to the 1981 Census, over forty one per cent of the Indian population in Britain is in the 0-19 age range (CRE 1985:4). In the study of Hindus in Britain this generation merits particular attention. With such a high proportion of the population in full time education, teachers and other concerned adults may have a more significant role to play than they realise in the moulding of British Hindu traditions.

☐ Religious Transmission

Clearly Hindu tradition has remained alive in the alien cultural environment of the United Kingdom. But what of the transmission of Hindu culture from an adult generation to children and young people, especially to those born in Britain? For many Hindu parents in India, the religious upbringing of children is a natural and partly unconscious activity, centred on the home but fostered by many aspects of cultural life such as temple worship and festivals, as well as street processions and religious dramas associated with the latter. Although religious teaching is excluded from the curriculum of Indian state schools, Hindu symbols, concepts and rituals nevertheless pervade the environment in which most children grow up, though, of course, such exposure in no way guarantees children's knowledge of the meaning of customary religious practices (Holm 1984; Jackson and Killingley 1988).

In Britain Hindu children have restricted access to the features of their ancestral tradition described above. They are exposed to non-Hindu influences through their schooling, through peer groups and through the media, and they are likely to encounter hostility to their parental religion and culture from some elements within British society. So, how far and in what ways is the Hindu tradition being perpetuated among the young?

According to many Hindu adults in Britain their children know little or nothing of their tradition, and there is relatively little in the anthropological literature to challenge this. The literature on the religious lives of children of any faith growing up in this country is small and there is a dearth of literature on the transmission of Hindu culture from one generation to the next in India or amongst Hindu communities overseas, including Great Britain. Inherent in this situation was a challenge to explore and document the transmission of Hindu culture to children in Britain and to discover if, indeed, the tradition was dying out.

We discovered a lively interplay of influences shaping the growing generation of Hindus in Britain. Among the factors at work in nurturing children as Hindus are the performance of rituals in the home, the video and the formal education provided by concerned Hindu elders. Also the small input of Hindu material in school curricula plays its part. The purpose of this book is to share the findings of our research, knowing that this too will contribute, albeit only slightly, to the process which we are reporting.

Our findings may seem surprising in view of parental pessimism and in the light of a study which was conducted in Newcastle over twenty years ago (Taylor 1976). This was J.H. Taylor's study of Asian youths in Newcastle upon Tyne. Taylor interviewed the sixty seven Asian boys and young men who reached leaving age in Newcastle's schools between 1962 and 1967. He called these young people members of 'the halfway generation', since sixty two of them had been born in South Asia or East Africa and had moved with their parents to the United Kingdom at various stages. Fifteen of these young men were from Hindu families. All the Hindus were ethnically Punjabi and Khatri by caste, with fathers predominantly from urban backgrounds, and mostly in business or other non-manual occupations. Taylor's findings concerning these young men's knowledge and practice of their parents' religion seem gloomy. To quote:

> The young men ... had no knowledge of caste, the religion's most practical aspect. They showed no awareness of reincarnation or other aspects of Hindu philosophy. They could not understand the festivals or

the ceremonial. All that remained with them were half remembered stories from the mythology. These were seen as a mixture of fairy-tale ('kings and queens and how they lived')... and science-fiction: 'Fantastic stories', 'Gods flying to the moon'...(Taylor, p.101)

Six young men in Taylor's group regarded 'Hinduism' as unimportant and gave their lack of knowledge or their disagreement with some parts of the teaching as one or other of their reasons. There was also little evidence that the young men took much interest in Hindu practice. Taylor took as evidence for this the fact that twelve out of the fifteen had not visited the Hindu temple in Newcastle.

In spite of this apparent ignorance and lack of involvement in religious life, eight of the fifteen youngsters regarded 'Hinduism' as important to them: because they had been brought up as Hindus (3), because 'Hinduism' was the way of life in India (3) and because the religion told them how to behave (2). Along with other Asian respondents, all the young Hindu men considered respect for parents a centrally important value. Moreover, despite the fact that a majority did not disapprove of mixed marriages, most, in Taylor's judgement, were likely to accept a marriage arranged by their parents.

Obviously one cannot generalise from Taylor's findings. They are based on fieldwork done mainly in 1968 in one place and only among Hindu Punjabis. Further, only boys and young men were interviewed. One cannot help noting that Taylor sometimes did not formulate questions as well as he might have done, particularly on the subject of caste. In addition, his own rather generalised and Orientalist presuppositions about the nature of 'Hinduism', assuming the importance of temple worship and of philosophical beliefs such as reincarnation, distort his findings. It is a pity, for example, that no information was sought about private prayer, domestic ritual and other non-temple based practices. More and better questions might have yielded a fuller and perhaps more positive picture of the boys' knowledge and practice of their tradition than the one quoted above.

Taylor's research, of course, gives no indication of religious transmission among the majority Gujarati community. Neither does it deal with significant numbers from the 'African' communities which have been so influential in establishing Hindu tradition in the United Kingdom. It is certain too that during the last two decades Hindus have set up temples and organised religious events in a way then unforeseen. The findings reported in our studies no doubt reflect the growth of more self-assured, established Hindu community life which has developed during the crucial period of over twenty years since Taylor's research. They also suggest the need for more prolonged, responsive research techniques when exploring children and young people's experience of their religious traditions.

Research among Gujarati Hindus conducted within fifteen years of Taylor's had already indicated that Hindu tradition was not simply dying out. In the context of detailed study of two trading castes Maureen Michaelson observed:

> Eight years ago the young children of my acquaintance were almost without exception uninformed and ignorant about several aspects of ritual and religion. Today, as teenagers or young adults, these same people have gained an impressive amount of knowledge of at least the practical aspects. This has been learned informally, through the witnessing of the daily, weekly, monthly and annual cycles of events over a number of years. At all social and religious gatherings children of all ages, including the newborn, add to the general atmosphere of jollity, vitality and noise, and they remain at the celebration either awake or asleep until even the early hours of the morning. In addition the more 'westernised' people of my acquaintance, who previously shunned religious gatherings, have, since the birth of their own children, begun to take a more lively interest in religion generally, and to participate in the social and religious functions of their own extended families. (Michaelson 1984)

Otherwise in most of the published sociological and anthropological literature on Hindus in Britain, any mention of the transmission of culture from one generation to another has been incidental. Ursula Sharma's otherwise sensitive presentation of a Punjabi family hardly touches the question of the children's absorption of Hindu culture (Sharma 1971). Although material was available on the lives of Sikh children (Dosanjh 1969; James 1974), study of how and what Hindu children learn about their tradition has only begun relatively recently. The single exception is David Pocock's study of religious teaching material used with Gujarati children on the Swaminarayan sect in London (Pocock 1976).

During the 1980s while we were conducting our research, Heidi Larson was researching among Punjabi pupils in Southall (Larson 1988a; 1988b) and Penny Logan made a detailed study of the transmission of culture of Gujarati Hindu children in London (Logan 1988a; 1988b). Hugh Bigger investigated the nurture of children in the Hindu tradition in two sectarian groups (Sathya Sai Baba and Swaminarayan) in the north west of England (Bigger 1987) while Johanna Dwyer made a study of formal nurture of groups of Hindu children in Leicester (Dwyer 1988). Moreover, insights are increasingly available from studies of Hindu diaspora communities overseas. Steven

Vertovec describes the transmission of Hindu tradition in Trinidad (Vertovec 1987:159), while Raymond Williams makes valuable observations on the perception of South Asian religions in the United States (Williams 1988:30-31, 46-47). The present book offers a further contribution to the literature on the nurture of Hindu children outside India.

Notes

1. The eight to thirteen range was chosen primarily because it corresponds approximately to the years of schooling covered by students in our institution preparing to be primary or middle school teachers or specialist curriculum co-ordinators in religious education. The age distribution also complements parallel studies of fourteen to nineteen year olds being carried out as part of the Community Religions Project at the University of Leeds. We also hoped to be able to conduct studies of some of the same children when they became young adults. The fact that we focus on younger children means that certain factors — especially related to inter-generational conflict within families — figure very little in our work. Nevertheless there is a great deal of data relating to formal and (especially) informal religious and cultural transmission which contributes to an understanding of the evolution of Hindu life in Britain as it appeared in the 1980s.

2. In 1982 the number given by the Lord Mayor's Committee for Racial Harmony was 6,000. According to the Forward Planning Division (1989:36) there are 3,289 Hindus aged eighteen and over. Another 9215 residents may be either Sikh or Hindu, and a further 1,120 may be either Muslim or Hindu. This information was gleaned from the Electoral Register. As some South Asian names are common to Hindus and members of the Sikh or Muslim community, it is impossible to ascertain all Hindus' religious allegiance from their name alone. As over forty per cent of Britain's Indian population is in the 0-19 age range, Coventry's Hindus could number well over eight thousand.

3. For Balaknath see Sharma (1976). In popular iconography he is associated with the Sanskrit poet, Bhartrhari, an aristocrat who became an ascetic.

4. Knott (1986a) gives some details of the Brahmakumaris.

5. Juergensmeyer (1982 and 1988) gives an outline of Radhasoami.

6. Chapter eight provides information on these religious movements.

CHAPTER 2

Research Studies and Methodology

The present book results from three studies based in the Department of Arts Education at the University of Warwick.[1] The aim of all three was to learn about what we termed the 'nurture' of Hindu children growing up in Britain. Nurture was adopted, as an analytic term, from the American and British religious education literature and denotes the processes by which children born into a particular faith community acquire its characteristic practices and beliefs or some adaptation of them (Bushnell 1967; Hull 1984).

The first study concentrated upon the formal aspects of nurture; in other words the focus was on supplementary classes run by Hindus in which distinctively Hindu teaching was provided for children of their community. The second study, the largest of the three and the main source of data for this book, explored many more aspects of nurture — the values, myths and rituals which are integral to the children's total experience. This included supplementary classes — and, indeed, children's comments on religious education in the maintained school — but it primarily examined the role of the home, the temple and of community events in a web of cultural transmission. The third study continued this approach but narrowed its focus to two Punjabi communities.

Some findings of our study of the formal Hindu nurture are described in chapter ten. In 1983 a questionnaire was sent out to fifty five Hindu organisations and associations (Jackson 1985). Of the forty three organisations which responded, seventeen were running evening or weekend supplemen-

15

tary schools or classes providing teaching in Hindi or mother tongue. In 1984 ten organisations were visited. These were the Gujarati Education Society, Coventry, the Shree Sanatan Mandir, Leicester, the Vishwa Hindu Kendra, Southall, the Indian Volunteers for Community Service, Harrow, the Vishwa Hindu Parishad (UK), Birmingham and Bolton, the South East Hindu Association, Woolwich, the Arya Samaj London UK, Ealing and the Shree Kutch Satsang (Bhuj) Swaminarayan Temple, Bolton. In each case a forty five minute interview was tape recorded, usually with the person who had completed the questionnaire, and wherever possible at least part of a lesson with each group of children was observed and the literature used in teaching was noted. Unfortunately it was not possible to observe each organisation's classes over a longer period of time, or to speak to all the teachers involved, nor to interview the children. Nonetheless, the research demonstrated the diversity and the overlap of approaches to the formal transmission of Hindu culture in Britain. Some findings were published in Jackson (1985) and Jackson and Nesbitt (1986).

The work was followed by an ethnographic study of eight to thirteen year old children with the title 'Hindu Nurture in Coventry'. Research proceeded in clear but overlapping stages between January 1986 and January 1988. The first six months were devoted to an investigation of the complexity of the local Gujarati and Punjabi Hindu population. Through participant observation we built up an extensive network of contacts. These included Bal Vikas classes run by the devotees of Sathya Sai Baba and other worshipping groups, notably the Arya Samajis, the Pushtimargis and the International Society for Krishna Consciousness, as well as other more or less informal groupings. We were keen to meet Hindus from as wide a range of caste, regional and educational backgrounds as possible, and to identify their devotional orientations. For example, from literature and from our study of formal Hindu nurture we already knew that there are many followers of Swaminarayan in Britain (Pocock 1976; Barot 1981; Williams 1984; Dwyer 1988), but we found that there is no significant following of this movement in Coventry. During this period we established which movements were influential or numerically strong locally. We particularly noted the ways in which children between eight an thirteen years of age were involved in Hindu religious activities. Photographs and sound recordings were made. It was necessary to gain as comprehensive an overview as possible of the Coventry Hindu scene before proceeding to the second and third stages.

Stage two was the selection of a group of children whose lives could be followed in detail as the subjects of case studies.[2] In order to select a cross section illustrating the diversity of the local Hindu population, it was important to know what variables had to be taken into account. With the agreement of children, their parents and the Local Education Authority a semi-structured interview was tape-recorded with thirty four children in school. The list had been drawn up — on the basis of participant observation — to include Punjabi and Gujarati boys and girls between eight and thirteen years of age from families of as may castes and sectarian orientations as possible. With the intention of coming across hitherto undetected variables, and in the hope of finding children from 'less practising' families than those identified through primarily Hindu community events, all eligible Hindu pupils in one school were interviewed.[3] On the basis of these interviews and the previous participant observation, and with parental approval, twelve children were selected for follow up.

The third stage of the research, in which twelve children from a total of nine families (seven Gujarati and two Punjabi) were studied, extended approximately from November 1986 to October 1987. Regular visits to these children began at the Gujarati Hindu New Year which, in 1986, was on November 1st. The children were given diaries in which to record day-to-day happenings, particularly those which were distinctively Hindu in character. During fortnightly visits each child was interviewed informally about the diary entries, drawing out more detailed comment and explanation. Cultural events, religious gatherings and supplementary classes continued to be attended, and the children's degree of involvement recorded. Home visits allowed further photography, informal conversation with other relatives, and the opportunity to observe the domestic shrine, religious pictures and the Indian videos to which children were exposed. 'Focused interviews', with artefacts, pictures and slides used as cues, elicited much information. The children appearing under pseudonyms in this book were all contributors to the 'Hindu Nurture in Coventry' study.

Finally, in a third study, research was extended to include children from two more Punjabi communities, the Valmikis and Ravidasis. These are structurally distinct groups with their own places of worship, their religious 'movement' and caste being coterminous. Fieldwork for this study lasted from July 1988 to February 1989. Two interviews were conducted with each of twenty four children. In the first the questions covered children's daily life, special occasions, thoughts about the future and past. The second interview consisted of comments from the children on twenty five religious pictures which they were shown by a researcher. Further data were derived from participant observation in homes and places of worship and from the diaries which twenty eight children kept for three months. Some material from this final study is included, but for more detailed coverage see Nesbitt (1990 a and b) and Nesbitt (1991). The Valmikis and Ravidasis cannot be classified unequivocally as Hindu since many individuals perceive themselves as Sikh.

Observations in this book relate to children whose families described themselves as Hindu.

☐ Methodology

Studies of this type conducted by Religious Studies scholars often adopt a phenomenological methodology (e.g. Barton 1986; Bowen 1988). The main problems with phenomenology as a theoretical underpinning and method for the study of religions are twofold. First of all there is a presupposition that there are essences which are universal in human consciousness. In the work of many phenomenologists of religion this assumption is expressed in terms of essences (*eideia*) which are held to be universal in human religious experience. Much recent work in philosophy, the social sciences, cultural criticism and literary theory would question the existence of universal 'essences' common to widely varying ways of life and which can exposed through the application of a method (e.g. Wittgenstein 1958; Rorty 1980). The problem does not end here, for we do not only have to be cautious of our own and our contemporaries' tendencies in this direction. Earlier examples of culture contact have resulted in the projection of terms, assumptions and structures from one world view on to those of others, structures that have subsequently become embedded in literature and language and which have tended to be accepted as received truth or common sense. The emergence of the terms 'Hindu religion' in the eighteenth century and 'Hinduism' in the early nineteenth century are good examples (see chapter one). This is not just a matter of inadvertent misunderstanding, but results from an unequal power relationship. In periods of colonial expansion the on-going imbalance of power has permitted politically and technologically stronger cultures or groups to define weaker groups (Said 1978).

The second problem with phenomenology is the emphasis it places on the use of empathy as a means to understanding another's world. First the researcher is required to bracket out his or her presuppositions and then is expected to empathise with the subjects of study. It is clear from Said's discussion of the structuring of concepts in certain historical contexts (1978) that even a step in the direction of bracketing (*epoché*) requires at least some skill and knowledge. Pragmatically, researchers can try to be aware of at least some of their presuppositions and to hang on to that awareness (this might require some historical study as well as philosophical skill), but they can do no more.

Then there is empathy (*einfülung*). In van der Leeuw's words empathy is 'transposing oneself into the object or re-experiencing it' (1926 in Waardenburg 1973:401). The danger here is the inadvertent superimposition of the researchers' categories on to the subjects of study, with consequent errors of interpretation. We would argue that empathy becomes possible after one has grasped the 'grammar' of another's discourse. It is the tools for learning that 'grammar' that the researcher needs. In this respect we have found interpretive anthropology, in particular the work of Clifford Geertz, to be particularly helpful (1973; 1983). In Geertz's approach the art of grasping another culture can be summarised in terms of the application to the ethnographic process of what Dilthey called the hermeneutic circle. In his own fieldwork Geertz used the usual ethnographic methods of participant observation (but without the 'empathetic' emphasis of Malinowskian anthropologists or phenomenologists of religion), interviewing and documentary analysis. His ongoing approach to data analysis consisted in getting a sense of each part — each 'symbol', whether it be a word, image, institution or behaviour — by considering it in relation to the whole.

For us the 'wholes' were sometimes the cumulative Hindu tradition in general (Smith 1978) and sometimes relevant segments of that tradition, such as a particular *sampradaya* (religious movement) within the tradition or the tradition as generally expressed through a loosely knit group sharing a specific ancestral Indian regional and linguistic origin. The 'parts' were the concepts, rituals, icons, family relationships, modes of communication (e.g. stories, video), beliefs and so on of the children and parents in the families we studied. As our Appendix on field methods illustrates, we sometimes had the additional complication of children having a concept, but (very reasonably) finding difficulty in expressing it precisely in English terminology. In such cases our more general understanding of Hindu ritual proved helpful in interpreting meanings. By reflecting on the interplay between our evolving perception of the Hindu tradition (or the Sathya Sai Baba organisation or whatever) and the 'parts' — or as Geertz would say 'symbols' — revealed through observation or interview, we increased our understanding of both. Relating written sources — whether documents or books written by insiders or the scholarly works of academics — to our considerations was another important aspect of the methodology.

In learning the basic fieldwork techniques we found manuals such as Burgess (1984) and Spradley (1980) helpful. Our own modifications of some of these methods (especially the use of photographs and other visual material in focused interviewing and the use of children's diaries) are described in the Appendix to this book. Though these methods take us well beyond the good intentions of phenomenology, it has to be pointed out that there are inherent weaknesses in ethnographic approaches which need to be recognised. The following points are meant to counter any notion that we have produced an 'objective' account.

Firstly there is the obvious influence created by the ethnographer's presence in the field. This reduces to some extent over time, and there are 'triangulation' techniques for cross-checking information gained from one interview with another, or by the use of other methods such as participant observation. Nevertheless there is an undoubted influence. For example, the subject matter of the researchers' questions sometimes raised issues which only subsequently became high on the agenda of particular individuals or groups (cf Knott 1986a:3). The gender of the ethnographer is also a relevant consideration, both in the frankness with which informants would sometimes speak to a researcher of the same gender and in terms of access to particular events. Ethnic background and professional status are two further categories which sometimes influenced communication and access.

Secondly, the ethnographer's range of concepts and thought patterns also influence the way in which field notes are written, the selection of data from those notes, the English terminology used to interpret or 'translate' folk terms, and the subsequent structuring of reports and other texts. Geertz uses the term 'experience-near' for concepts which insiders use naturally to define their thoughts, feelings and so forth. 'Experience-distant' concepts, on the other hand, are those (in this case) employed by ethnographers often as analytic terms. We have already referred to our use of 'nurture', for example, as an analytic term connoting the formal or informal transmission of religious culture from one generation to the next. Through fieldwork we found that the Hindi term *bal vikas* (literally 'child development') was used regularly of formal 'nurture' classes within the Sathya Sai Baba organisation. *Bal vikas* expresses an 'experience-near' concept while 'nurture', though close in meaning, is 'experience-distant'. 'Multiple allegiance' is another 'experience-distant' concept, expressing the idea that some people attending devotional gatherings of one *sampradaya* might also participate in the devotional activities of other groupings. Many 'experience-near' concepts are listed in the glossary.

A key aspect of the art of ethnographic analysis according to Geertz, is to put 'experience-near' concepts in 'illuminating connection' with 'experience-distant' concepts to produce an interpretation of a way of life so that it is neither locked inside the conceptual framework of insiders nor bereft of the way of life's subtleties or tonalities (Geertz 1983:57-8). This is what we have tried to do, but we are conscious of the *artistic* nature of the enterprise. Other people might have done it differently. Take the chapter headings of this book. We remain true to the field data in selecting material which was of importance to insiders. It is doubtful, however, that insiders would have arranged the material in exactly the same way or used the same terminology. Our choice of subject matter and our approach to classifying material into chapters are influenced by our background in Religious Studies and also by a desire to help English speaking non-Hindu readers into the material. In considering some of the English terms used in the chapter titles, the reader needs to be cautious. A *vrat* is not a 'fast' as the word is used in ordinary English, nor a *sampradaya* a 'religious movement' in the general sense in which the term is used both in everyday language and in the social sciences. A Gujarati teacher in a supplementary school, acknowledging the *sanatana dharma* (eternal tradition), a Sai devotee, a Pushtimargi and a Punjabi follower of ISKCON would all have structured texts differently from us. They would also (probably) have written texts significantly different from one another. Further, an ethnographer with a background in sociology would, in all likelihood, have given less attention to the details of ritual and practice than we did and would have employed a different (though probably overlapping) range of analytic terms or 'experience-distant' concepts.

In short, we do not incline to the view that it is possible to write an 'objective account'. We acknowledge the cultural and academic influences involved in writing an ethnography, and especially that there are 'artistic' elements in the conduct of the fieldwork, the selection of data, and in writing ethnographic texts. In these respects we accept some of the observations made by writers such as James Clifford and Vincent Crapanzano, without concurring with their complete rejection of Geertz's hermeneutical approach to ethnography (Clifford and Marcus 1986). At the same time we would argue that ethnographers should always aim for the highest standards in doing their work, in terms of both sensitivity and method. Ethnographies are valuable sources, but they have inherent distortions and should be read preferably in conjunction with other texts, especially those written by 'insiders'. Further discussion of our field research methods can be read in the Appendix to this book, while a fuller discussion of Geertz's approach to ethnography is in Jackson (1993).

☐ The Children

Before moving to the main body of the book we must say something about the children who were the subjects of case studies and their families. To these children, who kept diaries for us and answered questions on our fortnightly visits, we owe a particular debt. We cannot give their real names, but refer to them in the text by pseudonyms.

All the families were owner-occupiers living in terraced or semi-detached houses. Two families lived in the South of the city, the others in the North where South Asian settlement in Coventry began and where many Hindu families now live. Deepak and Ritu's family lived outside the city boundary. All except Arun's family owned a car, but no household had two cars. Mridula

21

lived with her father's parents and his two sisters. The other children lived with their parents. All had other relatives — grandparents, uncles, aunts and cousins in Britain — and most lived within a mile or two of their own home. All the children attended county schools. During the research period Jyoti and Sanjay transferred to a Church of England aided primary school because it was near their new house. Ritu was preparing for the entrance examination to an independent school to which she went after the research period as her parents felt she would benefit from a more academically demanding school.

When research began Deepak was eleven and his sister barely eight. Like their young brother and sister they were born in the Midlands. Their parents had previously lived in New Delhi, the capital of India. Like many other Punjabi Hindus their father's family had moved there from further west when the state of Pakistan was created in 1947. The family is Khatri by caste. This is a Punjabi community which approximates to Kshatriya in the Sanskritic *varna* system. The Khatris constitute a predominantly urban, professional and business community in India. Both the children's parents had received secondary education and spoke English readily. During the research period father had a supervisory post in a food producing factory. Mother's domestic duties prevented her from going out to work.

Both parents were prominently involved in the Hindu Temple (Ram *Mandir*). Father was an office-holding member of the management committee. The Hare Krishna Movement (ISKCON) profoundly influenced their devotion and their understanding of their faith. During our research, which predated the opening of an ISKCON temple in Coventry, their home was frequently the venue for Saturday evenings *satsangs* (religious gatherings).

Sunil, Jyoti and Sanjay were also Punjabi. When our study commenced Sunil was eleven, Jyoti nine and Sanjay eight. They had three younger siblings, one born during the first year of our research. All the children were born in Coventry. Their parents had both grown up in Punjab, but now their father's mother and brothers all lived in Coventry. Neither of the children's parents was in paid employment. The family was much less involved in temple activities than Deepak and Ritu's. They were not associated with any religious movement such as ISKCON and their house was not a centre for regular corporate worship. However the children were familiar with devotional activity occurring at home and in the temple. By caste the family was Rajput, another community which may be classified as Kshatriya.

The other named interviewees were from Gujarati families and all had some family connection with South or East Africa. Bhavini, born in July 1978, was the youngest of our core group of children. She and her younger brother were born in Coventry, where her father's parents and brother also live. Both her parents grew up in Kenya and their family roots were in the

Kathiawar region of Gujarat. By caste they were Brahmin and members of Bhavini's father's family performed priestly duties in the Shree Krishna temple.

Bhavesh, who was ten when we began our research, was also a Gujarati Brahmin, from an Anavil Brahmin community. His family came from a different area of Gujarat, from the town of Valsad, south of Kathiawar. His mother had been brought up in Uganda and her close relatives had more recently moved to North America. During the research period Bhavesh's family left Coventry and settled in his father's home town in Gujarat.

Hitesh was ten years old and his family was from Surat in southern Gujarat. By caste they were Soni (goldsmiths) and in keeping with their ancestral occupation Hitesh's parents ran a shop specialising in the 24 carat gold jewellery which is given to Indian girls when they get married. When not at school Hitesh and his sisters would help in the shop. His mother had lived in Kenya, his father in Surat. The family's religious belief and practice was much influenced by the living Godman, Sathya Sai Baba.

Arun (twelve years) was also from a Soni family. His relatives in Britain and in other countries, including Canada, the USA and India, were jewellers and watch repairers. During the research period neither of his parents was in paid employment. His father had grown up in Aden and his mother in Uganda. The family originated from the Kathiawar region of Gujarat. His mother was deeply involved in the Shree Krishna temple's activities and in the *satsang mandal*, a group of women who met weekly for devotional singing and scriptural reading. The family was not associated with any religious movement, but Swami Satyamitranand Giri (see chapter eight) and Morari Bapu were held in particularly high esteem.

Sarita was ten when our research began. She had lived all her life in Coventry but her father was brought up in Gujarat and her mother in East Africa. Her maternal grandfather, whose family is from near Surat, was an office-holding member of the committee of the Shree Krishna Temple. By caste they were Prajapati, a community associated in the past with skills as artisans and builders. Her parents both went out to work and her maternal grandparents, with whom she spent much of her time, had a dominant influence on her upbringing.

The influence of grandparents was evident in the lives of the other two Gujarati children. The strongest religious input in Mridula's life was her paternal grandmother's daily devotion. In chapter eight this is described in some detail. Unlike the rest of our selected children, Mridula had spent the first years of her life in Kenya. In Coventry she lived with her grandmother and paternal aunts, behind the post office-cum-general store which they ran. Although her relatives visited India they had no relatives there. Her family originated in Kathiawar, Gujarat, and were Lohana in caste. In common with many others from this business community the family's religious allegiance was to Pushtimarg, the 'Way of Grace'. Because of her grandmother's involvement, local Pushtimargis would gather for *satsang* in Mridula's house among others. When research began Mridula was twelve years old.

Anita was nearly twelve. Her parents had come from South Africa, though the family's roots were in Gujarat. Her father was working as a bus driver, her mother in a factory. With them lived Anita's elder sister, their cousin and paternal grandfather. By caste they were Matiya Patel. Their lives were profoundly influenced by Sathya Sai Baba and for Anita devotion to him took priority over any consideration of caste. Every week fellow devotees gathered on one evening for *satsang* and on another for discussion in their living room which served as an unofficial temple.

When data supplied by children or their families is used, or when we make observations about the children and their kin, we use the pseudonyms as above so that readers can refer back to specific details of family background. Other children who were interviewed during the course of our three studies are not mentioned by name, but details of family background are given in the text when relevant to the discussion. The following chapters show how much the children and their families gave of themselves in contributing to our research. At the very least their contributions correct the view that British Hindu children are uninterested or uninvolved in their religious tradition.

Notes

1. The Religious Education and Community Project in an umbrella term for a series of linked studies based in the Department of Arts Education at the University of Warwick under the direction of Robert Jackson. We are grateful to the following bodies for supporting our research financially: the University of Warwick Research and Innovations fund for supporting our study on formal Hindu nurture, and the Leverhulme Trust for supporting both our studies on Hindu Nurture in Coventry and on Punjabi Hindu Nurture. The Religious Education and Community Project undertook a three year study of Christian, Jewish, Muslim and Sikh children funded by the Economic and Social Research Council (1990-1993). Part of RECP's work is to produce curriculum material, and in the context of the Hindu tradition see Jackson (1989 a and b) and Jackson and Nesbitt (1990).

2. Our own perception of what constitutes 'Hindu tradition' influenced our selection of the range of membership groups to which families were attached. The composite picture presented through illustrating tendencies and themes from across the case studies also inevitably reflects the researchers' view of the scope of Hindu tradition. Detailed reference at certain points in the book (e.g. chapter eight) to children from particular membership groups, however, gives some indication of their distinctive character. There is scope for further research on

children from particular membership groups. So far the Religious Education and Community Project has completed a study of Valmiki and Ravidasi children (Nesbitt 1990a and b; 1991).

3. Our methods of networking out from contacts made through various kinds of community events and of interviewing children, initially in schools in the main areas where Coventry Hindus reside, meant that we excluded certain families with a Hindu ancestry from the study. These would include a small number of non-Gujaratis and non-Punjabis with a parent working in certain professions — for example as doctors based in hospitals.

CHAPTER 3

The Self-perception of Hindu Children

☐ Introduction

In this chapter we examine children's perception of themselves and, in particular, what they understand by being Hindu. We note a few of the features of Hindu children's experience which combine, in the observers' perception, to give them a distinctively Hindu identity. Religious allegiance is only one part of children's personal and social identity, but a significant one. Sociologists and anthropologists who take a situational view of ethnicity (eg Barth 1969) and social psychologists writing about identity (eg Tajfel 1981; Weinreich 1989) acknowledge that an individual's dominant self-perception will be determined by changing contexts. For example, as Drury (1990) shows in the case of young Sikhs, in some situations individuals regard themselves as 'Indian', in others as 'Asian' or 'black' with reference to members of other groups. Similarly the individual's sense of belonging to a particular religious tradition may only surface in certain situations. How British Hindu children perceive their religious tradition and themselves in relation to it will profoundly affect the British 'Hinduism' of future generations. As Knott points out:

> What young British Asians and West Indians choose to do in the name of religion will contribute to the future face of British Islam, Hinduism, Sikhism, Black Christianity etc. (1986b:174).

27

Although not discussed in this chapter the children's sense of themselves as, for example, Coventrian or as pupils of a particular school should not be forgotten. They are influenced by pupils and teachers at school and this affects their image of themselves and of Hindu tradition.

☐ Religious Boundaries

It also needs to be recalled that both insiders and outsiders draw the lines between religious traditions in different places and in different ways. The examples of the relationship between Jains and Hindus and Sikhs and Hindus have already been referred to. Children at the boundaries between religions sometimes have a clear sense of their own identification with a particular tradition. In the case of the boundary between the Hindu and Sikh traditions, children from Valmiki and Ravidasi communities articulated their relationship to Hinduism as follows. In one girl's words:

> I know what culture I am, Hindu, but it's not as if we're restricted to Hindu because we believe in Sikhism as well. It's just one thing really. Everyone just parted it.

Another said:

> I say to myself I'm Sikh but like really I'm a Hindu. I'm a Hindu Punjabi, I do many things that Sikhs do. We go to a *mandir* but I call it a *gurdwara*.

Her brother also called himself Hindu Punjabi but associated himself with Sikhism both in describing his aunt (through a 'love marriage') as 'a Jat, a proper Sikh, not really a different community' and in relating that Guru Nanak said,

> 'Not just Sikhs can believe in me. Everyone can believe in me'.

Analogous to his 'proper Sikh' is a Ravidasi girl's reference to a film of a Hindu family which she had watched in a school religious education lesson. It showed 'true Hindus'. She added, 'We are more free than they are'. For the purposes of our research individual Valmikis and Ravidasis were included if they described themselves as Hindu.

A rather different complication in children's perception of themselves as Hindu is expressed by Sathya Sai Baba's devotees who see their faith not as Hindu only but as an affirmation of all faiths. Yet to our perception as researchers, the Hindu background of Sathya Sai Baba and of his devotees (in Coventry at least) as well as the concepts and the style of worship are unquestionably Hindu and justify their inclusion in an account of Hindu children. Further, the involvement of Sai devotees in more general Hindu community events and the use by some of them of the terms 'Hindu' and

'Hinduism' (Anita, for example, identified herself as Hindu) suggested that they should be included in our account.

Many of the experiences of Hindu children in Britain and the values expressed in family life are equally those of other South Asians, although Hindus may link them with Hindu tradition. Thus hospitality, respect for older people and consideration of the family's rather than the individual's interests, would also be prominent in an account of Sikhs, Muslims or Christians from the Indian sub-continent.

One way children identified themselves as Hindu was by contrasting the freedom which they felt that they had with the restrictions which they associated with Muslims ('they have to cover their legs') and Sikhs ('they aren't allowed to cut their hair'). In a Punjabi girl's words:

> If I was Sikh I wouldn't have this short hair. I wouldn't be wearing a skirt if I was a Muslim.

□ Religion and Language

Most of the children used the term 'religion' to cover the concept of 'culture'. 'Language' too was used by many to mean 'culture' and there was a tendency to use 'Hindi' (a north Indian language) for 'Hindu' and vice versa. This confusion may result partly from hearing their school teachers confuse these words. Between religion and other aspects of culture different individuals would draw boundaries at different points. In the case of 'Hinduism' such a distinction has little validity. For many of the children the distinction did not exist at all. One child's reference to having 'English religion food' in his sandwiches revealed how differently the word 'religion' can be understood.

The children clearly equated religion with the community of which they were a part whose prime characteristic was language. Children seldom acknowledged that someone with the same mother tongue might be of a different faith community. In Coventry most Gujarati Hindu children have not met Gujarati Muslims even though Coventry has a significant number of Muslim families with a Gujarati ancestry. Interestingly none of the Punjabis immediately gave his or her religion as Punjabi, although this conversation with a nine-year old Punjabi girl is representative of the confused categories of at least six interviewees:

> Q If somebody said to you, 'What's your religion?' what would you say? (Reply indistinct — either 'Hindi' or 'Hindu').
>
> Q What's the difference between Hindi and Hindu?

A   Well it's little bit the same — and Punjabi, because my friend she's in my class, she's Punjabi and I'm Punjabi and we speak the same language.

Q   Do you have the same religion as well?

A   Yes.

Q   And what's the name of the religion?

A   Punjabi.

Q   The religion? If somebody said to you, 'Are you a Christian or are you a Muslim?' what would you say?

A   I'm a Hindi.

Q   What do you think is special about your religion?

A   Well it's different than Pakistanis.

Quite apart from this girl's confusion of 'Hindu' and 'Hindi' her account of the relationship of Hindi and Punjabi is not surprising in view of the fact that many adult Punjabi Hindus whose mother tongue is Punjabi claim that their real language is Hindi. Thus Punjabi Hindu children grow up hearing and using Punjabi at home but, unlike Sikhs, they are told that the language which they should learn to read and write is Hindi. The reasons for this lie in the often troubled history of religious communalism in the politics of Punjab where Punjabis with a common mother tongue have identified with Urdu, Hindi, or Punjabi on the basis of their religious allegiance respectively to Islam, Hinduism or Sikhism.

Gujarati Hindu parents respect Hindi but do not devalue Gujarati in relation to it. Their children are as confused as the Punjabis about the relationship of 'Hindu' and 'Hindi' as this excerpt from an interview with a ten year old Gujarati girl illustrates:

Q   If somebody said to you, 'What's your religion?' what would you say to them?

A   Gujarati, and sometimes I say Hindu or Asian.

Q   Is there any difference between saying, 'I'm Gujarati' and saying, 'I'm Hindu?'

A   No. It's just like different languages.

Q   If somebody said to you, 'What do you think is special about your religion?' what would you say?

A It's just different from English people's. All it is is some of the words are same, some of the words aren't. Some of the words are the same as Hindu.

Q What do you mean?

A Like in Hindu you have different types of words and Gujarati's a different thing ... All it is is a different language. And some of the words in Hindu and some of the words in Gujarati they're both the same.

Q You're talking about language, but what's different about being Hindu from being Muslim or Christian or not having a religion?

A I don't really know.

The next quotation shows how for Anita's cousin 'Gujarati' and 'Punjabi' are terms parallel to 'Christian' and 'Muslim':

If they're Punjabi they'll go into a *gurdwara* — what do you call it? — a Sikh temple to pray. They'll sit down and this holy man would read it. If I went to a Christian house they'd go to church. If I went to a Muslim house they'll go to the mosque. But if I went to a Gujarati house they'd go to the temple.

Children work out the relationship of 'Gujarati' (a regional and linguistic label), of 'Hindi', a purely linguistic term and 'Hindu', a religious label, largely through contact with others including South Asians in school. This process of exploration emerges clearly in Larson's research on socialization and play among six to twelve year old Punjabi children in Southall (Larson 1988b). She shows how through conversation and crossing the boundaries between Sikh, Muslim and Hindu community life and by playing out parts of other traditions — for instance in school assembly, in plays about festivals or in giving Easter eggs or receiving *prashad* (blessed food) at the *gurdwara* (Sikh place of worship) — they work out what they themselves do and believe.

☐ Positive and Negative Perceptions of Being Hindu

Children associated various kinds of experience with being Hindu. Our selection of examples illustrates the contextual influence of family, wider Hindu social groupings within or beyond the caste or ethnic group, peer groups and school.

In describing their religion, children often referred to values and rules of conduct encouraged within the family and (in some cases) within supplemen-

31

tary classes. For example, one child who was influenced by the values of the Sathya Sai Baba movement said members of his religion would 'speak truth' and practise 'love, non-violence'. Another child said, 'you wear a sari if you're married, pray every day'.

Children said that if they went to live in a non-Hindu home they would miss their family, festivals and the domestic shrine (temple). They often commented on the fact that food would not be vegetarian in a non-Hindu household. These aspects figured so prominently in children's account of their lives that they are the subject of later chapters of this book.

Children also often associated being Hindu with enjoyable experiences. Children from a Gujarati background often referred to their enjoyment of the festival of Navaratri or Norta, a nine night celebration every Autumn. Depending on their specific background, children would participate in programmes of dance organised by their family's *samaj* (caste association) and by the Shree Krishna temple. Though children usually attend Navaratri as part of family groups, girls in particular had plenty of opportunities to meet friends and to participate in the traditional dances.

Although long religious ceremonies could be boring, children's attitudes to their religion were often enthusiastic. When asked what he would like a non-Hindu to know about his religion Hitesh replied:

> Well you might have a better time. If the English people tried to live in the Indian religion they might find it a little different and more exciting.

Anita said that in her Bal Vikas class:

> I heard that Hinduism was the first religion. Gandhi was a Hindu. You feel really good that you're a Hindu.

Talking about being Hindu another child said:

> It's nice. I enjoy going to *mandir* (temple) and praying and I just like being one.

Although most of the children we studied were too young to participate directly in Asian 'youth culture' activities, when they referred to them they sometimes associated them with religion. Children of the Valmiki and Ravidasi communities frequently mentioned *bhangra* dancing. *Bhangra*, the triumphal folk dance of Punjab, has been transformed by contact with Western pop music and is extremely popular with young South Asians including Gujaratis in Britain (Baumann 1990). A Valmiki Hindu boy who had experienced name-calling and stone-throwing articulated the way in which playing in a *bhangra* music group had boosted his self-esteem:

> I've gone a bit closer to my religion, yes, because like a couple of years back I just didn't like being an Indian because we used to get picked on. We used to be called 'Paki', but now I've gone close to it because new Indian music is coming out.

Day school provided another influence on children's perception of their Hindu identity, though the treatment of the subject was sometimes tokenistic. Some teachers' presuppositions about the nature of 'Hinduism' (eg perceiving the Hindu tradition to be a clearly definable 'religion', with a set of beliefs and a membership) often did not match children's experience in the home and in other Hindu-related groups. One Punjabi girl 'discovered' her Hindu identity from a non-Indian teacher after being questioned by her, then asking her mother about Divali, and reporting back to the teacher. This incident is one of several in which the children relayed questions, information or pronunciations relating to Hindu tradition from their school to their family. Most children felt encouraged by the schools' interest and respectful treatment of the tradition (see chapter ten).

Some children, from the minority of our interviewees who lived in the south of the city where the South Asian population is more thinly spread, seemed to have reservations about their ethnic and religious identity. Some children in this small group made an overt connection between being Hindu and being racially abused by some white peers. Children's sense of themselves as Hindu is inseparable from their perception of themselves as 'coloured' or 'black' with all its painful implications in a racist world. Bhavini remarked that at school, apart from a Punjabi girl, she had no friends 'because I'm brown'.

Self-image is built up from signals from those around. Questions about racial harassment revealed that signals are sometimes painful. Most often children mentioned being called 'Paki'. In particular two Punjabi boys who had moved from areas of high Asian density in the north of the city, to areas in the south had experienced name-calling.

> People make fun of my religion. They call me 'Paki'. I feel sad because it's not my fault that I'm Indian. I ignore them. Just walking down the street they make fun of our language.

However, only in Bhavini's case did a child's responses at all suggest that this antagonism made them wish to reject their language or culture.

☐ Caste

For many centuries Hindus' membership of a *varna* (Brahmin, Kshatriya, Vaishya or Shudra class) and *jati* (caste) has been integral to their self-per-

33

ception and the way in which others viewed them (Jackson and Killingley 1988). Upon their position in the hierarchy of *varna* and *jati* depended the range of people with whom they could eat and with whom marriage alliances were possible. Occupation and economic power were also largely decided by this. In Coventry, as we saw in chapter one, there are Hindu families from a spectrum of castes including both the lowest and the highest. Nevertheless British Hindu children seldom refer to caste by this or any other name. The children whom we interviewed showed no awareness of the implications of caste membership for ritual purity. When asked direct questions about caste they showed limited knowledge and little concern.

Deepak, for example, when asked to name his own caste, said unhesitatingly, 'Khatri — that means a fighter'. But when asked to name other castes he could only remember, 'there's Brahmins, Chamars, I think that's the last one' and he insisted that caste:

> ...doesn't make any difference to me. I don't believe in caste myself that much. In modern times like this the caste doesn't really matter.

Interestingly, in view of the fact that some Indians visiting from India quickly detect a stronger emphasis on caste among Indians living in the United Kingdom, the children felt that caste was more important in India than in Britain. In Deepak's words Hindus 'don't really have caste over here'. So, for example, according to Mridula her friend from the Kumbhar caste had been able to identify her immediately as a Lohana from her surname:

> She knows, because she's from India, so she knows more about the caste system than I do.

Generally it was the teenage children whom we questioned who were aware of their family's caste. Among Valmikis the older interviewees had experienced being identified as low caste by Asian pupils from other castes. One family defensively defined themselves as 'Hindu Punjabi' to avoid using the give-away title, Valmiki.

In general it is at the time when a marriage is being arranged for a member of the family that children become aware of the fact that it is acceptable for certain families to be linked and not for others. Children did not relate their caste to their parents' or ancestors' occupations or connect this with their own future careers.

Traditionally caste has played a decisive part not only in the selection of spouses and in matters of diet and ritual purity, but also in determining one's occupation. Although neither Arun nor Hitesh mentioned the word 'caste', both knew of many relatives who were goldsmiths, so carrying on the Soni caste's hereditary occupation. Arun had no first hand experience of the ancestral craft, but Hitesh and his sister spent much spare time in their parents' shop which specialised in Indian wedding jewellery. They felt under no pressure to be goldsmiths. It was simply the family's craft in which they were already experienced. As Hitesh said:

> If I wanted to go into computers, which I do, they wouldn't mind 'cos my mum said computers is quite good as well.

Although it is only in Soni families that there is an obvious continuity between the *jati's* traditional occupation and their work in Britain, for Brahmins too there is a certain continuity in the ritual domain. Although Bhavini's paternal grandfather served as a *pujari* (priest) in the Shree Krishna Temple, often assisted or replaced by her father's younger brother, she made no connection between being a Brahmin and being a priest. Bhavesh, another Brahmin, introduced the subject of caste of his own accord. While talking about diet he said that Brahmins pray more and do not eat meat:

> It's not very special, but it's something to be proud of. If you're one you got to be proud of it.

Thus any sense of caste hierarchy which British Hindu children have relates to the Brahmins and the lowest castes. This parallels development in countries in which Indians settled as indentured labourers in the nineteenth century (Vertovec 1988:161). Mridula reported a discussion with her Kumbhar friend about 'which caste was higher, after Brahmins, Lohana or Kumbhar. Mridula said that she thought that it was the Lohana who were 'next highest after Brahmins' but that it made no difference. She clearly had some sense of a hierarchy, but for her it was a matter of very little concern.

In the case of the Ravidasis and Valmikis one might have expected a higher degree of caste awareness because they belong to the congregations of places of worship specific to their castes. Undoubtedly their bonding as communities is reinforced by involvement in activities at the Ravidasi *gurdwara* and the Valmiki temple but younger children at least are unaware of the connotations of their caste or why they worship separately from Hindus generally.

Almost all their family's socialising is within the Valmiki or Ravidasi community respectively and children grow up secure in a network of caste fellows who attend the same temple and with whom they are increasingly aware of being related by blood or marriage. The term which Punjabis use for such a community of caste fellows interacting socially is *zat-baradari*. Other Hindu children in Coventry have no caste-specific public place of worship and their social network usually includes several castes.

As compared with Punjabis the Gujarati children generally had more caste-awareness as their families belonged to the *samaj* (association) appropriate to their *jati*. This is a national network. *Samaj* members gather annually for celebrations on one or more of the nights of the Navaratri festival. A bigger *samaj* would hire a hall for all nine nights. Children attended the *samaj's* annual function (a programme of cultural items such as dance, competitions and refreshments) and many shared other activities with fellow members of the *samaj*. Thus Sarita's family visited the Netherlands on a coach trip for Prajapati *Samaj* members. Mridula's caste, the Lohanas, held a St. Valentine's Day party. These instances aptly illustrate the flexibility of the *samaj* in its British setting. Newsletters, calendars and lists of members' names, addresses and telephone numbers are available to members. For many Hindu Gujaratis their *samaj* fulfils the same role as a club or an old boys' network.

Bhavini mentioned Brahma *Samaj*, the Brahmins' organisation. Sarita wrote about the Prajapati *Samaj* which consists of the artisan castes such as the Mistri (wood worker) caste. Arun's family attended functions organised and patronised by a Soni *Samaj*. The local divisions of the Soni (goldsmith) caste are specific to their area of origin in Gujarat. Whereas the Parekhs are Surat Soni, the Lodhias are Kathiawari Soni. There are also Patani Sonis. Bhavesh's mother mentioned Coventry's newly formed Desai *Samaj* for the Anavil Brahmins. Previously for five years they — the families with the surnames Desai, Vasi, Naik and Mehta — had met with those from Leicester.[1]

In an attempt to explain the meaning of the Prajapati *Samaj* Sarita called it:

> our community — like in the Hindus they have like different religions again — they divide it into a few parts. Like we're in the Prajapati *Samaj*. They're all different *samajes*.

Anita, whose personal view of *samajes* was very critical (see chapter eleven), spoke about the Matiya Patel (or Matiya Patidar) *Samaj*, and mentioned the smaller community of Pardi Patels, the people from the same villages in Gujarat as her mother's family. She and her elder sister entered the dance competitions organised by these two societies.

☐ Gotra and Got

Children are not only born into a *varna* and *jati* but also into a *gotra* (Punjabi *got*). This means an exogamous clan. A *jati* (*zat* in Punjabi) may consist of many *gotras* or *gots*. The marriages of members of any *gotra* can only be approved if they are with members of certain other *gotras*. Often the name used as a surname is the *gotra* name. However our interviewees made no mention of their *gotra*, with a single exception. This girl, a Ravidasi, said:

36

My *got* is K... I never use it though. I have a cousin whose name is Mina C ...; C ... is her *got*. *Got* is your family name which has travelled down from your ancestors into your family. It's like a sort of precious stone that belongs to your grandma and her grandma. It doesn't make no difference to me but when you actually get married then the *got* have to be matched. I'm not sure if they have to be matched or have to be different. I just don't understand that but it's something to do with the *got* and that's what the *got* is for.

She was referring to the fact that in her community (as among many other Punjabis) no one is supposed to marry into the *got* of his or her father, mother, maternal or paternal grandmother. But *got* was of little importance in her perception of herself.

She did not connect this or any aspect of her family experience with 'caste', about which she had learned in religious education classes at school.

There's priests at the top, I think, then there's warriors and there's (another group) under warriors and another one of them, lower life which is insects and that.

☐ The Influence of India

By contrast with the general haziness about caste we were struck as observers by the degree to which all the children, whether their parents had migrated to Britain from India or from some other country, shared a sense of being Indian. They most commonly distinguished people in Britain as 'Indian' or 'English' rather than using terms such as 'East African', 'Asian', 'black' or 'white'. In some contexts they referred to their mother tongue, whether Gujarati or Punjabi, as 'Indian', perhaps because Westerners, including teachers, talk about 'speaking Indian' without realising that it means as little as 'speaking European'.

Many children spoke of themselves as Indian, regardless of where they or their parents were born. A girl who had never been to India and whose mother grew up in Singapore said she was Indian:

because I came from India, I came from Delhi — our family came from Delhi, ancestors from Punjab — all over India I think.

Apart from school and the mass media the sources of children's information and impressions of India were chiefly videos of Indian films. A twelve year old girl who had not seen India and whose father had lived in Kenya said that she thought of India:

sometimes when I watch Indian films I think they've really got a good life. They show the really beautiful parts of India and I wish I was there.

She added that films also showed:

the tops of roofs, the *bustees* and all the small villages because some people are really poor, and I think about them and I think, 'O God, if I was born there what would I be like if my parents didn't move here?'

Children's views of India were also based on what relatives who had lived in India or visited India told them. Even when these accounts were off-putting children felt bonded with India. In Sarita's view:

The Indians' real country is India and I think that every person in the world, if they live in another country, then they should at least visit that country once, the one that they really belong to. I don't want to (visit India) but I think I should. It's like Muslim people, they should go to Mecca.

Excitement surrounds travel to India. As Anita explained, when people leave for India they receive gifts. She described how the sum of £1.25 and some sugar are given as *shakun* (a blessing) to anyone who is going to India.[2]

Sometimes children's relatives from India and elsewhere came to Britain. Some came to get married and live in Britain permanently. Sometimes the chief reason for coming was to attend a marriage or a funeral. When Deepak's father's younger brother died suddenly his father's eldest brother flew over from Delhi and spent three months with his relatives in the West Midlands. Such visits strengthened children's sense of relationship to family members in India who might otherwise seem little more than names on airmail letters. With them the visiting relatives would bring news and gifts. These observations accord with Kelly's account of 'transcontinental families'. This is based upon Muslim families in Gujarat and Lancashire:

The connections between kin in the different countries appeared to be well able to withstand long periods of absence. They were closely observed and checked by, for instance, grandparents who flew to join their sons and daughters on extended visits (1990:251).

Sarita wrote in her diary:

When people from India come I feel excited. If they're younger than my parents, then my parents have to give them something like a present. If it's a man they give a shirt. If it's a lady then they give a sari. I like it when they bring us presents like Punjabi suits, jewellery and bracelets in beautiful colours. I hope someone from India comes soon, because I can't wait for the presents and other things.

In all the families involved in the research, the children were probably aware that some relatives made frequent comparisons, both favourable and unfavourable between certain aspects of life in Coventry with life in Africa, India or North America. They knew that outside Britain the climate, customs and standards of hygiene differed. British norms were not absolutes. During the research period Ritu's and Deepak's cousins moved back to New Delhi. Their mother had found that housing and state education compared adversely with what she had experienced in Delhi. At about the same time Bhavesh's family left Coventry to settle in his father's home town of Valsad in Gujarat.

In addition to mentioning relatives in India (as all except Mridula did) all the children in the case studies mentioned relatives in other countries including an uncle who was studying in the USA, an aunt in Hawaii, parents who had grown up in Aden or Kenya and other relatives in France, Germany, Canada, Fiji and South Africa. Nonetheless in their perception of their religious identity India had a unique position.

Most significant in children's feelings about India were their first hand experiences. The majority of the children had visited India once. Even when the child concerned was not old enough to remember the period spent there the family's photographs, of a boy's *mundan* (a traditional head-shaving ceremony), for example, helped to establish a link in his mind between himself and India. A Punjabi girl, who was no longer so fluent in Punjabi, could hear her parents' tape recording of her as an infant speaking Punjabi at her grandmother's house in India.

In Britain children perceived themselves as Indian, but in India they were aware of a difference between themselves and native Indians. Anita referred to herself, her family and other overseas visitors to Puttaparthi (the headquarters of the Sathya Sai Baba movement) as 'foreigners'. These she distinguished in her comments from 'the Sri Lanka people' and 'the India people'. Swami (Sathya Sai Baba) had, she said, had a canteen built for 'foreigners' which served toast and spaghetti and where 'everything was clean'. Similarly with accommodation:

The Indian people stayed outside in tents, but there were frogs and we were not used to it. Only foreign people stayed in the Junior College.

Hitesh also alluded to the difference between people like himself who visited from Britain and those Gujaratis who lived in India:

You could buy Terry bars — milk chocolate with nuts — for 42 rupees. They rob you. There are no price tags. They know we're from abroad by our clothes and the way we talk. They talk full Gujarati. We use half and half (ie half English).

Children associated India particularly closely with their religion. As a thirteen year old Punjabi boy said:

I like the villages as well because they're nice and open. It sort of makes you feel like this is like your home — that's where the beginning of Indian religion is — there.

When Bhavesh's family moved to India during the research period he was sure that in India he would learn a lot more about Hinduism. All the children were aware of India as a place with importance for their religion. Some mentioned festivals which they had enjoyed in India. For instance Arun and his sister had vivid memories of celebrating the festival of Holi there. A seven year old remembered another festival:

I was in India when it was Mahashivaratri. We went where God was born. Then we had a bath up there.

Children also described marriages and *mundan* (head-shaving) ceremonies witnessed in India. Children remembered too their visits to holy places. Several Punjabi children recalled the mountain temple of Vaishno Devi in Jammu.[3] A Gujarati girl described bathing in the Ganges and climbing a special mountain with:

a temple at the top and priests all the way up and statues of gods and you pray as you go up.

For Anita the purpose and climax of visiting India was to be in the presence of Sathya Sai Baba. For Arun a high point was the opening of a temple in his uncle's native village in Kathiawar, Gujarat. There were:

lots of people ... a *murti* (statue) came by tractor. It was quite exciting and enjoyable.

Hindu children's cultural geography did not only differ from their non-Indian peers' in featuring India so evocatively. In Britain too they had their network of significant locations. The places which they visited most were those where relatives lived. Though increasingly dispersed the Hindu population is clustered in certain cities. Leicester, where twelve per cent of the population is Hindu (and most of the Hindus are Gujarati), plays an important part in the experience of Gujarati children. They look forward to visiting the street illuminations at the festival of Divali. They attend religious gatherings in its parks, temples and in houses and community centres. They grow up knowing that outside India the best saris and foodstuffs are available in Leicester. For

Valmiki children Southall, Bedford, Oxford and Birmingham are the places to be visited most as relatives are concentrated there.

□ Conclusion

Positively, for the group of children we studied, 'being Hindu' was associated principally with factors related to family life: with mother tongue, family values, the enjoyment of festivals, domestic worship, traditional food and interactions with relatives — whether living locally, in other parts of England or elsewhere. Beyond the family but within 'Indian' social networks, the caste helped to shape their outlook and self-image, though the concept of caste hardly figured at all in their understanding. Involvement in new musical syntheses associated with 'Asian' youth culture was also sometimes a factor in identifying positively with 'being Hindu'. We have also seen how a special relationship with India permeated their discourse, although Hindu children:

> are constructing a place for India in their mental map of the world different from the India of their parents. (Williams 1988:289)

Special though India remains it is not, for most British Hindu children, a place in which they have spent more than a few months of their lives. It is a place for visits but not a country in which to live permanently.

Negatively, a few children associated 'being Hindu' with racial abuse by white peers. This was especially the experience of children living in the south of the city where children with an 'Asian' cultural background represented a minority of any school class.

Most children recognised boundaries between themselves as Hindus and Muslims and Sikhs, for example by associating 'being Hindu' with freer attitudes towards dress and haircutting than those experienced respectively by Muslim girls or some Sikhs.

Notes

1. Anavil Brahmins cannot, according to Sarita's grandfather, participate in the Shivaratri puja. According to Majmudar:

    > The Anavils of South Gujarat are a different type of Brahmins (ie from outsiders accepted as Brahmins). Once connected with the Scythian invaders, they came from local non-Brahmin classes who were chosen by the northern invaders to be their teachers and priests (1965: 37).

2. This would be given to people travelling to other destinations too!

3. Visiting the mountain shrine of Vaishno Devi involves passing through a narrow tunnel. According to several informants the virtuous, however fat, could go through whereas the wicked, however slim, would get stuck.

CHAPTER 4

The Family: The Roles Which Children Learn

☐ The Scope of the Family

When we asked one nine year old Punjabi girl how many people there were in her family she replied, 'sixteen or seventeen — I don't know'. In this figure she was including her parents, her three sisters, paternal grandparents, her father's two brothers, their wives and children, all the people in fact who lived in her terraced house and the two next door to it. In Coventry some Hindu families live as joint families. This means that a married couple, their unmarried sons, married sons, daughters-in-law and grandchildren form a single household. Even if they do not all sleep under one roof the houses occupied by married brothers are often close and meals and child-care may involve the rest of the family.

Many Hindu children also have close relatives whom they seldom if ever meet because they live too far away, often in India or North America. In many cases family members travel between continents, especially for marriages. Contacts are maintained through letters, telephone conversations, gifts, photos and videos. Children experience their family as a large, cohesive whole even though it is spread over two, three or more continents.

By comparison with their non-Asian contemporaries Hindu children in Coventry spend a great deal of time socialising with kin. Especially at weekends and during school holidays they play, gossip, watch videos and go out shopping with cousins from Leicester, London, Birmingham and else-

43

where. They go to the same weddings and share similar experiences at school. They are brought up to regard cousins as their brothers and sisters. They grow up with a powerful sense of the family as supremely important, as the context and model of social life.

☐ Family roles

Integral to this awareness of the family is a sense of the expectations inherent in particular relationships. According to their sex, seniority and the relationship (by blood or marriage) in which individuals stand they have certain privileges and responsibilities. Among South Asians in Britain, despite such pressures as the impact of surrounding social mores, the complex traditional patterns of responsibility within the family persist, even if in a modified form. Any non-Asian who is accepted into a Hindu home is still likely to notice the significance of the family to all its members and the use of kinship terms to describe relationships with outsiders.

Hindu parents and grandparents, on the other hand, are noting a decline in traditional values. They observe the tendency of younger Hindus to conform to prevailing Western norms. They know that some elderly Asians are now being looked after by outside agencies, not by their own families, and that their children do not show as much deference to authority as previous generations did.

In assessing children's understanding and acceptance of roles based on gender, seniority and relatedness it is helpful to look at how they address and refer to others, at their involvement in family-based activity, particularly ritual, at the explicit instruction on their roles which they receive and at the accounts which they give of their responsibilities to others. Symptomatic of both the older presuppositions and their erosion is a change in the ways that children address and refer to others. It is South Asian custom to address people — whether or not they are family members — with words which express and so establish a relationship. These terms convey loving respect. An older Punjabi woman will refer to a younger one as *beti* (daughter), a young person from a Punjabi family will call a slightly older girl or woman, *didi* (elder sister). If a woman regards someone as a sister then her children will use the word *masi* (mother's sister) to address her. Hindu parents sorrowfully comment upon their children's tendency, in line with their non-Asian peers, to use simply a person's first name without adding or substituting *didi*, *masi* and so on. To their elders this seems disrespectful. Similarly if a child refers to one of the family's friends, Ashok Sharma, as Mr Sharma rather than 'Ashok uncle', 'Uncle Ashok' or by one of the Indian terms for uncle, this sounds unnaturally formal. By referring to him as 'Ashok' they sound rude, un-Indian, 'English'. If a child tells his mother that 'your friend' telephoned, instead of saying 'aunty telephoned', the mother feels acutely the individualism of the child's assumptions. In the past, parents explain, no one was 'my friend' or 'your friend'. Instead others were perceived as a part of the family and referred as 'brother', 'son', 'uncle' according to the relative age of the speaker.

Despite older Hindus' laments, the non-Asian is still, however, likely to be struck by the extent to which Hindu children do use such words, perhaps, like Ritu, referring to *bhaiya* (brother) rather than using a brother's given name, or calling their aunts *masi, mami, bua, chachi, tai* or other equivalents, the words which denote one's mother's sister, mother's brother's wife, father's sister, father's younger brother's wife and father's elder brother's wife respectively.

Children grow up hearing their parents using a much wider range of relationship terms than exists in English, a language which provides no way of distinguishing between different types of aunt, uncle, brother-in-law or sister-in-law. Hearing the words *bhabhi* and *nanad* or their equivalent the Hindu child learns how a woman should refer to her brother's wife or her husband's sister respectively. Children hear such words as *devrani* and *jethani* which distinguish a husband's younger brother's wife from his elder brother's wife. With the addition of 'ji', names and relationship terms convey more respect. Children frequently say 'Daddyji' and 'Mummyji'.

Since such practices are not reinforced in school, parents and the teachers in Hindu supplementary classes come to see the importance of encouraging children to address others appropriately. Anita's teachers in the classes which she attended insisted on the children addressing them as *bhai* and *ben* in keeping with respectful Gujarati convention. Thus their teacher Manjula Lad was never called 'Miss Lad' or 'Manjula' but always *Ben* or *Manjulaben.*

Such a wealth of terms to specify family relationships suggests a strong interest in family structure. Hierarchy would be a more appropriate word. This is extended to include all those who are not relatives, but who are regarded as such. Children become aware as they grow up that senior members of the family have precedence in conversation. Not only would Deepak show deference to his father but his father would treat his own elder brother with great respect. A daughter-in-law usually says little in the presence of her mother-in-law and of older women, let alone in the presence of her father-in-law. Those who argue and assert themselves are likely to be criticised for it.

☐ Ritual Reinforcement of Gender Distinctions.

Children are also used to a tendency, however slight, for segregation between the sexes, whereby men socialise with other males, women with their female acquaintances. In houses with two downstairs rooms, when guests call, the males will often socialise in the front room while their wives and daughters sit in the back room nearer the kitchen. This is by no means a hard and fast rule, but it is a familiar part of children's experience. At home, if there is a *kirtan* (hymn-singing session) or *satsang* (religious gathering) the men and women will tend to group themselves separately even though they are all in the same room. At religious gatherings in temples the men and women usually sit separately, although a husband and wife acting as *yajman* (hosts performing a *puja*) will sit together.

In some religious movements in which Hindu children participate, gender-based distinctions in particular spheres are marked. To take an extreme case from outside Coventry, in congregations of the Swaminarayan tradition the men and women are separated by a screen.[1] At the time of the Navaratri festival, when Gujarati Hindus gather in public halls to dance for nine consecutive evenings, the followers of Sathya Sai Baba hire their own venue and here men are not allowed to join in the dancing.[2] At the close of *arati* (worship in which a light is circled in front of the shrine) children in the *Bal Vikas* classes pay homage to Baba. Boys are taught to prostrate themselves full length, girls to press their foreheads on the floor from a kneeling posture. The reason given by the *guru* (teacher) leaves no doubt about the sexual associations:'The earth is female and two females together is wrong'.

However in the context of ritual and religious organisation, girls and boys can nonetheless pick up confusing messages about the relationship between the sexes. For example in the *mandir* the goddess, usually in the form of Ambaji on her tiger, is honoured as much as any male representation of divinity. The priest is, however, male. In a dramatic presentation of a myth a girl may play a male role such as Krishna and vice versa.

In a social event organised by Sai devotees, Bhavesh consented to be adorned as Rama's wife Sita, and was told that Sathya Sai Baba liked this. At large celebrations organised by his followers, the principal *gurus* who address the children have been women. Sathya Sai Baba is believed by his devotees to be the incarnation of both Shiva and Shakti, God in both male and female aspects.[3] In *bhajans* (hymns) on *Dasehra* day, for example, when Hindu devotion is directed to the goddess, Sathya Sai Baba is equated with the goddess as Sai Ma.

Despite these seeming ambiguities and anomalies, ritual behaviour often illustrates and affirms certain family relationships and the general emphasis on gender differentiation. Life cycle rites, festivals and other rituals tend to reinforce or celebrate certain relationships.

☐ Raksha Bandhan and Karva Chauth

Raksha Bandhan is a useful starting point. This annual festival, which falls usually in August on the full moon day of the lunar month of Shravan, is celebrated by Hindus of all ages. At its simplest the festival involves girls and women tying a decorative thread on the right wrist of anyone whom they regard as a brother. This category includes not only 'real' brothers but also male cousins and those for whom they feel sisterly affection. The sister gives her brother something sweet and he gives her a gift, usually of money. The sister may circle a *thali* (round metal tray) containing items (such as flower petals) used in worship in front of her brother's face and will probably mark his forehead with red powder and grains of uncooked rice.

The ceremony is minimal but its meaning is clear in so far as it emphasises the hallowed relationship that binds brothers and sisters throughout their lives. One Punjabi boy explained, 'It's the sister who thanks the brother for look aftering' (sic).

All the children whom we interviewed described the festival readily. It may be significant that the male expresses his care by giving cash, something concrete and measurable, whereas the girl adopts an attitude of gratitude and worship. The brother's gift indicates the strong protecting the weak, a relationship which, he is told, will continue after his sister leaves her parents on marriage to be part of another family; the sister ties a thread suggesting a linkage of dependency. Although children may not make a connection between this and the role which their *mama* (mother's brother) plays at their rites of passage, there is probably a cumulative effect. At a Punjabi boy's *mundan* (head-shaving) his mother's brother provides the boy's outfit. At a marriage children watch as the brides's *mama* gives the red and white wedding bangles (*churian*). Ritual obligations such as these confirm relationships, in these cases the brother-sister relationship, rather than suggesting that females *qua* females stand in a certain relations to males *qua* males.

Other ritual activities in which children are involved confirm women and girls in other relationships with a male counterpart. As we shall see in chapter five, wives often observe a *vrat* (vow involving abstention from certain foods) for the welfare of their husbands. On such occasions there is scope for even very young unmarried daughters to imitate their mother's behaviour. Karva Chauth, a Punjabi *vrat,* is a good example. On this day, which falls about eleven days before the all-India festival of Divali, wives dress up in bridal colours (red and gold) and after eating at dawn refrain from all food and drink until they sight the moon. Girls often fast and decorate their hands with *mehndi* (henna). They accompany their mothers to the temple to hear the *katha* (story) which is integral to the observance although they often cannot

47

understand much even if they concentrate. Like their mothers they sprinkle milk and water on the ground before they can break the fast.4

Fasts such as this suggest that in the husband-wife relationship the man's well-being depends upon the woman's behaviour, in this case self-denial. Children grow up imbibing this assumption. A popular taboo, widely known and not infrequently upheld, similarly adds to a girl's sense that on her behaviour depends her brother's welfare. If, according to many Punjabi girls whom we interviewed, a sister washes her hair on a Tuesday she endangers her brother.[5] Similarly, Anita, a Gujarati, mentioned that:

> If you've got a brother, on Wednesday you shouldn't wash your hair or your brother gets cursed. It's just an old Hindu belief.

Girls are encouraged by the festival of Raksha Bandhan to see their brothers as their protectors. By seeing their mother fast and by hearing, even if lightheartedly, that a brother's welfare is jeopardised if his sisters break the hair-washing taboo, they get a sense of female responsibility for the well-being of male family members.

☐ Rites Specific to Boys

Some children at least were aware of the importance attached to having sons but children also showed excitement at the birth of a girl in the family. According to Sanjay:

> When my mum went to hospital my sister was praying to get a baby sister.

However a boy's birth is often signalled by greater evidence of rejoicing than a girl's, especially if he is the first boy child. Sarita mentioned that when a boy is born 'the family call you to see' and Bhavini mentioned that *goyanis* (girls symbolising the goddess) are invited after the birth of a boy. Sanjay, Sunil and Jyoti knew that when a girl is born you don't have a party, but 'when a boy is born there's a party and the girls are given money'.[6]

Two life cycle rites also single out boys. These are the *mundan samskar* and the *yagnopavita*. The first is the shaving of a boy's hitherto uncut hair. The second is his investiture (if he is from certain castes) with the *janeu* (sacred thread). Boys seldom remember their own *mundan* but they see photographs and witness the *mundan* of younger boys. Arun's *mundan* at thirteen months was recorded on a cine film. Nowadays *mundans* are videoed (see Jackson and Nesbitt 1990 for an account of a *mundan*). The boy, as the centre of attraction, has new clothes and receives gifts of money. In some communities, his sister has to catch his hair as it is cut. She may receive a new dress or jewellery, and *gur* (brown unprocessed sugar) may be put into her mouth. Thus, by virtue of the relationship in which she stands to him, she too has a specific role to play. But she is the centre of no corresponding ceremony.

The *yagnopavita* ceremony is also specific to boys although fewer boys are invested with the *janeu* (sacred thread) than undergo *mundan*. Even among Brahmins this ceremony does not always occur. Of the children interviewed only Bhavesh anticipated a *janeu* although in Mridula's community boys are also given a *janeu*. Bhavesh and his younger brother received their threads in January 1989 after the family left Coventry and settled in Gujarat. The ceremony lasted all day and was held when their *mama* (mother's brother), who was living in America could be present.

The ceremony symbolises the boy's inauguration into a period of study and celibacy prior to entering upon the *ashrama* (stage) of married life and major family responsibility. However the ceremony is too cursorily and infrequently performed for children generally to be influenced by it.[7]

☐ Girls' Ritual Roles

Although there are no life cycle rites specific to them, girls are indispensable to certain religious ceremonies. By Punjabis as well as Gujaratis, young girls are regarded as pure and as embodiments of the goddess and so to be honoured as potential mothers. Deepak's father said that as they 'are the goddess', little girls do not wear a *pera* (protective thread) as their brothers do. He had also seen small girls who were possessed by the goddess during religious singing. They were able to give a true answer to any question about the past, present or future. Because of this association with the goddess, girls are confirmed in a sense of having ceremonial roles to play by virtue of their gender. Gujarati girls spoke of being *goyani*, Punjabis referred to being *kanjakan*.[8]

For local Gujarati (Brahmin and Soni) girls whose families originated from the Kathiawar region of Gujarat the invitation to be *goyani* would come when a woman had set up a temporary shrine in honour of Randal Ma, the consort of Surya Bhagvan, the sun god. This is done at the time of marriages, at the *simant* ceremony marking the seventh month of a woman's first pregnancy, and on the occasion of a *mundan* or *janeu* ceremony. As Bhavini wrote:

> I have been invited as a *goyni* on several occasions by my relations. People invite *goynis* on occasions — like if somebody is pregnant for the first time, after a baby boy is born, or if someone has fasted 16 Fridays for Santoshi Maa and their wish comes true.

Valmiki girls mentioned being *kanjakan* in connection with worship of the goddess. For example a woman might eat no meat on Tuesdays, Kali Ma's (the goddess Kali's) day, and then invite seven girls to be *kanjakan*. If a member of her family was suffering from chicken pox or measles a woman might invite one boy and six girls and give them a *chuni* (gauzy scarf), bracelets and money.

☐ Girls' Roles at Weddings

Young girls also have a specific role to play in marriage proceedings. In Gujarati marriages, when the bridegroom and his party arrive at the hall where the wedding is to take place, the men are greeted at the door by the bride's younger sister, cousin or niece. On her head she carries a bead-covered imitation coconut lodged in a bead-decorated pot. At this point, the girl may tweak the bridegroom's nose as a time-honoured practical joke. Inside the marriage hall, while bride and groom are sitting facing the fire, in some communities a young girl strokes their backs with a small pot covered with a green cloth. Inside the pot are moong beans (*mag*). This practice is referred to as *lunutarvi*. According to one informant it derives from an earlier period when the bridal couple were children and the marriage took place at night. A pot of coins would be rattled to keep them awake! The bride's sister might take her future brother-in-law's shoes and hide them. So, at their father's niece's wedding, Anita and her sister threw the bridegroom's shoes on the roof, and held out their arms sideways to block the doorway until he gave them some money. Anita's sister recalled how at one wedding there was a balloon full of water which popped over his head and Anita described how the bridegroom's feet were tied together without his noticing. When he stood up to hold the bride's hand he fell over pulling her over too. The fun and laughter encourage the continuation of such role-reinforcing pranks.

While describing marriages a Cutchi girl described a 'game' during the wedding.[10] This involves the youngest sister or cousin-sister of the bride-groom:

> There's this sort of string tied round the hands of the bride and bride-groom and she has to untie it. It's really good if you've got long nails. It's really easy, and they give you money for it. It can be the chosen one, but normally it's the youngest. It's just a laugh, like on birthdays when you get money, you get money for it. Otherwise it's tied there for the rest of their life if they don't get it off, because you're not allowed to cut it. It's got to be untied with a hand.

All this light-hearted involvement in an older relative's wedding gives girls a sense of their own role, distinguishing them from older women or contem-porary male relatives. Boys have fewer such roles to play on religious occasions. In traditional Punjabi marriages a small boy related to the bride-groom plays the role of *sarbala*. He is dressed in the same princely style as the bridegroom and seated on the mare which carries him to the wedding. In Britain the custom of riding a mare has lapsed, although the boy who escorts the bridegroom is still referred to as *sarbala*.[11]

There is no sign that ritual involvement instils in either girls or boys a sense of superiority or inferiority based on their sex. But it seems likely that rituals accentuate awareness of gender differentiation. Repeatedly children see life's progression through expected stages, and they become aware of specific relationships of obligation and reliance.

☐ Instruction

Children learn of the ideal behaviour for a wife, brother or son from the story of Sita, Lakshmana and Rama as recounted in the *Ramayana*. This sets women the standard of total fidelity and submission to their husband's judgement. There is also the story of Sarvan to illustrate a son's devotion to his aged parents. When they were too infirm to go on a pilgrimage Sarvan carried them in panniers hanging from a yoke on his shoulders (Jaffrey 1985:16-20).

Sometimes these responsibilities are taught explicitly. Among prayers displayed at the Bal Vikas camp in July 1986 was:

> *Mathru Devo Bhava*
> *Pithru Devo Bhava*
> *Acharya Devo Bhava*
> *Athithi Devo Bhava*

This was glossed in English as:

> Worship mother as God, father as God, Guru as God and guest as God. These are scriptural injunctions. God is pleased only if we do the above duties properly. Mother and father are visible, living Gods for they have given birth to our welfare and happiness. If today you show respect to your parents, your children will respect you and give you happiness in future.

☐ Observation of Parents' Roles

Children are further influenced by the example of their elders. Some might have echoed this eight year old Ravidasi girl's statement:

> Some people in my house work in the kitchen. Some, sort of all the girls, all the women and girls, just tidy the house and get all the dinner ready and my dad and all the other men get the *sharab* and everything for when people come... (*Sharab* is) whisky, gin and that.

This suggests a domestic division of labour along gender lines to which young children are accustomed. But it would be unfair to the evidence to describe a uniform scene of women doing all the cooking and serving their husbands and male in-laws. Jyoti was emphatic that her father was a better cook than their mother and it was he who taught his daughter how to cook. Neither he nor their mother was in paid employment. Nor were Arun's parents, although in their case it was his mother (with some help from his elder sister), who did all the cooking and domestic work. In other homes one or both parents earned money in jobs outside the home. This contrasted with some other South Asian commmunities (Nesbitt 1981).

☐ Job Expectations

Like boys, Hindu girls mentioned job aspirations, including being a pilot, which suggested that they and their parents expected them to have careers outside the home. Girls no less than boys enjoyed school sport, learned about equal opportunities at school and looked forward to going out to work. Anita was not alone in holding views that show the generational difference between her and her elders as well as influence of current thinking in the wider society.

> Some of the old people they believe too much. When you get married you stay at home, look after the kids. The men shouldn't do the work, only women should do the work. Now, to my grandad I go that 'It's got to be equal rights', and he goes, 'No, that's not right'. My grandad was in the beginning of the 1900s and so what his parents told him he's telling us and we don't agree with it because now you believe in equal rights, women's lib. They could have just as good a job as a man. Girls are equal with everything and some things they're even better.

Mridula's views were even less in line with traditional assumptions. She drew a distinction between, 'this country now', and 'India'. When asked whether someone who didn't wish to get married would be persuaded to do so by the family, Mridula said:

> But it still goes on in India I reckon. They want their kids to make a life out of themselves. They reckon marriage is the best way, where here nowadays we're saying that career, a job and that's the best way. It's up to the person herself or himself.

☐ Attitude to Marriage

When asked whether she herself wished to marry, Mridula said:

I don't want to get married. It depends on your luck as well and your husband. If you get on well with your husband, if he doesn't keep saying that you've got to follow his family's rules and do as his mum and dad say, you get on fine. As long as you don't tell him that he's got to follow your mum and dad's rules as well, it's all right. But if one side says, 'You've got to listen to what I say', it wrecks the marriage, and so I wouldn't get married.

Further research would be required to determine any correlation between age, Gujarati or Punjabi 'ethnicity' or other factors and the children's thoughts about getting married. Mridula's sentiments may not have differed markedly from those of her elder relatives as she had been brought up by two aunts, one single and one divorced.

Nevertheless the children generally took it for granted that they would get married in due course and they were very aware of gender-specific responsibilities. Interviewees articulated clearly the gender-differentiated family roles which lay ahead of them. Quotations from just two, Deepak (as noted in chapter two, a twelve year old Punjabi boy of Khatri caste) and secondly a nine year old girl of Valmiki background, sum up the expectations of all:

You've got responsibilites. When I grow up my parents will be old. Then they can't take care of themselves. They need someone to take care of them. Then my two sisters will marry, won't they, so it'll be up to me.

I'm not looking forward to being married. I want to stay at home and look after my parents when they're old. If I married I would have to live in a different house and only visit sometimes. I suppose I'll have to. Everyone does.

Perhaps when they are a few years older girls will be more aware of possible tensions to be faced in accepting both the equal opportunities approach and the traditional family roles.

☐ Behaviour Expected of Girls

Certainly the older girls whom we interviewed were aware of the behaviour, including diet, expected of them as they grew older. Girls also voiced awareness of stricter rules for clothing as they got older. Two Punjabis referred to this. One mentioned that in front of visitors she must wear a *chunni* (a gauzy scarf integral to Punjabi suits). This girl also remarked that, as a prospective job, 'modelling some clothes would not be respectable' and that she must do something which 'the boy's side (ie her future in-laws) would approve of'.

Although girls wear Western fashion, skirts and trousers, they accept that sometimes, especially for such occasions as marriages, *satsangs*, and other corporate religious events they will wear Indian clothes. The Punjabis, like their mothers, wear a *salvar kamiz* or *kurta pajama*, two types of tunic-like top and traditional trousers, often with a *chunni*, although they seldom use this to cover their heads. Often these suits are made by their mothers. With Gujaratis too 'Punjabi suits' have become popular in recent years for girls (although not so much for married women). These suits, ready-made and stylish, dispense with any head covering. The Gujaratis' regional dress is the *chaniyo choli*, an embroidered full length skirt with a brief blouse. A decorative *chunri*, a length of lighter-weight material, is draped over the *chaniyo choli*. Girls enjoy wearing these on festive occasions. After marriage Hindu girls realise that their mother-in-law may well influence what they wear. On her may depend the extent to which they are expected to wear a sari. As one said, 'If you're Hindu you wear a sari if you're married'. Clothes are a topic of more consequence and comment for girls than they are for boys and are one of the ways in which the gender boundary is marked.

Some earlier studies of Hindus and 'Hinduism' have been completely male, brahminical and middle class. Partly in reaction to this imbalance, women have written recently about Hinduism, stressing the key role of women in the perpetuation of Hindu tradition. For example a journal for teachers of religious education focused upon women and included contributions by V. Sharada, Penny Logan, Carrie Mercier and Rashmibala Pandya on the role of women.[12] It would be untrue to the evidence, however, to suggest that in general either boys or girls are more steeped in ritual observance or more aware of expected roles simply by virtue of their gender.

☐ Conclusion

To date, as noted in chapter one, little has been written about the religious upbringing of Hindu children either in India or elsewhere. Children's experience of their tradition has received little attention in studies of Hindu communities and children have not been taken seriously as informants by many ethnographers. Penny Logan's research in London from 1984 to 1986 is a notable exception (Logan 1988a and b; 1989a). She notes gender differences in her description of children's lives. In writing of fasting, for example, Logan observes:

> Girls tend to know more about these matters than boys, due to their closer involvement in domestic work... Girls are also more expert in this domain, because they may well fast themselves (Logan 1989a:51-52).

The Coventry findings have corroborated Logan's observations as far as particulars such as fasting were concerned. But they have also shown that the level of engagement with Hindu tradition varies not so much with gender as with individual and family preference. Gender did not determine the degree of involvement in daily worship at the home shrine or in temple activities, but, as we have noted, on certain occasions there are ritual roles for boys and girls which are gender-specific. These commence before the children concerned can remember, but by watching other children in these roles, and seeing photographs and videos of occasions in their own infancy, children's awareness of gender distinctions is reinforced. However a greater degree of differentiation need not mean correspondingly increased discrimination, at least in the eight to thirteen year old age group. Girls participate fully in both religious and school activities. The possible disjunction between gendered role models and expectations at home and assumptions both voiced and implicit among teachers and peers is examined elswhere (Nesbitt 1993).

Social life frequently involves kin, rather than unrelated friends, even when family members are widely dispersed. Observation suggests that through their involvement in family life children became increasingly familiar with the roles expected of them as sons and daughters. They gradually realise the privileges and obligations associated with seniority in the family and within specific kinship ties such as the relationship of niece or nephew and maternal uncle. Among children of the age group under observation roles are enjoyed or simply taken for granted, although some girls feel foreboding about their lives after marriage. So far as the present is concerned children had few complaints more serious than an occasional boy's grumble about having to give his sister money at Raksha Bandhan.

Notes

1. The followers of Swaminarayan maintain strict segregation of the sexes. On his visits to Britain no woman is allowed to come into contact with Pramukh Swami, the head of one branch, the Akshar Purushotam Sanstha.

2. At other Coventry venues eg the Shree Krishna Temple and the halls hired by caste societies some men and boys join in some of the *dandiyan* (stick) dances.

3. According to one of the *gurus* Baba was hailed as Shiva Shakti after appearing to be half paralysed. This was because long ago Rishi Bharadwaj went to Kailash to see Shiva and Parvati and cursed her because the intense cold had left him paralysed. A god alway takes on a devotee's suffering. So, by being half paralysed Baba showed that half of him was Shakti (Parvati). This phenomenon of having both a male and female half is described by Haraldsson (1987: 107).

4. See Jaffrey (1985: 16-20) for one version of this story.

5. Hershman provides a detailed account of the treatment of hair by Hindu and Sikh Punjabis:

> No Punjabi woman will wash her hair or clothes on Tuesday (the most ill-starred day of the week) unless she wants to commit sorcery with the water dripping from her hair which is especially empowered on that day. (1974:281)

6. Another occasion for celebrating the arrival of a son during the previous twelve months is the Punjabi festival of Lohri which usually falls on January 13th. In Britain the festival is marked in a more cursory way than in India, but a small fire is lit and the baby is held up carefully near the flames while seasonal Punjabi sweets are dropped on the fire and distributed.

7. Boys in Britain often receive their sacred threads from a visiting spiritual master such as Swami Satyamitranand Giri at a corporate public event. Bhavesh was twelve but, as was apparent in the large scale *yagnopavita* ceremony which was conducted in Leicester in May 1987, candidates can range in age from infants to young men. On the day of a marriage the *pandit* often invests male members of a Brahmin family with the *janeu* (sacred thread).

8. *Kanjakan* (singular: *kanjak*) are mentioned by Hershman (1977) who also describes the association between pock diseases and the goddess (p 63). For an account of *goyani* see Logan (1989a).

9. For details of the Santoshi Ma cult see Chapter five.

10. In other communities it is the bride and groom who compete in untying each other's threads.

11. But see Nesbitt (1980) for mention of Bhatra Sikhs who continue this practice.

12. See Erricker and Barnett (1988) and McDonald (1987).

CHAPTER 5

Food and Fasts

☐ Ideas about Food Preparation

What Hindus eat and their ideas about food are a significant strand in Hindu tradition. As Mridula said, by implication contrasting Hinduism with Sikhism:

> If you're Hindu, being religious or not shows in your food, what you cook, not (in not) cutting your hair.

The divergence between the children's homes and the rest of their environment was particularly obvious in the area of food. Much of the food prepared at home differs from food at school and elsewhere in its ingredients, spiciness, smell, consistency and colour, and the manner in which it is presented, served and eaten, using the right hand rather than cutlery. These are the aspects on which children may fear their non-Asian schoolmates' suspicious or derisory comment. The different underlying assumptions dictating how foods are prepared, and when they are eaten or avoided, are less immediately obvious and children may have difficulty in articulating them. Hindu children are faced implicitly, and sometimes explicitly, with presuppositions about food of which their non-Asian teachers or peers usually have no inkling.

When Mridula described her grandmother as 'very religious', the way in which she elaborated this statement shows the centrality of food-related assumptions to her concept of 'being religious'.

> She doesn't let anybody eat on her plate, she doesn't let anybody touch her plate. She takes her food out before we have our food. Whether she

57

eats it before us or not she takes it out of the pan, and keeps it separate from ours. (Otherwise) all the food would become the same. She says we don't wash our hands, we've got dirty hands. And she has a bath every day and we're not allowed in her room with our shoes on.

Here Mridula was describing the concept of *jutha* (*ethu* in Gujarati).

Jutha food has been rendered impure by contact, however indirect, with another's saliva. But that does not mean that the term refers only to hygiene in the Western sense. Clearly food in which others had dipped cutlery which had touched their mouths would be both *jutha* and unhygienic. But *jutha* refers also to the food left over on someone's own plate and, as Mridula's comments on her grandma's practice shows, the concern for ritual purity goes beyond the requirements of Western food hygiene. Indeed followers of Pushtimarg and some other Hindu sects may refuse to accept cooked food from all but those whom they know to observe the same strict rules.[1]

At the other extreme a Valmiki Hindu contrasted her community with others who would not share even a friend's plate, because the food would be *jutha*. What is significant is that despite the dissimilarity of practice both girls shared a concept regarding food which is unfamiliar to non-Asian peers and which both regarded as part and parcel of religion. For Anita the *jutha* principle was not only observed in food preparation at home but was also a subject of instruction in Bal Vikas classes.[2] Her *guru* emphasised that when serving food the spoon must never touch people's plates. If it did so the food would become *ethu.*

In Bal Vikas Anita and her friends received instruction on food, health and hygiene. They learned that a prayer must be said before eating (see chapter seven). They were taught that food is affected by the thoughts of the cook. This point was illustrated in the story of a *sannyasi* who committed theft as a result of eating food prepared by someone whose mind was intent on stealing.[3]

Anita also heard in Bal Vikas that food must be eaten on the day on which it is cooked. In the climate of the Indian plains, particularly before the days of refrigeration, this was clearly advisable for health reasons. The reasons given by the *guru* were 'scientific'. He explained that obviously the mould which appears on stale food must be present before it can be seen by the human eye.

Hindu children not only have a shared awareness of religiously acceptable practices for preparing and serving food. They are also aware that food falls into different categories, some of which are more acceptable than others in religious terms.

☐ Classification of Food

Although children did not use this classification, in Hindu tradition foods are divided according to their *guna* (inherent quality). These qualities are *tamas* (darkness or dullness) *rajas* (activity) and *sattva* (purity). So *tamasik* foods are ones which increase sloth and lust. This category includes flesh and alcoholic drinks. The diet of a strict vegetarian consists of *sattvik* foods such as milk products and pulses which advance the consumer's spiritual progress.[4] Those who eat *sattvik* food are believed to develop *sattvik* qualities.

According to traditional medicine all foods are also classified as 'hot' or 'cold' because of their intrinsic properties and effects. This classification is widely accepted in South East Asia too. The terms 'hot' and 'cold' have nothing to do with the temperature at which food is served or with its spiciness. Peanuts are 'hot' and so are popular in India in winter. They would be avoided if someone was in a 'hot' condition such as pregnancy or during very hot weather. Oranges are 'cold' so orange juice would be less appropriate in winter than summer. Gujarati cuisine differs from Punjabi, and there are many variations within each of these regional styles, but underlying both there is a shared understanding of the significance of categories of food.

☐ Meat

When asked during interviews in 1986, 'What would you notice most if you lived in a non-Hindu home?' many children referred to meat consumption. More children said that beef, rather than meat in general, should be avoided. As reasons for avoiding beef, children referred to the cow as holy, as a mother, as associated with 'God' and 'Krishna' and as the giver of milk. According to one thirteen year old Gujarati girl:

> The cow's holy, and you're not supposed to throw milk away, because that comes from the cow. We wouldn't let it (go sour). Normally if we have too much milk we make yoghurt out of it.

Some children mentioned the nastiness, from the animal's point of view, of being killed. In the words of one Gujarati boy who attended Bal Vikas classes (run in accordance with the teaching of Sathya Sai Baba who preaches strict vegetarianism):'Would you like to be killed, because really you might one day be a chicken'. The effect on the killer or consumer of the slaughtered animal was also mentioned: 'If you eat pork, right, you'll be like a pig'. This may determine a person's future birth. In the words of a Punjabi girl:

> My uncle told me, if there was an animal and I killed it and ate it myself, then in my next life I would be the animal and the animal would be the person who killed me, and I'd see how I like it.

In practice, however, not only some of the children but also their elders frequently ate meat.

Children are faced within their own community with a variety of responses to the question of meat eating. It is far from being simply a divergence between a Brahminical Hindu culture at home and Western culture outside. This came over clearly in the words of a teacher at the Sri Sathya Sai Centre, Bradford:

> A lot of parents tend now to be non-vegetarian. Coming to England they've become non-vegetarian. The kids want to become vegetarian because I've taught them. They say, 'Why do you not eat meat?' so I explain to them. A lot of the kids have become vegetarian (whereas) in India it's fashionable to eat meat now.

Clearly it is the religious movements, rather more than Brahminical culture which are emphasising vegetarianism. Thus, for example, the grandma of a Punjabi boy from a very low caste who 'just started believing in God so much that she became vegetarian', was greatly influenced by the teachings of Radhasoami.[5] A Punjabi Hindu mother from another low caste had become totally vegetarian after hearing the preaching of Darshan Das, a Punjabi *sant* (religious leader) based in Birmingham.[6]

The impact of *gurus* and religious movements on people's attitude to diet was noticeable. In the Ayra Samaj, Ealing, teenagers were encouraged to make speeches during the weekly Sunday programme. Speaking on vegetarianism a girl gave many reasons, some based on scientific research. Her statement that Jesus was a vegetarian reflected the view (also voiced by some Sikhs with reference to Guru Nanak) that no one so holy could conceivably have eaten flesh. Followers of Radhasoami and Darshan Das avoid non-vegetarian food and stress the importance of avoiding meat.

In some castes meat-eating is expected and accepted. Sarita's grandfather commented that 'we' (ie members of the Prajapati caste) 'eat meat and drink'(ie alcohol). He added that members of the caste would ask for vegetarian food, for example, on air flights simply to avoid being given beef.

It is sometimes assumed that the lowest castes eat meat whereas the highest castes do not.[7] However the Kshatriya (warrior) castes have a tradition of meat eating whereas (though ritually ranked below them) the merchant castes of Gujarat do not. Children's home diet depends more on the family's allegiance to a particular spiritual teacher than on caste.

Both vegetarianism and non-vegetarianism can be justified by reference to Hindu scripture and its divergent interpretations. Thus a Valmiki Hindu girl expressed her family's view of history disenchanted with Brahminism:

Some people don't eat meat or beef or egg. In olden days people used to eat beef but someone just came to India and just made up that your mother gives you milk and the cow gives you milk so if you eat meat that's from a cow then you're going to eat your mother. And I don't think that's really good because in the olden days people just used to eat beef and the priests, the pandits, they used to eat beef themselves. They didn't let anyone else eat beef because the cow gives you milk and if everyone starts eating it then all the cows will be finished. My dad told me.

In other words the speaker is reporting a low-caste argument that beef-eating is primordial and therefore right. It is implied that Brahmins prohibit this, using specious arguments to do so, in order to keep beef for themselves.[8]

Latitude where meat eating is concerned is not traditional for the Brahmin castes, but many Brahmins are happy to have adapted to British norms. It is not unusual, especially outside the home — and of course outside any religious context — for a Brahmin knowingly to eat meat including beef. However, Bhavesh, a Gujarati Anavil Brahmin, said:

Brahmins don't eat meat. There's lower classes that eat meat. You pray more. The lower classes, they forget because they eat meat and they drink.

Bhavesh was attending Bal Vikas classes and so the family's traditional attitudes were reinforced by the teaching of Sathya Sai Baba. In Coventry, children like Anita who were present at the Dasehra celebrations of Midlands Bal Vikas groups heard a *guru* from Wolverhampton say:

My own son was eating meat. Baba asked my son, 'What does Sai Gita (ie Sathya Sai Baba's pet elephant) eat?' He said, 'Grass'. 'Yes,' said Baba. 'She is always with me. The lion eats meat and stays far away in the jungle.'

Here the message is clear: carnivores are less close to the divine than herbivores are.

ISKCON's teaching also totally prohibits non-vegetarian food. The movement has published a book of vegetarian recipes (Adiraja dasa 1984). All the children who were interviewed whose families were associated with ISKCON said that meat should not be eaten although not all adhered to this in practice. Deepak said:

I've heard some Hindus eat beef. They shouldn't really because they're cows. But if you go to any devotee of ISKCON they'll always say 'No meat'. It's the regulation, they keep it, because you're killing an animal which is God's. We're all the same really, but it's even more important not to eat beef than other (sorts of meat) because it (ie the cow) gives you the milk.

☐ The Meaning of 'Vegetarian'

As taught by teachers in these movements and as understood by Hindu families in Britain, vegetarianism means avoidance of any food that contains animal flesh or fat or any fish or eggs. It does not mean being vegan, as dairy products are highly regarded. Fish is not part of the traditional diet of the Hindu Punjabi or Gujarati families who have come to Britain. When asked if Gujarati Hindus ate fish Arun's mother said she thought that 'low castes' did. Eggs are not eaten by Hindu vegetarians although some would eat cake which they knew to contain egg. Two Gujarati children who attended Bal Vikas mentioned eggless birthday cakes — one (Anita) for a celebration of Sathya Sai Baba's birthday, the other (Bhavesh) for a family birthday party. Since the age of seven, he said, he had only eaten cakes made without eggs.

Pushtimargis, such as Mridula's grandmother, are strictly vegetarian. The word by which they themselves and other Gujaratis refer to Pushtimargis is *'vaishnav'*, a word for a Vaishnavite or follower of Vishnu, and in common parlance this word is used with the meaning of 'vegetarian' as in *'vaishnav bhojan'* i.e. vegetarian food. Mridula's grandmother herself was 'a proper vegetarian', she ate no onion or garlic, carrots or red water melon.[9] Because of the association with blood certain reddish foods are avoided by adherents of some religious movements although Mridula's grandmother ate red chillies and tomato puree. Onions and garlic are widely believed to increase lust.

Mridula was used to these dietary restrictions and accepted that they were 'religious' in nature but was perplexed by them. When a Pushtimargi teacher came to Mridula's house and answered devotees' questions the question uppermost in Mridula's mind was 'why are we forbidden to eat carrots?' She could understand why non-vegetarian food might be taboo, even why onions and garlic were forbidden, but why carrots and watermelon? Nor could she explain why Pushtimargi leaders ate only food cooked in coconut water, never in tap water. The juice from an unripe coconut, a popular beverage in India, is regarded as pure whereas tap water may have come into contact with polluting substances.[10]

Mridula's comments also introduced the factors of age, sex and initiation with reference to diet. Mridula said that she was allowed to eat meat but that as she grew older she would have to stop, according to her grandmother. This, Mridula remarked, was more the case for girls than for boys. Her grandmother's attitude reflects a widely-held belief in India that after puberty a girl's sexual instincts are increased by eating flesh and other *tamasik* food. It was since she 'had *brahmasambandh*' (initiation by the *guru*) that 'they think

I should stop'. Like her aunt she had taken *brahmasambandh* apparently primarily to be able to assist her grandmother in preparing and serving food for other Pushtimargis who would not accept food from an uninitiated person.

☐ Foods Eaten by the Children

Aware though she was of the dietary implications of her religion, Mridula showed a readiness to eat Western food, whether or not she liked it, rather than make a fuss. This attitude she contrasted with a non-Indian friend's attitude to Gujarati food. For instance Mridula enjoyed a dish which her grandmother makes from green bananas fried with sugar but the English friend said she wanted chips and beans instead. By contrast, although Mridula did not like hamburgers she would eat these when her friend prepared them.

Many children and their elders accept that they will follow different norms inside the home from those operating outside. Many eat meat outside but would not expect it to be prepared in their family's kitchen. Where parents or supplementary class teachers explain dietary rules and give reasons the children more readily uphold these even in school. Arun, Bhavesh, Hitesh and Anita were vegetarian at home and outside.

☐ Food and Water used in Ritual

In the domestic shrine and in the public temple, offerings (*naivedya*) to the deity will be *sattvik* substances — milk, Indian sweets, nuts, sultanas, sugar crystals (*misri*), fruit and it is these which (as *prashad* or a sign of God's grace) will be taken and shared afterwards. A *thali* (circular steel tray) of cooked food will be offered for God's blessing before the family and others present are served at the close of corporate worship in the home. Such food is always vegetarian.[11] In anticipation of chapter eight, it is worth noting that one substance consumed after worship by devotees of Sathya Sai Baba is a fine, white powdery ash, *vibhuti*. Whereas other substances consumed in a ritual context are also eaten as part of people's normal diet, *vibhuti* is a substance of a different order.

Water may also convey divine grace. In particular the water of the Ganges (*Ganga jal*) and the Jamuna river. Holy water is kept in a metal vessel in the domestic shrine. A few drops will be added to the tap water which is distributed at the conclusion of worship. Gujaratis celebrate a joyous *loti utasav* (pot festival) when a container of hallowed water from India is ceremonially opened by hammering a nail through the metal sealing the top of the pot.[12]

☐ *Amrit*

This word, from the same Indo-European root as 'immortal', is used by Punjabis for holy water. For Sikhs it denotes especially the sweetened water with which candidates are formally initiated into the Sikh community. Punjabis also use the term *amrit* for water which has been kept under the 'platform' supporting the scriptures while they are being read aloud. One ten year old Valmiki girl's mother kept a bottle of this in the domestic shrine. She would sprinkle some around the house and give some to anyone who was afraid.

Another Valmiki girl mentioned that at the Golden Temple there is:

> precious water. It's like *amrit* and they duck themselves under it. They drink it. You can get *amrit* in this country as well. It's like when mum went to Maharaj. He gave her some.[13]

The girl's mother said that after more than a year they still had plenty and 'it hadn't gone green or anything' The holy water must, she said, be kept in a clean place, and must not be touched by a menstruating woman. In these ways *amrit* resembles other holy water such as *Ganga jal.*

☐ Periodic Abstinence

Whether their families were strictly vegetarian or not, children were accustomed to the fact that at certain times only particular foods, all of them vegetarian, were appropriate. For example Valmiki Hindu children said that one day each week (Tuesday or Thursday) was the day for family worship and that no egg, fish or meat would be eaten in the house on that day. When one Rajput girl proposed making ice-cream at home the following Monday her mother reacted immediately. In her family meat eating was traditional and her husband's take-away sold meat curries, but ice-cream requires eggs and on Monday, Lord Shiva's day, she would not like to have any non-vegetarian food in the house. Deepak's cousin said she was not a vegetarian, but she would not eat eggs on a Tuesday.

In school a child may avoid eating something, usually because it contains eggs, fish or meat, which would be acceptable on other days of the week. This can be a source of bafflement to non-Hindu staff whereas Hindu adults and children accept that on particular days only strictly vegetarian food is appropriate.

Children were familiar with the foods that marked particular festivals. Punjabis have corn meal *roti* and mustard leaf followed by *khir* (rice pudding) at Lohri, for instance. Festivals not only mean special delicacies or seasonal dishes, they also involve self-denial as many Hindus abstain from specified foods on these days.[14] Usually adult members of the family observe this more assiduously than children, but thanks to teachers in supplementary classes, roles may be reversed. Thus the Director of Vidya Vihar, a Hindu supplementary school in Harrow, mentioned the case of one pupil who had learned about the key features of the festival of Mahashivaratri in class on the preceding Saturday. When he came downstairs on Mahashivaratri day he found breakfast laid as usual, but he refused to eat. In answer to his parents' enquiries he explained that he had learned that on Mahashivaratri only fruit, nuts and milk were allowed. His family were impressed and joined him in keeping the religious rules.

☐ *Vrat*

In many Hindu families some members observe stricter dietary rules on one day of the week or for a certain period than at other times, and usually only one meal is eaten on the days concerned. This is in observance of a *vrat*, a 'vow'. A *vrat* usually entails abstention from certain foods for a specified period, the reading or hearing of the relevant *katha* (story) illustrating the importance of keeping the *vrat* and the performance of the appropriate act of worship, followed by distribution of specified foods. Most *vrats* are observed by women although some, like the Saturday *vrat* for Hanuman, are kept by men. The goal is family welfare — in most instances the husband's (Bhattacharya 1957). Thus Arun's mother was 'fasting' in the hope that her husband would find a permanent job. The fast for the goddess Jivantika Ma, mentioned by Bhavesh's mother, is kept by Gujarati women in the hope of bearing children or for the good health of their children.

The word 'fast' was often used by children to translate '*vrat*' although in English fast has the meaning of abstaining from all food (*upavas* in Hindi). Sunil and Jyoti did not use the word 'fast' but '*barat*' (pronounced rather like Bert with a Scottish 'r'), the Punjabi form of *vrat*.

In Coventry many *vrats* are observed by Hindus. There are weekly, monthly and annual *vrats* and ones which are not dependent on the calendar. Shah's Pan House, a local Gujarati retailer's, stocks booklets containing the *kathas* and ritual requirements for a dozen or so *vrats*. For example the *Saptvar Vrat Katha* is a Hindi booklet containing details of the *vrats* that are kept on particular days of the week.

Not only do the names for the days of the week indicate — as in European languages — association with divinised planets, but for each day of the week there is an appropriate story and ritual procedure relating to a certain deity. Individuals may observe one day's *vrat* weekly throughout much of their lives or for a previously determined number of weeks or until a wish is fulfilled. So, for example, many women decide to observe the *vrat* of the goddess

Santoshi Ma (the 'mother who gives contentment') on successive Fridays.[15] Arun's mother fasted on sixteen successive Thursdays, praying to the revered saint, Shirdi Sai Baba.[16] On the Fridays of the lunar month of Shravan, Bhavesh's and Anita's mothers observed the *vrat* of the goddess Jivantika Ma. *Ekadasi* is observed twice a month. Known as *agiaras* by Gujaratis, this is the eleventh day of either the waxing or waning half of a lunar month. It is of particular importance to Vaishnavite Hindus.[17] A thirteen year old Gujarati girl was aware of the connection between the phases of the moon and fasting, although her statement shows confusion over the actual day on which *ekadasi* is observed:

'It's when there's a full moon or half moon. That's called *ekadasi.*'

Other *vrats* occur annually. Examples are the *vrats* of Karva Chauth, which falls between Dasehra and Divali, and Jaya Parvati which is observed during the summer month of Asadh (June — July).[18]

The observance of *vrats* is part of Hindu pragmatism, an attempt to strike a bargain with a deity, so bypassing the otherwise unavoidable effects of *karma*. This is clearly expressed by Deepak who had heard a lecture on *ekadasi* delivered by a follower of ISKCON.

It's a day on which fasts are kept. It was derived a long time ago. You can't eat grains. You can have fruit, a glass of milk and you can eat once or twice in that day. You can get rid of all the bad things you've done in your *karma*.

Many people may also believe that by observing a *vrat* associated with a deity they acquire the qualities of that deity.[19]

Many Hindu adults regard *vrats* as unnecessary or as misguided superstition. Anita had clear views on the subject.

I don't do *vrats* because I think that means you're always asking God for something. I think he's given you enough — food, clothing and so on.

The degree to which children were involved varied but they all accepted as a natural part of life that at certain times someone in the family would be abstaining from particular food neither for medical reasons nor to lose weight but as a religious act.

They were often only vaguely aware of *vrats*, sometimes remembering the name, sometimes only a salient feature, usually dietary. They hardly understood or remembered anything of the stories which their mothers read as an integral part of the *vrat*, even in the case of Arun who heard the *katha* of the Dharamraja *vrat* daily for six months and was fully involved in the surrounding procedure. Before having tea, and well before the children had to leave for school, his mother would read the *katha* each morning. Arun's role was to keep punctuating the narrative with the word '*dharamraja*'. Half the *punya* (merit), which is believed to accrue from faithful observance of the *vrat*, would pass to whoever did this, his mother explained. She and Arun had to hold five rice grains, stained yellow with food colour, in their right hand. After the *katha* they threw these to the birds.

On the dietary aspect of *vrats* children had a great deal to say. In part this was based on observation of the older relative who was keeping the *vrat*, as, for example Arun's sister on their father's Saturday *vrat*: 'He's only allowed to eat dinner one time and he's just allowed things like crisps and tea'. Similarly Hitesh had this to say about his grandfather's Saturday *vrat*: 'He can't eat any salt, he can't eat bread. He can only have tea and he can only eat once. He can have fruit.'

Sometimes children spoke from personal experience of keeping the dietary requirements of a *vrat* which a relative was observing. Hitesh had tried fasting with his grandfather on Saturdays but said: 'I started feeling really hungry because you can only eat fruit and fruit makes you even hungrier.'

Some Punjabi girls kept the Karva Chauth *vrat* with their mothers. Before dawn wives can have something to eat and drink. This food, which is consumed before the *vrat*, is called *sargi* and, for young wives, it should be food sent by their parents. Through the day they are allowed to consume neither solid nor liquid. For this reason Jyoti described Karva Chauth as the day 'when my mum couldn't drink water'. A Valmiki girl said that she had started keeping the fast the previous year, but:

> I won't next year because you have to get up at 4 am (and eat). After that you don't even have water. If I was at school I wouldn't do it because if we're fasting on a school day we have to miss all athletics. It's a rule at our school.

In the case of some *vrats* the observance is ineffectual unless children are feasted in the prescribed manner at the conclusion of the appropriate period of fasting. Many children mentioned being involved in this way. Both boys and girls had been invited for the meal which must be provided by any woman who has completed her sequence of Friday *vrats* in honour of Santoshi Ma. In the *katha* it is specified that eight boys must be feasted and they are depicted on some calendar pictures of the goddess.

Most importantly — and the story is a cautionary tale reinforcing this prohibition — on the Fridays of the fast nothing at all acid such as tomatoes or apples may be eaten.[20] If the children who had been invited to eat swallowed any sour substance on the final day, or even bought anything at all sour with any money they received, the fast would be invalidated. To quote Arun's sister:'We're allowed to eat, but not anything with lemon in.'

Similarly, as described in chapter four, other *vrats* in honour of a goddess require the participation of *goyani* (the Gujarati term for young girls or married women who are not menstruating) or *kanjakan* (the Punjabi word for prepubertal girls) who are ritually fed before anyone else can eat. In her description of being a *goyani* Anita described being given the ritual meal by the hostess:

> They usually put lots of food inside your plate, you know all the nice things. Then the person who's actually doing the *goyani* (ie the hostess) she comes round taking a bit of your *chapati* with some rice pudding — *khir* and that — and then she puts it in a little plate, and you can only break your fast after that, and after that really you can eat anything.

In such cases the hostess had to take a small amount of *chapati* and rice pudding from the plate of each of the girls. As they represented the goddess, their *jutha* (left over food) was her *prashad*.

The foods required or forbidden on *vrats* vary considerably. On the days when Arun's mother fasted and prayed to Shirdi Sai Baba she would eat only once and the meal consisted of spinach and *khichri* (lentils and rice cooked together). The meal to which friends and relatives were invited at the conclusion of the *vrat* included, as prescribed, *khichri,* spinach and thick brown *rotlo* (*chapati*) made from millet flour.

On *ekadasi*, according to a Gujarati girl: 'You only eat fresh things. You can't eat onions or garlic.' According to Deepak, who did not himself observe the *ekadasi vrat*:

> You can't eat any grains. You can have fruit, a glass of milk and you can eat once or twice in that day.

On *ekadasi* Arun had special food cooked by his mother — potato crisps, shredded much finer than those that are commercially available, and a mixture of yoghurt, potato and chopped peanuts.[21] Foods such as these, which are generally acceptable when someone is fasting, are called *pharari* (Logan 1989a).

Sometimes the words which Gujarati children used for particular *vrats* were Gujarati terms for the dietary requirement. Thus Hitesh and his sister used the name '*aluna*' for the Jaya Parvati *vrat. Aluna* means 'no salt'. Anita used the Gujarati words for 'cold food' to refer to Shitala Satam, a *vrat* on which no food can be cooked.

Children were also aware of other aspects of *vrats*. They mentioned requirements not related to food. So Anita explained that on the days of the *vrat* of Jivantika Ma her mother must wear nothing yellow, and so had to remove her *mangalsutra*, the necklace of black beads and gold which was given to her on her wedding day.[22]

Children frequently mentioned the gifts which they would receive at the conclusion of a *vrat* in which they were involved. Speaking about being a *goyani* at the conclusion of a *vrat* to the goddess Anita said:

> The girls usually get *supari* (betel nut) with a five pence coin wrapped with a handkerchief and a little bowl.

She also mentioned that married women who acted as *goyanis* would be given '*suhagan*', the items signifying the status of a wife such as *sindur* (the red powder with which married women may mark the parting of their hair), a red blouse, a necklace, mirror and comb.

From their experience of Karva Chauth Punjabi girls described the procedure. Jyoti and Ritu said that their hands had been patterned with *mehndi* (henna paste). Ritu described how in the evening her mum's friends came to visit. In the house they had passed a round tray around, counting the number of times they did so. Each of the three women had a plate which was filled with almonds with an oil light in the middle. Someone told the story which, Ritu thought, was about a woman pretending to be a man's wife.[23] They had sung a song, then gone outside to 'spill water', pouring it from a glass.

The children realised that the *vrats* were observed with a purpose. Concerning Karva Chauth a Valmiki Hindu girl wrote in her diary:

> A wife fasts for her husband to give him a long life. She has to wait until the moon comes out. Then she can break her fast.

Asked why his grandfather fasted on Saturday Hitesh said:

> My grandad told me it gives good luck if you do it for seven weeks. My grandad keeps going but my uncle did it for seven weeks and he still hadn't got any luck.

In some cases failure to observe certain requirements was seen as likely to cause misfortune. For example, although she had reservations about her own performance of *vrats*, Anita was aware of a connection between the *vrat* of Shitala Satam and her father's well-being. Shitala is the goddess associated with pock diseases.[24] Anita knew that her father could bathe only in cold water on the day of the *vrat,* and no cooking was allowed. Otherwise he would 'come out in spots'. She explained:

> You have to turn off the gas where it's controlled. Shitala Ma comes as a visitor in the night and sits on the gas.

Anita described Randhan Chhathh, the eve of Shitala Satam, as the day when 'you make lovely things' to be eaten cold the next day. In general children spoke positively about *vrats*. Involvement, to whatever degree, strengthens their sense of solidarity with older relatives and peers who are also participating. On Karva Chauth Punjabi girls feel a challenge similar to that experienced by Muslim children during Ramazan (Ramadan). They also enjoy having their hands decorated with *mehndi*. Gujarati girls enjoy the climax of the Jaya Parvati *vrat*. Hitesh described this, saying that his sister and female relatives would:

> all go to my cousin's house, all the women and they watch a film all night.
> It's something to do with the religion or sometimes they just buy a normal
> Indian film.

This all night session of Indian films from about 10 pm to 6 am, the climax of the *vrat*, is a recent development, popular with the girls concerned, but not approved of by all adults.[25]

☐ Conclusion

On the subject of food generally, although many of the children sometimes ate Western and Indian non-vegetarian food, the majority nevertheless perceived their diet, with an emphasis on vegetarianism, as a key feature of their religion. They shared a common awareness of an association between their religion and patterns of food consumption and avoidance.

Although some Western foods are vegetarian and *sattvik* by the strictest Hindu criteria, there is little sign of the range of foods associated with ritual extending to include these. Plain unflavoured potato crisps and boiled fruit sweets at children's events are, so far, almost the only change in this direction. As with dress, so with food, a line is increasingly apparent dividing the everyday, secular and Western from the special, religious and Indian. Even in families who readily socialise in Western style their ritual occasions will be distinguished by vegetarian foods prepared in the style traditional in Punjab or Gujarat.

As far as *vrats* are concerned our observation suggests that, in general, British Hindu children are familiar with the idea of *vrat* although the observances of different families and of their individual members differ widely. Adults mentioned more fasts than children did and could give more details than children.[26] Children tended to know some of the requirements but almost nothing of the *katha* (story) related during each *vrat*. Children noted and accepted uncritically that individual adults would change their regimen — from non-vegetarian to vegetarian or from the restriction of (say) a Tuesday to the lack of taboos on the following day of the week.

It seems likely that many children will adopt some variation of this flexibility, much as girls change from Western to Indian dress as the context demands. It is unlikely that the growing generation will altogether abandon the practice of *vrat*. This is partly because they have happy memories of *vrats* as special occasions shared with members of their family and community. Some women are aware that regular abstinence, like Western dieting, can contribute to health and a slim figure. Most importantly, when a family is beset by trouble which doctors and others seem unable to dispel, the observance of *vrats* can reduce individual frustration and despair, giving members a sense of helping through their disciplined, self-sacrificial action. Furthermore *vrats* are responsive to current trends as shown by the all night film session with which the Jaya Parvati *vrat* often concludes.

Notes

1. For a fuller account of Pushtimarg see chapter eight.

2. For Bal Vikas see chapters eight and ten.

3. Belief in the importance of a right state of mind while cooking was expressed by Arun's mother who gave this as one reason for listening to tape-recorded *bhajans* in the kitchen. Similarly another mother (a Pushtimargi) explained the reason why she avoided eating any food which might have been prepared by a menstruating woman was that during her period, a woman's thoughts may turn to sex. According to Lannoy, ingested food is believed to transmit certain qualities in the nature of the donor and the cook (1971:151).

4. For further discussion of the Hindu analysis of diet see Jackson and Killingley (1988). Khare (1976) provides a more detailed study of Hindu gastronomic belief and practice. On the more general issue of Hindu attitudes towards the environment, see Jackson and Killingley (1991).

5. For Radhasoami, also mentioned in chapter eight, see Juergensmeyer (1982 and 1988).

6. Darshan Das, a controversial Punjabi religious leader, was killed by Sikhs in Southall in 1987.

7. Srinivas (1967) argued for a process of Sanskritisation whereby members of an upwardly mobile lower caste emulate ideal Brahmin behaviour. In this process their adherence to a vegetarian diet is a significant factor.

8. We are grateful to Dr Dermot Killingley for his analysis of this interpretation.

9. Compare Stevenson (1971:241) 'neither are vegetables (served) whose juice is red, such as beetroot or tomatoes. No strict Brahman would eat onions or garlic'. Similarly some Jains avoid red foods.

10. Strict Namdhari Sikhs avoid tap water for fear of its possible contact with leather washers.

11. Arun's mother had heard of meat being offered at Taljapur as *naivedya* (offering) and of goats being killed in Calcutta. Worshippers of Kali in Bengal often offer a goat for sacrifice and Brahmins eat the meat.

12. See Jackson and Nesbitt (1990:40).

13. The Golden Temple (Harmandir Sahib) in Amritsar, Punjab, is regarded by Sikhs as their holiest shrine and is respected by Punjabi Hindus. 'Maharaj' is an honorific title bestowed, in this instance, on Darshan Das.

14. For the dietary implications of Navaratri see Logan (1988a).

15. For an excellent, detailed description and analysis of the relatively recent cult of Santoshi Ma see Brand (1979).

16. For details of Shirdi Sai Baba see Sahukar (1983).

17. Several adult informants mention *ekadasi* and heaven almost in one breath. For instance according to one of the *gurus* at Anita's Bal Vikas, people say that you go to heaven if you observe a fast on *ekadasi*. Arun's mother mentioned that it is good to die on *ekadasi* or on Janmastami as heaven's gates are open on those days for the spirit of the deceased to go 'straight to Vaikunth', the *svarga* (heaven) where Vishnu dwells (Stevenson 1971:197).

> The days are not only holy, they are also the luckiest in the month, and hence they are the best days on which to die, and on which to be born. (Stevenson 1971:261)

18. Karva Chauth, a *vrat* observed by Punjabi wives, including many Sikhs, falls between Dasehra and Divali on the fourth day of the dark half of the lunar month of Kartik. The *vrat* of Jaya Parvati lasts for five days, beginning in the bright fortnight of the month of Asadh. For details see Logan (1989) and Bryant (1983:193).

19. This was a point made by Jacqueline Suthren-Hirst who quoted a Hindu girl's words: 'I'm going to fast for Durga when I'm older so I'll be strong and kind' (personal communication).

20. The *katha* translated in Brand (1979) and Howell (1975) and discussed in Kurtz (1984) is available in a booklet, entitled in Hindi *Story of the Friday Fast* (*Shukravar vrat katha*). The booklet outlines the procedure to be followed eg *gur* (unprocessed sugar) and chickpeas are to be offered and no-one in the house may eat anything at all sour such as oranges. When the person's wish has been granted she must complete the fast by feeding eight boys. Because of the Hindi movie, *Jay Santoshi Maa*, children are more familiar with this *katha* than with the *katha* told on other *vrats*. For this reason the story is given here as an example of the genre. The story concerns a woman whose husband was treated badly by his mother. Eventually, realising that she only gave him his brothers' leftovers (*jutha*), he went to another country where he was given a responsible position. His wife fasted on Fridays, praying to Santoshi Ma for him to return to her. Her wish was granted but her jealous sisters-in-law tried to thwart her and told their sons to disobey her, so that she could not conclude the fast appropriately. As a

72

result her husband was taken away by soldiers, but when she managed to conclude the fast to the goddess' satisfaction, happiness was restored to them. The booklet also includes songs to be sung when food is offered to Santoshi Ma and when performing *arati* (rotating the oil lamp in front of her picture).

21. Arun's mother referred to the fact that some people (her own mother for example) would abstain from salt. They would use 'bitter salt', a traditional alternative to sodium chloride.

22. The *katha*, as related by Bhavesh's mother, concerns a virtuous woman who refused to wear yellow.

23. An English version of the story which Ritu mentioned appears in Jaffrey (1985:75-79).

24. For the association of Shitala and pock diseases see Hershman (1977:63). The association in the minds of children growing up in Britain is probably almost non-existent in most cases, but a Valmiki girl made the traditonal connection between Mata (the goddess) and rubella and measles:

> If someone has measles all the girls get together — one boy and six girls. The boy washes the girls' feet. The mother gives the girls dinner, a scarf, bracelets, money — like £1. It's *mata*, German measles.

25. According to Bhavesh's mother, before the days of videos, the women and the girls used to dance and sing all night. Anita's father felt that the religious character of the *jagran* (vigil) had been lost in watching popular movies.

26. Arun's mother mentioned Rishi Panchami, Divaso or Evrat Jivrat and Dhro Atham. Rishi Panchami falls on the fifth day *(pancham)* of the bright fortnight of the month of Bhadrapada. Semolina, rice and potatoes can be eaten. Divaso or Evrat Jivrat falls fifteen days after Jaya Parvati. If a woman observes this *vrat* she must stay awake throughout the following night and day. Stevenson (1971:323) describes Dhro Atham (Durvastami). *(Dhro* is a type of grass used in *puja*). Deepak and Ritu's mother recalled the *vrat* of Ahoi Mata. For their children's welfare, women make a picture of Ahoi Mata and fast until they see the stars .

CHAPTER 6

Festivals

☐ Festivals: a Changing Role

Excited crowds, multicoloured clothes and exuberant outdoor celebration make Hindu festivals a memorable experience for the visitor to India. At Holi the unwary traveller may be bombarded with water balloons, drenched with coloured water or worse. At Divali fireworks explode unpredictably in the streets. The tissue paper kites, flown hazardously from flat rooftops at Makar Sankranti, flutter impotently for weeks thereafter on the overhead wires that have broken their flight. Transiently in the bazaars there appear stalls heaped with vivid powders for Holi or laden with inventively decorative threads to adorn male wrists at Raksha Bandhan. Vendors sell unglazed clay saucers, destined to be oil lamps that light goddess Lakshmi's footsteps on Divali night, or sweetmeats distinctive in form and flavour for whatever festival is imminent. Society is briefly transformed. The year is punctuated by many opportunities to celebrate.[1]

For Hindu children in Britain festivals are fewer and even the major festivals are a more muted experience, but significant nonetheless as enjoyable extras to the lives that they share with their contemporaries.[2] They are also recurrent reminders of a distinct group identity. For Hindu children in a country where Hindus are only a small proportion of the population, festivals accentuate the experience of being in a minority whose special days pass unnoticed by society at large. This is a markedly different experience from the relaxed abandonment and self-confidence of festivals in India where society often seems totally immersed in the celebration.

75

For the interested observer in Britain festivals are hospitable, relaxed opportunities for noting the persistence and adaptability of Hindu tradition. At festivals the processes of cultural transmission, which will be discussed in chapter nine, come more sharply into focus. Ethnic and sectarian groups are both united and differentiated by the details of their observance. Children learn the ancient stories and wear new outfits. In many cases their sense of belonging not only to the Hindu community but to a particular Hindu community — whether based on a region of India, sect or caste — is enhanced.

☐ Uncertainty of the Calendar

Since the dates of Hindu festivals are decided by the lunar calendar, their dates according to the Western calendar move year by year. As a result the children have no sense of a secure, easily remembered, annual sequence of celebrations. Many children are unsure of the month of the Western (Gregorian) calendar in which even familiar festivals are likely to fall. They seldom know the names, let alone the sequence, of months in the Hindu calendars which are consulted by older relatives.[3]

☐ Difficulty of Celebrating

Even among those Hindus for whom a particular festival is important only a minority may be able to celebrate it as school holidays and holidays from work seldom coincide with Hindu festivals. Whereas in many *gurdwaras* Sikh festivals that fall on a weekday are celebrated on the following Sunday, Hindus usually do not make this concession to the British working week. As a result only a minority of those who would otherwise do so may be free to celebrate even a major festival. The birth of Rama is believed to have taken place at noon. So if the festival falls on a school day, children of school age cannot be present for the midday celebration in the temple. By contrast, almost everyone can attend the celebrations of Navaratri because they are held in the evening, mostly starting around seven pm and lasting for three to four hours, and so not clashing with most people's work. Perhaps, too, one reason for the children's familiarity with Raksha Bandhan, a festival which shows no signs of decreasing in popularity, is the fact that it falls during the summer holidays. Rathayatra, a chariot festival observed for the most part in Britain by those with leanings towards Krishna Consciousness (see chapter eight) is organised to fall on a Sunday during the school holidays. Cultural programmes are also often organised on a weekend close to a festival day.

☐ Inclusiveness

Unlike Hindu festivals the date of Christmas by the Western calendar remains constant from year to year. Unlike Hindu festivals it is marked in Britain by a national holiday and dominates pupils' activities especially in primary schools. So Hindu families are more aware of Christmas than of any other annual British festival, hence the tendency to explain Divali as 'our Christmas'. Hindus are happy to share in this midwinter season of generosity and family gatherings. Children also mentioned Easter, Mother's Day, Father's Day, Halloween and Guy Fawkes Day, all part of the primary school cycle of events.

Children are encouraged to share in these occasions. Like birthday parties Christmas, above all, has become part of the family's annual calendar of reunion.

> My friend Sharon is not allowed to celebrate Christmas because she is not allowed by her religion. I can't wait until it really is Christmas.

Here a Valmiki Hindu girl was contrasting her relative freedom with the restrictions on Sharon, a Jehovah's Witness. By contrast with Sharon she had an Advent calendar with chocolates in it and was singing in her school's Christmas programme.

All the Hindu children who were interviewed spoke enthusiastically about Christmas. Together with Divali it topped their list of favourite festivals. Sarita mentioned having more presents than at Divali. Bhavini had enjoyed a Brownie Party, presents and the school lunch of 'turkey, jelly and mince pies'.

Food (for the non-vegetarians English-style roast chicken or turkey), gifts and family reunion characterised children's experience, as did the build-up in school of Christmas quizzes, plays and making Christmas cards and decorations. Christmas trees stood in their families' brightly decorated living rooms for about a month and everyone rushed about shopping. Whereas at Hindu festivals children may have new clothes to wear and the gifts appropriate to each festival, such as money for girls at Raksha Bandhan, at Christmas children get all sorts of toys and other items wrapped in colourful paper.

The children knew the story of Jesus but celebrated Christmas as a secular festival. They did not go to church and there was no recognition of Christmas in the temple, though in at least one home the domestic shrine was decorated and, as we shall see below, for Anita's family Christmas had a religious content.

☐ Diversity

Apart from Christmas, and on a lesser scale other non-Hindu festivals such as Mother's Day and Father's Day, the festivals which Hindu children in Britain celebrate vary according to their parents' region of origin in the Indian subcontinent and the *sampradaya* or particular 'sectarian' tradition which most influences them. As this in some instances is closely linked to their caste (*jati*) it is also true to say that certain festivals or ways of celebrating them are caste-specific. The name by which families know a festival may be different for Punjabis and Gujaratis. The festival's details differ from one regional, sectarian or caste group to another.

☐ Regions of Origin and Regional Names

In Coventry the few Bengali Hindu families celebrate Saraswati Puja on the day when Punjabis may recall their celebration of Basant Panchami in Punjab. Maharashtrians remember the excitement of Ganapati Puja and Tamils miss the colours, sounds and tastes of Pongal. For the much larger Gujarati and Punjabi communities there are festivals and fasts (as we saw in chapter five) peculiar to their region of origin in India. Thus Punjabis do not celebrate Jalaram Jayanti and Gujaratis do not observe Lohri.[4]

Gujarati children talk about Norta, using the vernacular name for the nine nights of Navaratri (the Sanskrit name for the festival) that precede the victorious tenth, Vijay Dashmi or Dasehra. This period is generally known as Durga Puja by Bengalis, who commemorate the goddess Durga's triumph over the buffalo demon, Mahishasur.

Depending on their dialect Punjabi children are more likely to say Rakhi or Rakhri than to use the Sanskrit name Raksha Bandhan. Another day on which sisters honour their brothers is known as Bhaiya Duj by Punjabis and Bhai Bij by Gujaratis.

☐ Regional Emphasis: Holi

Some festivals are celebrated by both Gujaratis and Punjabis but differ in detail and impact. For example on the night of Divali only Gujarati business men assemble to have their new account books blessed by Shri (Lakshmi). Holi also exemplifies this regional differentiation well. This falls on the day of the full moon of the lunar month of Phalguna which overlaps March and April. The festival of Holi generally makes more impact on Britain's Gujaratis than on Punjabis, because of the Gujarati practice of lighting a Holi bonfire.[5] For Gujarati children the festival is more complex and memorable than it usually is for their Punjabi counterparts. Some Gujarati families lit fires at home. Many gathered at the Shree Krishna Temple. All the Gujarati children in the research families participated there.[6]

Just outside the temple wood was stacked in a wigwam-shaped pile, with a shelf around it (for roasting coconuts) half way up. Ganesha *puja* was performed at about 7.30 pm, the couple performing the *puja* having made the highest bid for the honour. After this preliminary *puja* the fire was lit, sometimes with a pennant flying on top of the timber.

If a baby has been born during the previous year in a Gujarati family it is customary to carry the child around the Holi fire, a ritual which is believed to confer a blessing. So Sarita described how her grandmother had carried her cousin round several times 'for good luck'.[7] Whether or not a child has been born during the previous twelve months, someone from each family carries a *loto* (pot) of water or milk and water with a coconut lodged in its neck, and popcorn, roast gram and *jawar* (millet). They walk round clockwise, spilling the water and throwing the coconut and some of the popcorn into the fire. When the coconuts are cooked they are retrieved from the fire with the help of a long stick. Each family (according to Arun's mother) offers half 'to Holi' and the other half is shared as *prashad*. Sarita said that this was the only time of year when she had cooked coconut to eat. Bhavesh mentioned the belief that when the flag fell down from the top of the bonfire the people who lived in the direction to which it pointed would be lucky. Inside the temple in 1987, when the fire had burned down, a *prashad* of popcorn and dates was distributed, an aspect of Holi particularly appreciated by Bhavini. Children's faces are often marked with a smudge of ash from the coconut. This, Bhavesh's mother explained, is like ash from a *havan* (ritual fire), bringing good luck and blessing.

For the Punjabis, on the other hand, Holi in Britain has a much lower profile, though it is marked in some instances by a 'cultural programme'. In 1987, for example, a few Hindu children from Coventry participated in a celebration at a Birmingham temple and watched girls dancing in a pink cloud as they threw red powder over each other.

☐ Sectarian festivals

Followers of different guru-led movements or *sampradayas* observe distinctive festivals in addition to those celebrated by their fellow Gujaratis or Punjabis. Just as Hindu festivals affirm children's sense of belonging to Hindu society, so these annual events strengthen their identity with the *sampradaya* and provide opportunities for learning more of its saints and founders. In chapter eight Rathayatra, Easwaramma Day and other sectarian festivals are described. As many Hindus are influenced in Britain by spiritual teachers with whom their families may have been less acquainted in India, some children in this country celebrate certain Hindu festivals that would not figure in the lives of their relatives who live in India.

Festivals can be occasions for projecting and promoting a group's image among non-members. It is often on such days that the Lord Mayor or some other local dignitaries are invited to a public function. Speeches are made, videos are recorded and the occasion and the community reach a wider public.

Valmik Jayanti demonstrates the efforts of a community which has been oppressed for centuries with poverty and association with a ritually polluting occupation and which is still suffering from the prejudice of higher caste Punjabis. By identifying with Valmik (or Valmiki), a figure revered by other Hindus, Valmikis provide their growing generation with a proud self-image. Valmik Jayanti, celebrated as the anniversary of Valmik's birth, draws community members together for congregational worship on a larger scale than on most other Sundays and instils a sense of caste identity and solidarity. As the following account shows, the celebration of even this non-Sikh anniversary is strongly influenced by Sikh practice in Coventry.[8]

Valmik Jayanti falls during the lunar month before the major Sikh festival of Guru Nanak's birthday on the full moon day of the month of Ashvina, and it is celebrated on the following Sunday. This marks the end of a week during which the *Ramayana* is read daily, but not continuously, in the Valmiki temple. The children stand in the street watching as men climb a ladder to the roof to replace the flagpole, now wrapped from top to bottom in a new red cloth and topped by a triangular pennant, also of new red cloth, on which the Valmiki emblem — a bow and arrow — stands out in silver. This one ceremony is akin to the hoisting of a *nishan sahib* at the festival of Vaisakhi outside the Sikhs' gurdwaras, but the red colour distinguishes the cloth from the saffron colour used by the Sikhs. The flag brings particular excitement to the family whose womenfolk have stitched it and to the family who go home with the treasured cloth from the previous year's flag. One young woman said that they might trim a small child's clothes with pieces of the used flag as *rakh* (protection).

At the 1988 celebrations children wore a ribbon round their necks to which a colourful emblem was attached. This consisted of a picture of Maharishi Valmik surrounded by thirteen circles each of which contained an Indian religious symbol, such as the Hindu *om*, the *khanda* (double edged sword) of the Sikhs, the wheel of Ashoka, a mace and a *swastika* (an auspicious Hindu sign). Such imagery might mean little to children but the central position of Maharishi Valmik made a clear visual point. The celebrations on the Sunday following Valmik Jayanti drew a large congregation. The usual weekly worship was extended with speeches and hymns in praise of Maharishi Valmik.

☐ Guru Ravidas's Birthday

Similarly for Ravidasi children, some of whom regard themselves as Hindu, the Sunday of (or following) Guru Ravidas's birthday is the religious high point of the year, the day when their families are most likely to attend the *gurdwara*. The anniversary falls on the day of the full moon of the lunar month of Magha, approximately February. There is a similar feeling of joyful reunion and of community pride. Video and sound cassettes of hymns in honour of Ravidas were on sale outside the prayer hall in 1989. Thus certain annual festivals strengthen and celebrate the children's identity as members of distinct Valmiki and Ravidasi communities.

☐ Sectarian Emphasis

Valmikis, and members of other caste and sectarian groups, celebrate the major festivals of the Hindu cycle such as Divali, but in some cases with emphases distinctive of their particular community. The festival may also mark a significant stage in their own local history. Thus in 1988 Divali marked a higher point than usual in the lives of Coventry's Valmiki children. Some of them presented songs and dances in their newly opened community centre in the course of a cultural event which was recorded by a television crew.[9] In the prayer hall a passage was read from the *Ramayana* and the point was made that but for Maharishi Valmik, the composer of the *Ramayana*, there would be no Rama and no Divali. Children from other communities would not hear this particular interpretation.

When Coventry followers of the International Society for Krishna Consciousness (ISKCON) contributed to Holi celebrations in Birmingham the aetiological myth of the triumph of the virtuous Prahlada over his evil uncle was retold (see below), but with a sectarian slant, for it was made clear that Prahlada was saved because he knew and repeated the *mahamantra*, 'Hare Krishna, Hare Krishna, Krishna Krishna, Hare Hare'.

In the case of the Hindu spring festival of Holi, sectarian emphasis leaves its mark. For devotees of Pushtimarg (see chapter eight) excitement builds up during the previous month. So Mridula was aware of the approach of Holi as the *satsang* group, of which her grandmother was a member, gathered with greater frequency than during the other months of the year. Her grandmother and her Pushtimargi friends met in each other's houses for *satsang* — singing in praise of Krishna. During this month a woman of the house would liberally streak the other women's faces and white cardigans with *kanku* — red powder). Popcorn was showered over each woman too.

For Sathya Sai Baba's followers (Sai devotees) Navaratri has distinctive features. In addition to the pictures of the goddess, with which Gujaratis in general decorate the polygonal shrine (*garbi*), the apex of the Sai devotees' *garbi* bears emblems of the world's major faiths. As noted in chapter four, men and boys there do not join in the dancing as they do at other venues. The concluding day of Navaratri, Dasehra, also takes on distinctively Sai characteristics. In *bhajans* (hymns) Sathya Sai Baba is equated, as 'Sai Ma', with the goddess, the focus of Hindu devotion on that day. Dasehra is also celebrated as the anniversary of the *samadhi* (merger with the divine) or physical death of Shirdi Sai Baba, the saint of whom Sathya Sai Baba claims to be a reincarnated form.

For Anita and other Sai devotees Christmas, too, has a particular religous significance. At Christmas time the supplementary Bal Vikas class which she attended sang carols in old people's homes and children's homes. They planned to entertain the elderly and the handicapped. Her family were joined by others for a Christmas *bhajan* singing session. A swing for the baby Jesus was hung up in the front of the shrine just as it would be for the birthdays of Rama and Krishna on Ramanavami and Janmashtami respectively. Anita knew that in Prashanti Nilayam, Sathya Sai Baba's headquarters in South India, Christmas was celebrated and Baba himself would appear to the crowds through silver doors which were opened on high days. The distinctive emphasis of Sathya Sai Baba's devotees results from the belief that Sathya Sai Baba is Jesus just as he is, for example, Vishnu, Shiva, Parvati and the Buddha incarnate.

☐ Adaptation to the British Environment

From their relatives' descriptions, from their own visits to India and from video films, children realise that in Britain festivals are more low key than in India. This is especially true of Holi. An uncomprehending non-Hindu majority, inclement British weather, expensively decorated and upholstered homes, the constraints of work and school all combine to rule out the messy, anarchic merriment of Holi as it is in India. Syringes of coloured water and skins and clothes dyed almost black by repeated drenchings are not part of most British Hindu children's first-hand experience of Holi.[10]

Divali's fireworks fare better, probably because of the proximity of November 5th. Fireworks are available in abundance and neighbours find nothing untoward in firework parties taking place during late October and early November. Elements of Divali disappear, however. For example the Indian custom of leaving a door or window open for Lakshmi, goddess of prosperity, to enter the house and shower her blessings, has understandably declined in Britain. Nonetheless, a Valmiki Hindu boy mentioned the goddess (*devi*) and reported that before going to sleep he and his family light candles:

the *devi's* meant to turn the candle out and then you know that she's come like to your house. Last year it did actually go out because, when we were going to sleep, there was like a bit of wind and it just went out. My mum would usually say that that's the *devi*, when the wind comes in.

As the following account by another Valmiki boy shows, the customs of lighting up the house, having Indian sweets and enjoying letting off the fireworks with the rest of the family persist, ensuring Divali's continuing popularity. He wrote:

It was Divali today and I went to school. When I came back from school I went to get some fireworks. My mum and my grandmother went to get some new pots and pans and some candles; when we got home we lit the candles all over the house in every room and we lit some *dive* (oil lights) on the doorstep. Then we prayed and blessed the Indian sweets. After that we went to my grandparents' house. There we lit lots of candles and lights. I called my cousins over to light the fireworks because there was so many.

☐ Formalisation

As the earlier reference to a Holi dance performed in a temple suggested, Hindu festivals have lost the spontaneity as well as the high profile that they have in India. Instead they are domestic affairs which have also become occasions for organised cultural programmes, usually held indoors in temples or hired halls.

For parents and grandparents serving on temple management committees or teaching in supplementary classes (see chapter ten) festivals are ideal opportunities to involve children in drama and dance. They are occasions for increasingly self-conscious transmission of Hindu myth and values to the younger generation. On Janmashtami children, including Ritu, perform plays from the cycle of Krishna stories — for example the story of Dhanna and of Govardhan Hill.[11]

On Divali in 1986, after evening Lakshmi *puja* in the temple, *arati* was sung to Lakshmi and the singing programme began with Deepak accompanying a Divali song on his *dholki* (drum). A group of girls who attended elementary Hindi classes in the temple premises, sang a Divali song:

ghar ghar dip jalao ki aj divali hai,
khushian khub manao ki aj divali hai.
nae khilone,nae kapre pehno,
ladu pere aur jalebi
ji bhar bhar ke khao.

aj divali hai,
sach tha jita, jhuth tha hara.
yah din hame bataya
sachi rah par chalne wala
ram bhagat ho jaye,
aj divali hai.

An English translation is:
Light lamps in every house, because it is Divali day,
Rejoice and be happy, because it is Divali today.

Play with new toys, put on new clothes,
Eat sweets as much as you can,
Because it's Divali today.

This day reminds us of the victory of truth over untruth.
Whosoever follows the path of truth,
Becomes the devotee of Rama,
Because it's Divali today.

Similarly in 1987, at Ramanavami, pupils from the Hindi class read verses from Tulsi Das's *Ramayana* and these were explained in Hindi by two senior girls.

In the same year the children attending the two Bal Vikas centres presented a cultural programme on the Sunday before Ramanavami. This was well attended and greatly enjoyed. Several months later Anita wrote:

We had a programme of Ram Navmi, in other words Lord Rama's birthday. Invitation cards were sent out and many many people came. We first had *bhajans* and then we had some plays, speeches and dances. My friend and I done a dance of Lord Ram.

Those attending supplementary classes are more likely to take part in such readings, singing, dance or drama marking the festival and are likely to be more aware of the festival than other children are.

☐ The Role of Maintained Schools

Simultaneously with the increasing organisation of festival programmes in which children play a key role, many British schools also began seeing festivals as pegs for the multicultural curriculum. Whereas Hindu parents are motivated by the realisation that their children will grow up in ignorance of their cultural heritage unless a concerted effort is made, school teachers have a different basis for concern. This is the awareness that children are growing up in a multicultural society and that, if this is to be a harmonious whole, then children from all cultural backgrounds should be enabled to share and value one another's traditions. Although school teachers and Hindu parents have different reasons for involving children in Hindu festivals these are not incompatible. Their efforts interact and can be mutually supportive. (See chapters ten and eleven for more comments on the role of maintained schools in the nurture of Hindu children.) When festivals become part of the school curriculum Hindu pupils and parents are often faced with what is alien to them. Unless the teacher is South Asian, the pronunciation of names can be a casualty. Sometimes too, not always wittingly, teachers introduce an element which is drawn from a regional tradition with which local Hindu families are unfamiliar.

When Coventry teachers introduce Holi they generally recount the Puranic story of Prahlada, with which many Hindu children are familiar. This is the tale of the virtuous young prince Prahlada who courageously carried on worshipping Vishnu despite the edict of his father, the King Hiranyakasipu, that everyone must worship him instead. The king, infuriated by his son's disobedience, could find no way of destroying him. So he asked his demonic sister Holika for help. Believing herself invulnerable she sat on a funeral fire with Prahlada on her lap but, whereas he survived unscathed, she was reduced to ashes. The association of Holi with the Prahlada myth was reinforced in those schools which used the Holi pack produced by the Coventry-based, LEA-funded Minority Group Support Service. This includes a lively version of the story.

In Mridula's school, by contrast, her teacher introduced Holi with a reference to the Krishna myth. As a clue to 'what special day' — apart from St Patrick's — was to fall that week he had told the class the story of Krishna stealing the brightly coloured *saris* of the maids while they were bathing. According to Mridula the bright colour of their clothing was the link with Holi, the festival of colour. Mridula found the teacher's introduction acceptable, perhaps because of Pushtimargis' emphasis on Krishna. This would have been equally acceptable to Bhavesh, whose mother had told him that:

> When Krishna was small he used to throw cream or milk over the ladies. And he thought it was fun so he threw colour over them.

However to some Hindus, including the teacher in one supplementary class who was interviewed, the association of Holi with Krishna is unfamiliar.

☐ Using English to Describe Festivals

When festivals are brought into the curriculum of schools or English medium supplementary classes, children may find it easier to articulate in English the principal features of the celebration. The verbal translation of Hindu experience into an English account meaningful to non-Asians is a complex one. Rahsha Bandhan exemplifies this. As we saw in chapter four, it reaffirms a Hindu view of family relationship, annually celebrating and strengthening the bond of affection between brothers and sisters of whatever age. Cousins (cousin brothers and cousin sisters as they are called in Indian English) are not distinguished from siblings. In essence the celebration is simple. Sisters tie an ornamental thread (*rakhi*) around their brother's or male cousin's right wrists, and they put a sweetmeat in his mouth. The brothers and cousin brothers reciprocate with a gift of money. If the relatives cannot meet them the sisters send the threads by post. In its most basic form a *rakhi* is a red thread tied by a sister around her brother's wrist on Raksha Bandhan day. Usually nowadays the thread is attached to a colourful, round decoration, consisting of tinsel, plastic, beads or other materials, often in the form of a flower or bearing some religious motif such as a *swastika* (the ancient symbol associated with Ganesh and good fortune) or an *om* sign.

Here are some of our interviewees' efforts to describe a *rakhi* in English:

'a red string'
'a string with a flower on it or some kind of picture'
'It's sort of like a material thing, like a watch'
'this kind of rope and it's got a pattern on it'
'sort of a string'
'There's this kind of bobble'
'It's a rope and we have like a flower in the middle, nice pattern'
'these special bracelets which are made of string'
'sort of a band, sort of like a bracelet that is made of thread or something like that'
'like a watch but it's really a pattern thing'
'these ropes and we get little thing pattern things on them'
'like string bracelet'

One boy resorted to the Gujarati word '*phumtu*' (a tuft, tassel).

Not only was there difficulty in describing the *rakhi's* appearance but also in explaining what is done with it. None of the children spoke of tying it around the boy's wrist. Instead they said:

'tie it round your brother'
'tie this kind of thing down the brother's hand'
'you get it all tied up'
'we tie sort of ribbons that go round the hand'
'she puts something on our hand'
'put it round his hand'
'we tie them round our brothers' hands'

The possibilities for misunderstanding or misinterpretation are obvious. There is a good case for producing curriculum resources grounded in the experience and vocabulary of British Hindu children so that teachers have access to reference material that relates to the lives of Hindu pupils.[12]

☐ Norta: Festivals as Enjoyment

An aspect of religious activity which is sometimes forgotten or regarded as irrelevant is pure enjoyment. If this chapter has eclipsed the happy anticipation and the pleasures that make festivals festive, then it is time to look at Norta, the Gujarati celebration of Navaratri every Autumn. For all the Gujarati children Norta (Navaratri) is a period of heightened activity and communal enjoyment.[13] Literally 'nine nights', Navaratri commences a month before Divali and ends with Vijay Dashmi or Dasehra, the victorious tenth.

To quote Arun's older sister:

> We dance in our best *saris* for the evening. The temple is usually crowded and looks very colourful. The thing I always look forward to is the stick dance. We have two circles of people who move in different directions and they hit sticks with the people opposite. These nine days are the most marvellous days in the year, because we meet new people. You get to know them better and you dance and sing.

For girls the chance to wear new outfits each evening adds to the excitement. Traditional Gujarati dress consists of decorative maxi skirts (*chaniyo*) worn with a brief, close-fitting blouse (*choli*) and co-ordinated length of flimsier fabric (*chunri*) which is drawn down over the right shoulder and secured at the waist back and front. As an alternative they may wear *saris*, but 'Punjabi suits' consisting of long tops (*kurta* or *kamiz*) and trousers are increasingly popular with girls and with some young women. The length of the *kurta* and the cut of the matching or contrasting trousers (*pajama* or *salvar*) is dictated by the trendsetters in Bombay.

On some or all of the usually nine evenings families — from babies to great grandparents — gather for dancing which climaxes in *arati* at about 9 pm. The children's families do not go to the same venue every night. There is the pull of Rugby and other nearby places, particularly Leicester where new dance styles originate. Within Coventry the caste associations hire premises where members and their families celebrate. Coventry members of some communities — Arun's Kathiawari Soni community for example — do not gather separately in Coventry but on occasion join their community at its venue in Leicester.

The dances are circle dances with a temporary shrine, the *garbi*, to the goddess in her many forms in the centre. Some dances are *garba* — women's dances accompanied by clapping, and words expressing devotion for the goddess. The others are *ras*, circle dances associated with Krishna and the *gopis* (girls who herded cows). In *ras* the participants, male and female, move in concentric circles, one clockwise the other counter-clockwise. Each dancer strikes sticks (*dandiya*), which are often brightly striped and the size of two foot lengths of broom handle, against those of the dancer opposite. The footwork and stickwork provide scope for considerable panache.

The music may be recorded but it is usually live and provided by a group consisting of singers, percussion and harmonium or electronic keyboard usually amplified to a point that makes conversation impossible. The group includes the children's older relatives. Bhavini's mother sang with a popular local Gujarati group. As each dance continues the pace quickens. The tempo and volume show the influence of discotheque music. The trend is towards 'disco-*rasgarba*'. Children dance, caught up in the rhythm and beat, but with little idea of the words.[14] At about 9 p.m. everyone stops dancing for the *arati*. The women nearest to the *garbi* rotate their gleaming *thalis* to the powerful rhythm of the song invoking the goddess in all her aspects.[15] Anita sums up the Norta experience in her own words:

> Navaratri means enjoying yourself, meeting friends getting hot, staying up late and it's just fun.

☐ Conclusion

Several important aspects of Hindu festivals are the subject of other chapters of this book. Chapter four has drawn attention to the role of certain annual celebrations in the life-stages and gender-awareness of boys and girls. Chapter five has reminded us of the relationship between diet and the ritual calendar. Chapter eight will further illustrate the festivities distinctive of particular guru-led movements in Britain. In chapter nine the role of story drama, music, dance is further explored. As festivals traditionally involve the expressive arts they are welcome opportunities for concerned adults to involve children in presentations, usually with a mythological content. This often occurs in the context of the supplementary classes which are discussed in chapter ten. Some schools are now, to a degree, shaping tradition, especially at Divali.

Stories, in many cases aetiological myths, cluster around festivals. In these myths certain moral and social values are assumed. With each successive year of the participants' lives they are reinforced. The stories of Prahlada's vindication (recalled at Holi) and Rama's reinstatement (celebrated at Divali) suggest the tendency of righteousness to suffer but finally prevail.

It is harder to find ethical meaning in, for example, the Holi-related stories of Krishna dancing with the local cowherds' wives. Here the myth, unless interpreted allegorically, is more akin, in its reversal of approved norms, to the stories of love marriage so popular in Indian movies.

In some cases it is the manner of celebrating a festival, rather than the associated story, which perpetuates values. Thus children's actions at Raksha Bandhan, in Britain as in India, are an expression of the sanctity of the brother-sister relationship. In the normally unchallenged hierarchy of an Indian village, Holi is a brief burst of role reversal and equality with the young playing pranks on the old, with members of the highest castes at the mercy of the lowest and, in certain areas of Uttar Pradesh, the men beaten up by their wives. In Britain, however, for reasons considered above, Holi has lost its anarchic and equalising role. Arguably, in a less hierarchical society the social function of Holi's excesses is an anachronism.

In this chapter we have noted both the persistence and the adaptability of the Hindu festival calendar in Britain. To longer-established celebrations birthdays and Christmas have been added. For some widely observed festivals the adherents of a *sampradaya* may teach their children a specific significance or justification.

In conclusion, their festivals survive principally because Hindus, not least the children, enjoy them. In Britain they have largely lost their outdoor character, and, with occasional exceptions such as Leicester's (and recently, on a smaller scale, Coventry's) Divali lights, they almost escape the notice of the non-Hindu majority. For Hindus they are annual opportunities for cultural affirmation. In this situation concern for their children is a dominant motive and children are encouraged to play a public role. It is clearly apparent that in the adaptations to festivals made by Britain's Hindus, a major concern for parents is the cultural identity of their children.

Notes

1. Major festivals are outlined in Jackson (1986) and Kanitkar (1984).

2. See also Jackson and Nesbitt (1989a) for reflections on festivals in the lives of British Hindu children, and Jackson (1989) for photographs showing Hindu festivals in Britain and in India.

3. Logan (1989a) sets out clearly the nature of the Gujarati calendar. Jackson (1989a) provides a photograph of the block, tear-off calendars which are in general use by Gujarati Hindus. For a summary of the Indian calendrical systems see Jackson (1986). More detail is provided by Basham (1967:494-497).

4. Lohri is briefly described in chapter four, note six. Jalaram Jayanti is celebrated in memory of Jalaram Bapa, a saintly nineteenth century merchant from Virpur in Gujarat. See Jackson and Nesbitt (1990: 45) for a story associated with Jalaram Bapa.

5. This is not a uniquely Gujarati custom. In the Indian state of Uttar Pradesh, for example, bonfires are lit.

6. See Jackson (1976) for an account of the celebrations of Holi at this temple, and especially for its connection with mythology. Bennett (1987) also briefly describes the celebration in Coventry in an account written for children. See Marriott (1968) for an evocation of Holi in North India.

7. Similarly (according to a Brahmin woman) a new bride may walk around or a mother who has prayed for her sick child's recovery (as she had done on one Holi) will carry the child around the fire on the next Holi.

   A woman of *darzi* (tailor) caste fasted on Holi until she went to the temple in the evening. This, she said, was to extend her son's life. Every Holi she had *mag* (moong), lentils, cooked with chillis to eat in the evening. Arun's mother recalled Holi in Uganda, with a big fire beside the temple. Women would carry a baby round this fire and sprinkle water one or four times in a clockwise direction.

8. See, for example, the account of Vaisakhi in Cole and Sambhi (1986).

9. It was televised in *Encounter*, Central Television, March 1989.

10. See Jackson (1976) and Marriott (1968).

11. In 1986 children acted the story of Dhanna, a very poor man whose devotion to Thakurji (Krishna), in the form of a stone, was so great that the god appeared before him. A version of this story is related in Macauliffe (1978). The story of Krishna lifting Mount Govardhan, and so showing his superiority to Indra, is told and illustrated in Vitsaxis (1977).

12. Attempts at this are Jackson (1989a) and Jackson and Nesbitt (1990). For an account of the process of writing these books see Jackson (1989b).

13. For an excellent study see Logan (1988a).

14. The following are *garbo* songs recorded 15th October 1985, translated by Mrs Hansa Mehta:

1. Mataji has unique strength.
   You kill giants and evil spirits.
   You ride with your weapons.
   Even the gods want your *darshan* (a
   glimpse of you).
   You come from high mountains and the sky
   above.
   You are the queen, your light flashes
   forever.
   The beauty of your forest Girnar is
   unique.
   Men and women come to you with faith.
   Your flag rises up in the sky.
   Your devotees call you.
   Everyone sings *arati* and experiences your
   darshan and gets what they want by
   singing your name, Amba.

2. Amba Ma's *garbo* is jingling and jangling.
   A jeweller comes to her door.
   He brings a pair of ankle bells (*janjri*).
   A shopkeeper comes to her.
   He brings two *saris* for her.
   A gardener comes to her.
   He brings flowers.

3. The goddess Mahakali comes down from the
   mountain to Gujarat. She dresses up in beautiful clothes.
   Her *sari* shines.
   She wears anklets and toe rings.
   She wears bracelets on her arms and rings
   on her ten fingers.
   Her earrings adorn her and the fifty-one necklaces around her neck.
   Her nose stud adorns her. She wears jewellery down her parting.
   She wears vermilion powder in her parting.
   On her plait is a cobra decoration.

15. In this hymn to the goddess, sung during *arati*, each of the fifteen days of this
    half of the lunar month is related to her glory. It begins:

    Victory to Primordial energy that dazzles the cosmos, and enlightens the
    learned.
    Victory to Mother of the World.

    On the second day (of Navaratri) I know your two aspects, Shiva and Shakti.
    Brahma, Ganapati and Shiva sing your praises.
    Victory ...

On the third day, you occupy the three parts of the Universe (Earth, Space, Heaven). You help me to cross three places (and achieve *moksha*).
Victory ...

On the fourth day you are Mahalakshmi
with four arms, filling all creation in
four directions, but manifesting
yourself in the South.
Victory ...

and concludes:

Whosoever sings this *arati* of Shiva's
Energy will gain happiness and good
fortune, says Swami Shivananda.
Shiva and Amba will remove your sorrow.
Victory to the Mother of the World.

[For this translation we are grateful to V.P. (Hemant) Kanitkar.]

CHAPTER 7

Prayer and Worship

☐ Children's experience

None of the children expressed any doubt that God or gods exist. All mentioned praying. Their references to God and to praying were as matter of fact as their accounts of school sports, eating or watching television. They not only mentioned the religious activity of relatives but spoke from their own personal experience.

They referred to prayer at the domestic shrine, to their peace of mind after reciting sacred words, with or without a *mala* (rosary), and to visiting the temple to pray. They described occasions when sheets were spread over the living room carpet and friends and relations gathered in their house for a corporate act of worship. These were sometimes *pujas* which required the presence of a Brahmin priest to guide their parents through the words and offerings demanded by the rite in question. Children also witnessed and participated in a range of activities which could be described in English as prayer, since they were ways of praising and petitioning God. Of these the *vrat* (vow) has been examined in chapter five.

The children frequently referred to the experience of worship in the home, but their recollection of particular forms of words and comprehension of their literal meaning was not as general as awareness of appropriate body movement and familiarity with the sounds and scents of *puja*. Nevertheless in this chapter we include the verbal content of some prayers which were widely used, and discuss the rich significance of the sacred syllable *om* and of *mantras* (sacred syllables, words and phrases) with which children were

93

familiar. By repeating these with a pure heart many Hindus not only experience inner peace but also believe that they will acquire merit to offset the effects of bad deeds committed in this or a previous life.

☐ A Temple in the Home

For celebrations in the home to which others were invited, a special shrine would be installed. Thus, when Bhavini's mother hosted worship of Randal Ma a special shrine was set up for the day to house the images of the goddess. Such days occurred rarely in any household.

In every home, however, there was also a space that provided a continuing locus for prayer and worship, a visual reminder of religious identity. This was the domestic shrine, and when children referred to 'the temple' it was often this which they meant, and not the public place of worship. For both the home shrine and the public temple the Hindi word would be *mandir*. In some homes the shrine would escape the notice of the casual caller. In others it dominated the living room. In all the homes visited during the research one part, however small, was permanently set aside for worship. This might be an entire upstairs room, a cupboard upstairs, a glass fronted cabinet downstairs or a grouping of religious pictures in the kitchen. Some people had constructed their own shrine — usually a rectangular plywood box. Each shrine was decorated and in it were pictures of gods and goddesses or small three-dimensional images of them as well as other items used in worship. These would usually include a *diva* (lipped clay bowl used as an oil light), a hand-bell, joss sticks, a container of holy water, a book of prayers and maybe a coconut which had been used in a ceremony at the temple or elsewhere. The catholic inclusiveness of many family shrines is apparent in the description which Arun wrote in his diary of the shrine in the living room:

> **Our Beautiful Shrine**
> In the corner of our living room there is a glass cabinet. It has been made into a shrine. Each of the glass shelves is covered with pink material. The top of the cabinet is covered with red material and on the material there are photos of Laxmi, Radha Krishna, Ambaji and Nine Durgas, and a small photo of Rama, Hanuman and Sita. In the top corner of the shrine is a statue of Lord Krishna. It is about 12 inches high and I got the statue for my birthday present. In the middle there is a book called *Devi Bhagvat*. In the top shelf in the cabinet there are photographs of Bhuvaneshvari Maa, Maha Kali, Khodya Maa with a crocodile, Ambaji, Gayatri Maa, a six inch tall statue of Krishna made out of clay, with cows as well. Two pots made of copper are filled with holy water from the river Ganges and Yamuna.

Arun goes on to describe in equal detail the contents of the second and third shelves which included three-dimensional images (*murtis*) of gods and goddesses, a picture postcard of Krishna, photographs of saints and *gurus,* a book of *bhajans* (hymns), and the implements and materials needed for *puja.* The gods and goddesses Arun mentions include major deities (Lakshmi, Shiva, Kali) and deities local to Gujarat such as Bhuvaneshvari Ma and Khodiyar Ma. Some are especially linked with his family — Tulja Bhavani, a form of the goddess Uma; Mal Bapa, a cobra who is worshipped as the family's *kuldev* or divine patron of their lineage; and Sura Pura Bapu, a holy man long revered by relatives of the family. The photographs he mentions are of contemporary spiritual leaders, Morari Bapu and Swami Satyamitra-nand Giri, who visit Britain annually.

Some households had fewer items grouped together as a focus for worship. Some had shrines devoted to the divine reality in one form above all. These were Bal Krishna (Krishna represented as an infant) and Sathya Sai Baba in Mridula's and Anita's homes respectively.

The procedure was similar in all cases. Before praying the children would make sure that they were clean. They all removed their shoes to go up to their 'temple'. Usually a grandparent or parent took the lead in worship but on occasion children might do so themselves. Sunil was used to circling a smouldering stick of incense clockwise in front of the pictures of deities in the family shrine which occupied a cupboard on the landing. He knew the details of family observance; for worshipping Shiva-Shakti, for example, they put mustard oil in the *diva* but for Sheranwali Ma they used *ghi* (purified butter). He knew how their mother made wicks for the *divas* by twisting pieces of cotton wool, and that the burned wicks must not be thrown away, but stored in a box until they could be put in the canal.[1] Children observed and copied the reverent behaviour associated with the shrine. At the least, when in front of the shrine, they put their palms together with the fingers pointing upwards in a respectful greeting to the deities. The Punjabis called this 'doing *jay*' since '*jay*' ('long live', 'praise to') is the salutation addressed to the gods with this gesture.

☐ Domestic Worship

As the contents of every shrine differed, so did the pattern and words of each family's worship. But all the children were united by the experience of growing up in homes in which a certain place and certain times were channels of God's blessing. Food offered at the shrine became *prashad* (blessed food, 'god food') to be received in cupped hands with the right over the left. Books kept in the shrine were religious, printed in an Indian language and understood only by older relatives. The degree to which the domestic shrine and domestic worship impinged on children's lives varied from family to family.

Children were familiar with *puja* and *arati* as ways of worship. *Puja* is the term for worship which involves singing and more tangible offerings to God. These usually include water, light, flowers, fruit, nuts and sweets, for God is welcomed much as an honoured guest would be. *Arati* marks a climax of worship. Details of procedure vary from one household or temple to another, as do the words of the *arati* hymn. But there is a common feeling of gladness as a bell is rung insistently, and everyone chants a special *bhajan* while an oil light is circled repeatedly, in a vertical clockwise motion, in front of the religious picture or image on which devotees' attention is focused. After this the lamp is brought to the participants in turn for them to share its blessing (the hands are warmed over the flame and then pressed against the eyes and forehead), and the *prashad* (usually sweets or fruits that have been offered at the shrine) is distributed before everyone disperses.

Ritu and Deepak's family gathered daily at about seven in the evening, the time of *sandhya* (twilight) for fifteen minutes worship. They would squeeze into a small upstairs room in which the shrine, an oblong, open-fronted plywood box, was fixed to the wall facing the door. Sitting cross legged on the floor parents and children sang together to the accompaniment of Ritu's harmonium and Deepak's *dholki* which he struck with his hands at both ends, while their little brother moved about happily. Deepak and Ritu took their turn at standing up and moving a *thali* (round steel tray) in front of the shrine, and ringing the handbell vigorously as they all sang in joyful and rhythmic unison. On the *thali* would be a burning joss stick and a small lit *diva*. As singing ended one of the family brought the *thali* to each of the others to extend their hands to the light and draw them back over eyes and head, so sharing the blessing. First one of them would waft the light over baby brother's head. With a small spoon Deepak or Ritu would distribute holy water to the family so that each of them could drink a few drops after receiving it in cupped palms. Then everyone received a handful of sultanas and almonds or other *prashad*.

Most children are not involved in such frequent, detailed acts of worship as Deepak and Ritu although many have similar experiences on occasion. Such worship is a time for being together, content and at ease within a framework of words and with a shared grammar of behaviour. The relaxed reverence shows in gesture and posture, the visual arrangement of pictures, the sweet pungency of incense, the build-up of the *arati* hymn, the taste of shared *prashad*. All these, together with the sounds of invocations and praise, add up to a happy, multi-sensory experience.

Assessing the degree to which children acquire or remember the words of prayers and hymns is an inadequate measure of children's experience of worship. However, as many of the children showed familiarity with certain sacred formulae, it is useful to examine these, while not forgetting the predominantly non-verbal impact of worship on children's lives.

☐ Mantras

Children often referred to repeating a sacred formula (*mantra*). They might do this on a daily basis at the shrine and also recite it at some critical moment. For instance Deepak described how:

> When we have sports I always chant a *mantra* for good luck. We had high jump yesterday and I forgot to chant (before) one of those jumps and I failed it. (Then) I said, 'Hare Krishna Hare Krishna' and I jumped over it.

Children usually do not know what the words of their prayers 'mean' but they testify to the peace of mind which they experience. In the words of a Valmiki girl the formula which she recited made her:

> feel calm, relaxed, and I feel I've done what I'm supposed to and I can do anything I like (afterwards).

Deepak said that repeating his *mantra* on each bead of his 108 bead rosary every day 'puts me in a nice religious mood' and Sarita said that after reciting the Gayatri *mantra*, an ancient Sanskrit prayer, each morning with her grandmother she feels happier in the knowledge that God will help her.[2]

Ritu said that she repeated the Gayatri mantra:'When I'm in trouble I say it and I have good luck'.[3]

The children had learned these formulae and, in some cases, how to use a rosary (*mala*) from grandparents, parents and the teachers of supplementary classes. Often they could recall unaided only a few words, but they were used to hearing the sound of the prayers in their appropriate ritual context. The Gayatri *mantra* is the prayer which is most widely known and it is used by children of diverse regional and sectarian backgrounds. It permeates both Gujarati and Punjabi families, including devotees of the living god-man Sathya Sai Baba and adherents of the Arya Samaj, a movement rejecting the use of images in worship.

No translation can convey the layers of association that the prayer has gathered over the centuries. Children (like most Hindu adults) could only guess at the literal meaning. They could not translate it into English or into their Indian mother-tongue nor did they know it was called Gayatri *mantra* or that it was in a language called Sanskrit. But this does not mean that they were out of line with the Hindu tradition. Knowledge and correct repetition of *mantras* (words and phrases charged with sacred power) are of more importance to many Hindus than a intellectual understanding of their 'meaning'. Children had encountered the Gayatri *mantra* in many contexts. Arun daily saw the words in both Devanagari and Roman script inscribed around the face of the living room clock:

Om bhur bhuvah svahah
tatsavitur varenyam
bhargo devasya dhimahi
dhiyo yo nah prachodayat.

The boys who received the sacred thread (*janeu*) during a grand scale *yagnopavita* ceremony in Leicester in 1987 heard continuous amplified recitation of the Gayatri *mantra*. In his diary Arun described two *yagnas* or *havans* (ceremonies centred on a fire in which recitation of the Gayatri *mantra* was central). One occasion, a huge *yagna* for world peace, included a highly elaborate ritual. According to Arun:

> The priest said the *mantra* 1008 times and the people had to put the herbs (in the fires) 1008 times. There were 1008 different names of Gods and Goddesses (each spoken) with the Gayatri *mantra*. The people had to say (this) from a special book.

Implicit in this vast exercise, which took place in Abbey Park, Leicester, on May 31st 1987, was the belief that recitation of the Gayatri *mantra* on this scale would help bring about world peace. The *yagna* lasted from nine am until five pm and involved 4032 participants and possibly as many onlookers.

In some cases, children repeated the *mantra* regularly in specific ways. Those attending the Sathya Sai Baba organisation's classes recited the words in unison, usually five, eleven or twenty-one times during each session. They did so sitting cross-legged on the carpet with their eyes closed and their palms upturned on their knees. Anita and her family would recite the Gayatri *mantra* twenty one times during morning worship. Some children learn to repeat the *mantra* on a rosary, once on each of the 108 beads. Before she left for school Sarita would pray in this way with her grandmother. When she reached the tuft, after 108 beads, she would stop, then repeat the cycle once or twice more. She also recited the Gayatri *mantra* on Sunday mornings at the Gujarati school.

A Gujarati girl summed up the importance of the Gayatri *mantra*, as compared with other prayers, in these words:

My mum knows everything... she says if you just learn this one (i.e. Gayatri *mantra*) you don't need to learn other ones.

☐ Hare Krishna Mahamantra

Children of devotees of the International Society for Krishna Consciousness (ISKCON) gave priority to the Hare Krishna *mahamantra* (literally 'great' *mantra*):

Hare Krishna Hare Krishna Krishna Krishna Hare Hare
Hare Rama Hare Rama Rama Rama Hare Hare

From Good Friday to Easter Sunday (28-30 March) 1986 the Ram Mandir rang with these words. This forty-eight hour long feat was publicised as 'chanting for peace'.

For Ritu and Deepak, and others who are involved in ISKCON, these words constitute the most powerful of *mantras*. As Deepak said:

It's a *mantra* that everyone can join in, simple, but highly effective. It's a prayer that means a lot of things. Like if you say 'Ram' once it's equal to a thousand times of Vishnu. And Krishna's higher than Ram, so that's even more than Ram.[4]

The unique value of the *mahamantra* was dramatised in English plays presented by ISKCON devotees and their children. Such plays were popular with a wide range of Hindu families as they felt that their children could come to enjoy and understand something of an often less easily intelligible Hindu heritage. For example, children from Coventry acted a sketch as part of the programme to celebrate Holi in the Shree Geeta Bhavan Mandir in Birmingham on 14th March 1987. In this a more educated passenger berated a boatman for his ignorance of many things. Eventually the passenger tumbled into the water and as he could not swim he drowned. Despite all his knowledge, he did not know the one thing vital for saving his life. 'So it is with the Hare Krishna *mahamantra*, which is the only knowledge necessary for life.'[5]

In 'Sanatan Goswami and the Magic Stone' which was performed in St Peter's Hall, Coventry on 11th January 1986, children saw a poor man who was desperate to marry a beautiful princess. To further his quest he was searching for the most valuable thing in the world. After many adventures he met Sanatan Goswami who offered him a touchstone which would turn everything to gold. With this the poor man's dreams came true, but he and the princess led a sad, quarrelsome life. Then he remembered that Sanatan Goswami had kept the touchstone not in a safe place but in his rubbish dump. Surely, he reflected, this must indicate that he possessed an even greater treasure. On returning to Sanatan Goswami he learned that this 'most valuable thing is chanting the Hare Krishna *mahamantra*; it is so easy, anyone can do it'.[6]

Repeating the *mahamantra* is indeed so easy that, to the family's delight, Deepak and Ritu's younger brother could say the words when he was only one year old. Children heard or joined in the singing of the *mahamantra* to several tunes and rhythms in both the Shree Krishna Temple and the Ram Mandir. As demonstrated by the fact that it was sung by children who attended the 1985 Bal Vikas Summer Camp, this *mantra* is widely used outside circles that identify with ISKCON.

☐ The Rosary

The rosary (*mala*), is widely used by Hindus as an aid to prayer, since they undertake to repeat *mantras* a certain number of times, and it is easier to keep count with the assistance of a string of beads.[7] It is familiar to many Hindu children from its use in domestic worship. Children also see it in some pictures (of Guru Nanak, for instance) and it features in the popular story of the Gujarati saint, Jalaram Bapa. He received a *mala* (rosary) and *jora* (bag) from God after demonstrating his total devotion — even to the extent of entrusting his wife to a stranger who asked for a guide. The stranger turned out to be Lord Krishna who had been testing Jalaram Bapa's trust.

The precise form of the rosary and the manner in which it is used vary from family to family, but the beads are generally of wood and number 108 and there is a shared belief in the spiritual benefit to the individual of repeating a particular formula in this way (see Blackman 1925 for a detailed study of rosaries). Pushtimargis for example, recite '*Sri Krishna sarana mama*' (I take refuge in Lord Krishna) as they tell their beads.

The word generally used for a rosary is *mala*. (To non-Indian ears the Gujarati form sounds more like 'mara'). Some children are familiar with its use, but as with so many items which they use only in the context of their home or the temple they do not know the equivalent English word. 'Necklace' is often the word they select when asked to use an English term. In ISKCON the rosary is called '*japa* beads'.[8]

Deepak said that if he were living in a non-Hindu household his 'beads' would be what he would miss the most. He explained how to recite the *mahamantra* with the help of a rosary. When he reached the bead nearest to the tuft he passed his fingers to the bead on the other side and recommenced. He said he would never touch the central bead 'because it is Krishna'. A duplicated colouring sheet used with children during the weekly ISKCON *kirtan* shows an outline drawing of the *japa*. The beads are shown with the small bag in which devotees carry them.[9]

Children referred in English to the practice of 'telling one's beads' in various ways e.g. 'doing the necklace'. One Punjabi girl said that among the requirements for becoming a *Guru* is the obligation to 'do sixteen rounds' i.e. daily rosaries. (ISKCON believers in Britain are exhorted to complete sixteen rosaries daily and a string of sixteen beads hangs from the bead bag to facilitate keeping count).[10] It was not only children influenced by ISKCON who used a rosary. Struggling to describe domestic worship a Gujarati girl said:

> If you finish the books... you put a necklace, but you don't put it on. It's round and then there's a 'leaf' and then when you stop there, then you got to go over it again.

In Bal Vikas children learned to say *'Om Sri Sai Ram'* on each bead, moving one at a time towards them with the index finger. Each child brought a rosary of 108 wooden beads in a cloth bag. The *guru* showed them how to hold the rosary up between the thumb and middle finger of the right hand, so uniting God with the *jiva* or *atma* (both could be translated 'soul' but see glossary), for, as Bhavesh explained, using notes in his Bal Vikas notebook to aid his memory, the thumb represents God, the index finger is *atma* or *jiva*.[11] The middle finger is *sattva* (active), the fourth finger is *rajas* (hyperactive) and the little finger is *tamas* (dull). He knew he should say his *mala* twice a day, but admitted that he did not do so.

Dry chickpeas can also be used as a counting aid when praying. In speaking about praying, Mridula decribed one of her grandmother's Pushtimargi *satsangs*. At these the women each took 'a pile of chickpeas' from the contents of a jar. Every time a woman had read the requisite amount she would take a chickpea, then resume reading. This each did many times. When she had used up all the chickpeas she put them in the middle of the floor. Then each woman would take some more chickpeas and they remained sitting until the whole jar had been used up.

☐ Prayer Before and After Sleeping

Children were sometimes encouraged to repeat holy words in bed, especially if they were sleepless.[12] Sunil would say the words *'Om namah Sivai'* (respects to Lord Shiva) over and over until he fell asleep. When Arun had a bad night his mother advised him to say, *'Sri Ram'* and since then he had, she said, slept soundly.

On waking in the morning some children are encouraged to recite:

karagre vapate Lakshmi
karmule Sarasvati

karamadhye tu Govind
prabhate karadarshanam.

Arun's mother does so and wrote the words in Roman script to enable him
to read them more easily.

This is an invocation to Lakshmi, Saraswati and Govinda (Krishna), each
of whom is associated with one part of the hand. As translated for children
attending classes in the Shree Sanatan Mandir, Leicester it reads:

> In the front part of the hand (the fingers) there dwells the Goddess of
> Wealth, Laxmi. In the base of the hand (the wrist) there lives the Goddess
> of Knowledge and Wisdom. In the centre of the hand (palm) is the place
> of the Supreme Personality of Godhead, Lord Shri Krishna, and so I
> worship the hand at the time of sunrise.[13]

The prayer was among those displayed in Gujarati (written in Roman Script)
and English during the Midland Bal Vikas Camp 26th July 1986. Below it
was written:

> You say this prayer in the morning and so when you are about to do a
> bad deed during the day you will stop and remember you are insulting
> these gods and goddesses.

Anita and her family repeated a much longer prayer entitled the Sri Sathya
Sai Suprabhatam each morning when they prayed daily at five am. *Su* means
'good', '*prabhatam*' means morning. An English translation of the first verse
is as follows:

> O! Son of Eshwaramba. O! Resplendent One. Dawn is breaking in the
> East. Awake, O Lord! to perform Thy daily duties.[14]

Anita's cousin knew that when praying in the morning it was good to invoke
Ganesh first. She explained:

> We have to mention Ganesh *slok* first. He's the first you know, how can
> I put it? We should say his *slokas* first before we begin the rest. Cos he's
> the sort of main god.

☐ Mealtime Prayer

Before meals a small minority of Hindu children say a grace. For pupils of
Bal Vikas this is a verse which affirms the presence of the Lord (*hari*) in
everything. It begins '*hari data hari bhokta*'. According to Bhavesh's Bal
Vikas notebook the English translation of the verse would be:

Hari the Lord of all beings is the giver, the enjoyer and the food itself. The body of the vipra is Hari. Hari is the one who eats and also who feeds. A vipra is one whose mind has become illumined with the brightness of divine knowledge and wisdom.[15]

This prayer was prominently displayed, in Roman script, above the food distribution point at the 1986 Bal Vikas Summer Camp.

Before eating their strictly vegetarian packed lunches the pupils of Vidya Vihar, the Saturday school run by the Harrow-based Academy of Vedic Heritage (see chapter ten), recited a verse which begins: *'Om saha nava-vatu...'* In English this prayer from the *Sama Veda* means:

May God protect us both, Guru and student (follower). Nourish us that we may work together with vigour and our endeavours shine. May we hold no malice towards each other. Om peace, peace, peace (Dave 1987:7).

☐ Prayer in Supplementary Classes

Prayer plays a significant role in supplementary classes (see chapter ten).[16] Even classes whose aim was not to teach religion as such, but to give instruction in an Indian language, often began and ended with prayer. Prayers also figure in the books which are used with pupils. These are the so-called 'secular' prayers of the type used in state schools in India where pupils of all religious backgrounds pray to God and the names of gods and goddesses are not used. Here, for example, is an English translation of a rhyming Gujarati prayer:

O Father, to you we bow.
We are your children and we sing your praises.
Please look after us.
Make us wise so that we do good deeds
and choose the right path.
May we have peace in our hearts.[17]

Many classes were religious in content and context — some being held in a temple building with adults coming in to pray. In Hindi classes in a temple in Woolwich, children sang a prayer which can be translated as follows:

O God, Giver of bliss, grant us knowledge
and remove our vices.
Take us into Thy care that we may become virtuous and peace-loving, protectors of the religion and brave. Always do we serve our teachers with love.

May we speak only the Truth, eschew lies
and maintain unity within ourselves.
Let us abuse no being, (even by mistake — in error).
Let our lives become Divine
and may we ever sing Thy praise. (Dave 1987:4).

In Coventry, Gujarati Hindu children including Sarita attended classes held in a large comprehensive school and community college. Prayer was a conspicuous element in these weekly sessions. All assembled on Sunday mornings in term time at ten am. Standing, with palms together, teachers and pupils first chanted a prayer beginning: *'gurur brahma gurur visnu'*. This prayer means:

The preceptor is Brahma, the preceptor is Vishnu,
The Guru is Lord Shiva.
The Guru is the supreme absolute.
I bow to my respected teachers.

Following it the children chanted a popular Sanskrit verse ascribed to Ramanuja, which is frequently sung at the end of *arati* in the temple. An English translation of the verse is:

You are my mother, you are my father,
You are my kin, you are my friend,
You are my knowledge, you are my wealth,
You are my everything, my God.

Following this they might chant lines translated by Dave (1987) as:

O Lord! Lead me from falsity to truth,
from darkness to light,
from death to immortality.
I am (alone without you)
O Lord! Bless me that I may see Thee.[18]

In classes intended to provide religious as opposed to linguistic instruction, prayer forms much of the content. In these classes children became familiar with the sound of the prayers through repeating them. Teachers also explained the meaning in English.

For Gujaratis the language of some prayers is their mother tongue. Below is an English translation of a Gujarati prayer which five year olds sang in 1985 at the Gujarati school's parents' evening in Coventry.

We are your children,
we are praying to you.

Dispel our troubles.
You show love to us.
You keep the light of love
between man and woman
and take the world forward.
My boat of life
is in the middle of the water.
Take it to the shore.
You are very merciful
We keep remembering you.
You give us peace of mind.[19]

Since Punjabis and Gujaratis often use Hindi in worship their children too learn Hindi prayers. The issue of language is not as thorny as it might seem since the key words in Sanskrit such as peace (*shanti*) and joy (*anand*) are used in India's modern languages. Many of the prayers cited above are learned by children in Sanskrit although most children have no tuition in the language. Children sometimes know a Sanskrit verse (*sloka*) without knowing the name of the language. As a Punjabi girl said, decribing the hymns which her family sing each day:

There's hard prayer in there and I can't understand. I've forgotten (what language they are in) I think they're not Bengali, but there's another one that I don't know what language it is but it's near to Bengali.

Deepak and Ritu were encouraged to learn Sanskrit verses from the *Bhagavad Gita*. Some of the prayers which children learn to recite are requests, sometimes for enlightenment (eg the Gayatri *mantra*), for forgiveness or for happiness as in the one beginning '*Om sarve bhavantu sukhina*'. Here is a rendering in English:

Let all be happy.
Let all be healthy.
Let all see the good.
Let no one be host to misery
Let everyone be happy.
Let everyone exercise equality.
Let Divine Joy engulf the world.
Let peace prevail throughout the earth.
Om, peace, peace, peace.
(Dave 1987: 6)

Many of the prayers which children learned were expressions of respect for God and for the *guru* (spiritual teacher). Terms for light, love, truth, mercy, peace, knowledge and life recurred. Above all, the prayers cumulatively impressed on children's understanding the concept of a supreme power which could be described in terms of the finest attributes, for example, 'God is true', 'the giver' etc. Prayers tend to repeat names or epithets for God rather than concentrating on aspects of the Divine-human relationship.

Many of the prayers learned by children were simply affirmations of the divine principle, using the traditional titles for the deities which have passed unchanged from Sanskrit into modern Indian languages. There is no one word for this divine power, but a multitude of terms. The names for the gods and goddesses of the Indian pantheon with their epithets are used in prayer. When the pupils of Vidya Vihar assembled on a Saturday morning, for example, they chanted a prayer which Dave translates:

> Auspicious Lord Vishnu,
> he with the eagle-emblemed flag
> with eyes of white lotus,
> he who is the sacred place itself.

At their annual parents' evenings Gujarati children in Coventry recited the invocation to goddess Saraswati. This *sloka* is translated in Dave (1987:6-7) as:

> She who is as fair as the jasmine flower, as the moon, like a snow white necklace, clad in white,
> whose hand is made beauteous in holding the vina.
> She who sits upon a white lotus
> is ever worshipped by Lord Brahma, Lord Vishnu,
> Lord Mahesh and yet more.
> Let this goddess, Sarasvati (goddess of knowledge) protect me, she who banishes ignorance.

In the Sathya Sai Baba movement's Bal Vikas classes, the supreme power was not only addressed in the Sanskrit epithets of Indian tradition but also prayed to in the form of the founders or leaders of the other major religious traditions. This *Sarva Dharma* Prayer (i.e. prayer of all religions), which is sung to a lively rhythm, has been translated as follows:

> O Lord! You are the Truth, you are Lord Narayana,
> You are the Supreme Teacher. You are Lord Buddha. You are Lord Kartikeya, Vinayaka and the Sun,
> The Purifier, You are Lord Brahma.

You are Mazad and Yahava,
You are Lord Jesus and Father.
Rudra (Lord Shiva) art Thou, Lord Vishnu.
You are Rama and Krishna, Rahim and Tao.
You are Lord Vasudeva,
You are the Universe entire and Eternal Bliss. Inimitable, Timeless and Fearless,
You are Lord Shiva within our souls. (Dave 1987:6)

□ Spontaneous Prayer

When questioned about prayer most children did not speak of praying in their own words. As one Valmiki girl said

> I wouldn't pray in my own words if someone was ill. I wouldn't have the words to pray in.

By contrast a Ravidasi girl explained:

> I say some words if I'm in trouble, I will say a prayer in Indian and in English...I'd say what my problem was, and I'd just talk for a bit as if the person was there with me and then I'd say 'amen' at the end...(I prayed like this) when my new cousin had Downes syndrome.

A *guru* at the Sathya Sai Cantre, Bradford said:

> I pray straight from the heart and I teach the kids that too. A prayer from the heart's more important — what you feel — rather than a prayer repeated.

It is probable that in their style of prayer children are influenced by encountering Christian practice. Certainly the *guru* quoted above had just mentioned using Christian prayers such as the prayer of St Francis of Assisi with his Bal Vikas class.

Sometimes it seemed that in describing their prayers to an outsider children were not repeating the words they would actually use but were providing an English prayer as a way of explaining their understanding of a traditional Indian form of words or gesture. So a Punjabi boy said:

> All I usually say is 'Dear God, will you forgive me' — something like that. (I do this) after I've done something bad or in the morning to a picture (he demonstrated putting his hands together in Hindu greeting then extending his hands to the picture, then putting them together again). I don't really say nothing, I just touch it just to say sort of like 'Good morning, God'.

☐ Silent Sitting

Children attending Bal Vikas, the 'child development' classes provided by followers of Sathya Sai Baba, practised 'silent sitting', a simple meditation technique (see chapters eight and ten). They sat, cross-legged on the floor with their eyes closed. One *guru* explained that at first the little children would scratch and fidget, moving their hands and heads. She would tell them to concentrate on not moving. Later on they would be encouraged to 'concentrate on their breathing or on a candle'.

Jumsai, a writer on human values from the Sathya Sai Baba movement, describes silent sitting in detail:

> Silent sitting means enabling the child to end his thoughts so that there is no wastage of energy, no noise within, only stillness and silence. It is in that silence that the intuition of a child comes.

> If you put a piece of paper in the sun nothing will happen, but if you bring a lens in between them, the paper gets burnt. The rays of the sun converge through the lens and develop the power and heat and energy to burn the paper. The paper is like a problem we may have. The lens is the process of silent sitting.

> If the children are too young, the teacher can paint a verbal picture for them — think of the fragrance of a rose, of the joy it gives, of a river, of a plant. The teacher must practise silent sitting at his or her own home for one or two minutes once or twice a day or as often as you can. (1985:18)

☐ *Om*

Before and after silent sitting the children in the Bal Vikas class chanted the sacred syllable om very slowly so that the sound reverberated. This is the opening syllable of many of the *mantras* which children use in worship at the family shrine or on each bead of the rosary (*mala*). Anita and her sister explained that they must repeat *om* twenty one times during their early morning prayers. In this way they were 'waking the god within the heart'. They went on to explain that *om* must be said at the beginning of every *sloka* (verse). As Anita explained, 'It is universal. It is sufficient on its own, but without it the sloka is useless. That is what Hindus believe.'

Indeed *om*, as their father explained, 'represents the whole universe'. Excited at what she had learned at Bal Vikas classes, Anita explained that the sages would concentrate on the dot which is part of the written Sanskrit character for *om*. As the *om* sound rose from the stomach, she said, the sound followed the outline of the *om* symbol, and ended in the dot with which it had

108

begun. She added that *om* is more correctly written *aum*, the letter 'a' being the last letter of Brahma, 'u' the last letter of Vishnu, and 'm' the first letter of Mahesh (Shiva). '*Om*', she summarised, 'is the creator, destroyer and preserver or sustainer'. Her father added that *om* is intoned at three levels; from the diaphragm it reaches the throat from where it rises to the top of the head 'which is Brahma'.[20]

Some children thought that *om* means 'peace'. This rendering presumably results from the frequent combination of *om* with *shanti*, 'peace'. Five children described *om* as 'God of snakes'. This would be a reasonable deduction as they hear Shiva (who is associated with the cobra) invoked by the words *om namah sivai*. Describing a picture of Shiva in his house one Gujarati boy said:

> Well, we got this other god and he's the god of snakes. He's got a snake around here, but the snakes don't bite him because the snakes know that he's a god so they don't bite.
>
> (Qu. You don't know what he's called?)
>
> No ... yes. I know what he's called. He's called *Om*.

Whatever their level of understanding of *om*, the children were familiar with it as a word used in prayer, a word of power. When Arun's great uncle died it was good, his mother said, that a relative was saying *om* in his ear.

☐ Conclusion

Hindu children speak unselfconsciously about praying. They use the term to describe the repetition of mantras and salutations to the deities. They mention petition and thanking God but this seems generally to represent the unspoken motivation behind offering a traditional form of words. They encounter nothing like the extempore vocal prayer of Protestant Christianity. Children accept that what matters is the correct repetition of sacred words and are not concerned about their literal meaning. They testify to the peace of mind that results.

The language of personal prayer may be English. The language of public prayer is always an Indian one — either Sanskrit or a modern vernacular. This contributes to a sense of distinct identity and of cultural continuity similar to the use of Hebrew by British Jews (Glinert 1985:9).

It seems likely that, as with previous generations, individuals devote more time to prayer when they face problems, such as coping with a handicapped child. At times of anguish or in old age, today's young Hindus are likely to turn to traditional forms of prayer for solace.

Notes

1. Coventry Hindus reported that sacred items, such as religious pictures and coconuts that have been used in a religious ceremony, must not be thrown away; they should be put in a river. The canal which runs across the north of Coventry was mentioned in this connection by other Hindus.

2. This is an ancient prayer for enlightement which occurs in the *Rig Veda* (3,62,10). It can be translated in English as:

    Let us meditate on the excellent splendour of the sun-god, Savitri; may he rouse our insights. (Jackson and Killingley 1988:96).

3. A Gujarati Brahmin adult, whose grandfather taught her the words as a child, mentioned deriving comfort from reciting them at times of stress. Arun's mother indicated that the *mantra* is believed to be beneficial even if the person who sees the words does so for the first time and reads them out with no knowledge of their significance.

4. Even to say the word 'Rama' accidentally or unthinkingly may give salvation' (Planalp 1956, II:360). Arun's mother also made the point that the name of Rama is even more powerful than Rama himself (cf Planalp op cit: 861).

5. This point is illustrated by a story from the Narada Parivrajake *upanishad* cited by Sastri (1963). Brahma requested Narada to teach this *mahamantra* as the simplest means for people to attain salvation.

6. For a similar story 'which comes down to us from the era of Sri Chaitanya's disciples' see Monks of the Ramakrishna Order 1974 : XX1-XXII. For the story of how Ravi Das ignored a philosopher's stone which turned all it touched to gold, with the words, 'only God is important and his name is the only good' see Briggs (nd : 207-211).

7. As Arun's mother mentioned, a rosary can also be used, for instance, to keep count when a holy book is being circumambulated a prescribed number of times.

8. *Japa* is a word cognate with *japna*. In several North Indian languages *japna* means 'to repeat' and is used for the contemplative repetition of God's name or a longer *mantra*. Gonda remarks:

    The repetition of mantras, and in general passages from the scriptures, spells, prayers, names of deities etc. in a murmuring tone is called *japa*'.(1986, chapter 10).

9. Stevenson describes one form of rosary bag and its use (1971:223 and 388).

10. On July 12th 1987 devotees and many others participated in a Rathayatra (chariot procession) through the streets of London. Children distributed free copies of *Rathayatra '87 Souvenir Magazine*. This gives guidelines on 'chanting *Japa*' including an illustration of 'How to use beads whilst chanting *japa*'.

    One may chant the *maha mantra* softly on beads for personal meditation. This is called *japa*. Using beads is very helpful for concentration. One can obtain a set of beads and, holding them as in the illustration, chant a *mantra*

110

on each bead, moving forward one bead at a time until all 108 beads have been counted on. This is known as one 'round' of *japa*, and practitioners of *japa* meditation chant a regular number of 'rounds' per day. There are no hard and fast rules as to time, place or speed of chanting. The main thing is to be attentive and listen to the sound of the names. The name of God is not a mundane sound vibration, it is one and the same with Him. (Kripamoya dasa 1987:24)

11. Stevenson remarks:

> If he uses a rosary, he tells the beads by passing them between his thumb and second finger, the rosary itself depending not, of course, from the inauspicious first finger, but from the second.(1971:223)

Anita's father explained the position of the hand in the meditation posture adopted by Sai devotees. The forefinger and thumb are joined. The thumb represents Brahma or Shiva and the forefinger is '*jiva*'.

12. Arun's mother spoke of reciting all the gods' names she could think of before sleeping each night. But her mother had cautioned that if anyone repeated the *Gayatri mantra* while lying in bed he or she would be a crocodile in his or her next birth.

13. For a variant interpretation see Stevenson (1971:210).

14. The verse in Gujarati is transliterated into Roman Script in Anon (1983: 8-11). The *suprabhatam* continues with eleven more verses. An English translation is also provided.

15. Stevenson reports:

> Food is Brahma, its essence is Visnu, the eater is Siva. He who dines realising this is free from the sins appertaining to eating. (1971:242)

16. The research on supplementary schools outside Coventry was conducted in 1984. For further details see Jackson and Nesbitt (1986).

17. Translated by A.M. Lakdawala.

18. These words are a Gujarati form of the words from the Brihadanayaka *upanishad,* which is also widely used in worship:

> O Lord, lead us from untruth to truth,
> from darkness to light,
> from mortality to immortality.

19. Translated by Jyoti Mistry.

20. Hoens (1979:103) quotes a similar analysis of *om* attributed to Vedantadesika, a fourteenth century teacher.

CHAPTER 8

Gurs, Babas and Religious Movements

☐ Introduction

Local tradition and family custom have for centuries provided Hindus with the supportive framework of an unwritten code of social behaviour. Myth and ritual have sacralised individual roles and points in the life cycle. Solace and inspiration could be found in devotional songs and, for the learned, in ancient scripture. In addition, individuals in every period have turned for spiritual sustenance and firm guidelines to living teachers, known as *gurus*. In the *guru* his (or, much less frequently, her) followers would sense a unique revelation of the divine. Members of successive generations have continued to worship some *gurus* long after their physical demise and people might also glimpse the divine in the *guru's* spiritual successors. This sequence of a *guru* whose disciples in turn become *guru* constitutes a *sampradaya* (literally 'handing on'). Many *gurus* have had only local followings. Some, such as Jalaram Bapa in Gujarat (1799-1881), have achieved regional status. Others, such as Sathya Sai Baba, have risen to national and international recognition.

The families of many Hindu children in Britain are strongly influenced by *sampradayas* or *guru* movements, though, equally, many are not, with some Hindus distancing themselves from certain movements. To understand their importance we must look at the contemporary British Hindu context. In British society there is no overall Hindu ethos. Previously accepted values are challenged; Hindu festivals are displaced. Individuals are caught up in

113

rapid change and recurrent perplexity. For many, fresh meaning and content is given to domestic and communal worship by the preaching of a *guru* or simply by coming into his or her presence and meeting his or her benedictory gaze, an experience known as *darshan*.

Gurus visit Britain to address often huge gatherings. Modern technology enhances their impact and increases their outreach as they can be seen discoursing on video cassette. Air travel and mass media are contributing to the energising vitality of a long established feature of Hinduism. Recent writers point to the unprecedented growth of *guru* cults in independent, urban India.[1] The factors of social mobility and dislocation which have made *gurus* increasingly popular in modern India are even more compelling features of diaspora Hindu life.

In this chapter we look at the range of Hindu religious movements in Britain with particular reference to the impact of three on children in Coventry. We note the part that *gurus* and their movements play in the religious nurture of Hindu children in Britain and this discussion continues in chapter ten.

It is important to emphasise at the outset that there is no English equivalent for '*sampradaya*'. The word 'sect' suggests congregations with a particular doctrinal stance meeting separately from other religious bodies. It is burdened with the history of Western denominationalism. The term 'movement' does not itself convey the centrality of the *guru* as a channel of divine influence and a guide to the individual human spirit's liberation from repeated rebirth on earth. Hindus may draw great inspiration from one *guru* tradition without having any sense that it is exclusive or that it is excluded from other Hindu traditions.

Religious movements play a significant role in the experience of Mridula, Deepak, Ritu, Bhavesh, Hitesh and Anita. At the same time all these children are involved in the life of a wider Hindu community. That this wider community is inclusive of these movements is made clear by pictures on the walls of the Shree Krishna Temple and the Ram *Mandir.*

In this chapter we look at children's experience of three *sampradayas*, and at the role played by the visits of India's spiritual giants. In Coventry fewer *guru* traditions are represented than in the larger Hindu populations of Leicester or London. In Coventry the Arya Samaj, a movement with predominantly Punjabi followers which emerged in the nineteenth century, is very small.[2] The Brahmakumaris are also few in number.[3] The various denominations of the Swaminarayan religion, though numerous in Bolton and elsewhere, are not evident in Coventry.[4] Jalaram Bapa, though respected by Gujaratis, especially those whose families originate from Kathiawar, has no public place of worship, as in Leicester.[5] Coventry does, however, have a substantial Valmiki community, all Punjabis of a single *shudra* caste. Valmiki children's experience is reported throughout this book. However, for detailed accounts of the community and of the children's involvement in religion, the reader must turn elsewhere.[6] Many Coventry Valmikis regard themselves as Sikh rather than Hindu and the issues involved fall outside the scope of this chapter. Punjabi Hindus participate in Radhasoami and attend the Bawa Balakanath temple. Both these extremely dissimilar congregations include many Sikhs.[7]

☐ Pushtimarg

For Mridula her paternal grandmother, radiant and whitehaired, exemplifies the religious life. She is a *Vaishnav* (a devotee of Vishnu), the name generally used by followers of Pushtimarg, the path (*marg*) of grace (*pushti*). This is the 'sect' to which many members of the Lohana (business) caste belong, though membership is not exclusive to this caste.[8] The founder of Pushtimarg was Vallabhacharya who died in 1532.[9] He urged followers to practise *seva* (loving service) to God in the form of Lord Krishna. This *seva* should be constant devotion without thought of reward and should involve body, mind and wealth. God blesses the devotee with his grace (*pushti*). This is contrasted with the way of discipline (*maryada*) symbolised by Rama, another human *avatar* (incarnation) of Vishnu. There is no hard and fast line between Pushtimargis and other Hindus, some of whom are profoundly influenced by Pushtimarg.

In Mridula's family some members, including herself and her younger brother, received *brahmasambandh*. This can be translated as 'connection with the Almighty' (Vaidya 1966). As far as Mridula was concerned it meant that her *guru* had whispered 'Sri Krishna' three times in her ear and that since then she had been able to help her grandmother more in serving guests, as other Pushtimargis would now accept food from her hands. Strict adherents will not accept food from others. Mridula explained:

> After *brahmasambandh*, if you are wearing the *kanthi* (necklace of beads made from the stem of the sacred *tulsi* plant) you can't eat meat or eat at anyone else's house except at the house of a person who had *brahmasambandh* from the same person as yourself. If you're not wearing it you are an ordinary person like me!

In the Shree Krishna Temple there are the three pictures, set side by side, which are to be seen in Pushtimargi homes such as Mridula's. On the left Vallabhacharya and on the right Yamunaji face inwards towards the central icon, a distinctive black form of Krishna, known as Srinathji. Yamuna, a goddess who is both river and queen, is highly regarded and the Pushtimargis' *arati* hymn is an invocation of Yamuna.[10] Mridula's family venerate Vallab-hacharya and they regard as *gurus* members of the Goswami family such as Indira Betiji, a female spiritual teacher whose religious base is in Gujarat, but who periodically visits Hindu communities in Britain and North America.

When the *gurus* come to Britain they visit Pushtimargi households includ-ing Mridula's. First the people who have gathered sit on the floor singing *bhajans*, then they ask the *guru* questions. Mridula referred to the *gurus* as 'Maharaj' and she said that she could not fully understand their homilies. She felt too shy to ask any questions herself as her Gujarati was too elementary. Sometimes Mridula's *guru* came to Coventry. She described meeting him and his children.

> We have to go there and when the time comes you touch their (the *guru's*) legs and leave some money there. They take that, they send the money off to India. Their children are quite friendly because we went some-where and some of us, a few girls, were left in charge of them. If we don't do what they tell you you get a telling off from your parents.

Since Indira Betiji would drink no tap water, but only coconut water, Mridu-la's aunts' shop did a good business in coconuts when Betiji came to Coventry. Even for washing up a linen cloth would be tied over the taps to filter the water.

Despite first hand experience there was little which Mridula could formu-late about Pushtimarg. She did not observe the dietary rules strictly (see chapter five) nor did she repeat the words which she had been told to repeat daily by her *guru*. She did not usually wear the *kanthi*, a necklace of beads cut from the stems of *tulsi* plants, which is the sign of *gurus* and people who 'have joined their little group'.

No supplementary classes are run by Pushtimargis in Coventry for their children nor did Mridula have books on Pushtimarg in English. But her knowledge of Pushtimarg, though not intellectual, was evident. She was acutely aware of her grandmother's consistent abstinence from forbidden foods, of her loving *seva* to lord Krishna and of her frequent participation in *satsang* (gatherings) with other Pushtimargis.

In the event of having to live in a non-Hindu household Mridula said that above all she would miss the daily devotions of Ba (Grandma):

> At home my gran would always have a bath and go into her room and pray and all that. I'd miss hearing all the songs she'd be singing because I quite enjoy that. I don't know the words but I enjoy the music. I just sit there outside the door. If I've had a bath sometimes I'll ask her (if I can go into the room). If she says 'yes' I sit there and sometimes help her out.

Ba joyfully and faithfully performed *seva* to Bal (infant) Krishna every day unless prevented by circumstances. If her Hindu calendar indicated an eclipse (an inauspicious day) she would do no more than replace the food she had offered to Krishna. Her *seva* consisted of expressing her love for Krishna in the same detailed service which a mother performs for her baby. A three inch long brass image of the infant Krishna in a crawling posture was central to this act of devotion which lasted several hours each morning.

After having a bath and putting on a clean *sari*, Ba would sit cross-legged on the floor of her bedroom in front of a wall unit. By her was a low oil stove on which she heated milk for Krishna. The lowest left hand section of the wall unit housed the image of Krishna whom she lifted tenderly from between the bedclothes in a small sewing basket which rested on an eight inch long bed. She kissed him and left him in the central section of the wall unit. Here on a miniature table were a minute *thali* and bowls of milk and almonds. After closing the door, hiding him from view, she would sit praying soundlessly on her rosary.

Having clapped twice to warn Krishna, she would open the door, remove the food and proceed to bath him in a small steel bowl. She dressed him in tiny pieces of cloth taken from a doll's chest of drawers and set him on a miniature sofa in the central section of the unit. Here she adorned him with necklaces, earrings and a crown, before setting a full size *thali* near him and closing the door on him to give him privacy while she prayed. Her worship included singing the *arati* addressed to Yamuna. Later Ba would give Mridula and others Krishna's *prashad*. This consisted of the almonds, sultanas, sugar crystals and dates which she had offered to him.

Like the other women in her *satsang* group Mridula's grandmother periodically hosted the *satsang* in her own house. These *satsang* groups consisted of about fifteen women sitting on the floor singing unaccompanied from hymn books. They might dance *ras* (circle dances in praise of Krishna), and perform *arati* in front of Yamuna, whose picture was hidden from view by a shawl held across the shrine. The women received in their mouths a spoonful of Yamuna water. Milk, flavoured with sweet spices, was shared and on special occasions the hostess provided a vegetarian meal.

For the month before the Holi festival, these *satsangs* were more frequent and lively than usual. Participants' cheeks and cardigans were stained with red powder (*kanku*). The hostess came round with a tray of *kanku* to daub the cheeks of newcomers amid banter and laughing protest. Everyone present was showered with popcorn.

Mridula was welcome to join in the *satsangs* provided she bathed and changed her clothes first. She knew and accepted the required behaviour but she could not define Pushtimarg in terms of its teaching or history because it had never been presented to her in this way. Above all for her it was simply her grandmother's way of life and a network of people whom she saw at *satsangs*.

☐ ISKCON — the Hare Krishna Movement

The International Society for Krishna Consciousness (ISKCON) is another *guru*-led movement.[11] Followers venerate the great saint, Chaitanya Mahaprabhu, a Bengali who lived at the same time as Vallabhacharya. He too presented *bhakti*, loving devotion to God in the form of Krishna. Like Pushtimarg, ISKCON requires strict vegetarianism. In Coventry some local families gather for regular *kirtan* (corporate hymn singing). They acknowledge a line of *gurus*, and give special prominence to Bhaktivedanta Swami Prabhupada (1896-1977) who travelled to America, founded ISKCON and wrote a commentary on the *Bhagavad Gita*.

Clearly, with its evangelising Western thrust, ISKCON's history differs markedly from the history of Pushtimarg. Not surprisingly the recent growth of Krishna Consciousness as a largely Western movement shapes its impact on children. So, for example, attractive books of Hare Krishna teaching are published in the English of native speakers. These publications, designed appropriately for different age groups, have an appeal beyond the movement.[12] Bhavini, whose parents are not associated with the movement, had an ISKCON colouring book.

The impact of ISKCON, unlike Pushtimarg, was apparent among Hindu families of diverse ethnic origin, whereas only Gujarati children in Coventry (indeed only children from one caste), described any experience of Pushtimarg. Hare Krishna *kirtans* (hymn singing and worship) drew both Gujaratis and Punjabis.[13] A few devotees of European and African descent were conspicuous at larger Hare Krishna events to which they came from outside Coventry.

With its professionally produced English language publications, the ethnic diversity of its devotees and its relatively high profile in the mass media, ISKCON has made some impact on Hindu families who had no association with the movement.[14] Arun's favourite key ring had been bought at Bhaktivedanta Manor, the mansion housing ISKCON'S temple and British headquarters. He was one of many who saw the Manor on television. Subsequently he wrote in his diary:

> On Monday 8th February we watched Blue Peter. It was about a temple in Watford called the Hare Krishna Temple. The man from Blue Peter went to the Temple and he wanted to become a producer so a camera crew went with him and he was allowed to film the Hare Krishna

devotees and their children who live there. The man from Blue Peter (Simon) directed the cameras and they filmed the people there inside the temple. They filmed them doing *arati* and praying to Lord Krishna because they believe in Lord Krishna a lot. Outside they filmed the garden and some peacocks and other wildlife.

Some Hindu adults were more negative, voicing criticism of the movement for its narrow interpretation of ancient texts and its drive to win converts. In this vein Mridula commented one day:

> I can't stand the Hare Krishna lot. They preach and preach and preach that you should become a Hare Krishna. I've been told these things by friends.

So much for the impressions of Hindu children who were not directly involved in ISKCON. For children such as Deepak and Ritu and their cousins the movement has profoundly affected their experience and understanding of Hinduism.

This was apparent when they and other children, whose families were involved in ISKCON, talked about their life as Hindus. As noted in chapter five they all stressed the importance of being vegetarian. They also talked about Krishna, and about their 'beads'. As noted in chapter seven, by their 'beads' they meant the *japa mala* or rosary on which ISKCON devotees daily recite the words:

> *Hare Krishna Hare Krishna Krishna Krishna Hare Hare*
> *Hare Rama Hare Rama Ram Rama Hare Hare.*

Chanting this *mahamantra*, dancing and eating food which has been offered to Krishna are the central requirements of ISKCON.

For children like Ritu and Deepak, Bhaktivedanta Manor is a special place for enjoyable family visits. The detailed service of devotees to the deities in the temple is an example of loving attention to ritual detail. Behind a wrought iron grille in the worship hall stand images of Sita, Rama, Lakshman and Hanuman and of Krishna's consort, Radha, all beautifully dressed, adorned and garlanded. Every day the deities are bathed, dressed, offered food, water, incense, light and flowers by the *pujari* (priest). At the opposite end of the hall is a life-size statue of Prabhupada.

Because thousands of Hindus flock to Bhaktivedanta Manor for Janmashtami, the celebration of Lord Krishna's birthday, it is an especially memorable occasion for the children who are present. 'On Janmashtami we feel so happy,' said Ritu. For Ritu and Deepak, in addition to the major Hindu festivals such as Divali and Mahashivaratri, there are ISKCON-related events to celebrate. The major festivals such as Holi provide opportunities for children to perform plays with a Hare Krishna message (see chapters six and seven).

Between January 1986 and August 1987 Deepak and Ritu's family participated in two local events organised by ISKCON — one a public function to welcome Srila Gurudev, then head of ISKCON in Britain, the other a forty eight hour session in the Hindu *Mandir* of chanting the *mahamantra* for world peace. Anniversaries such as the 'appearance day' (ie birth) of Swami Nityananda, a *guru*, and the 500th 'appearance day' of Chaitanya were marked as a reason for special rejoicing during weekly *kirtan*. But the undoubted high point of each year for the children was the Rathayatra. The Rathayatra is an annual procession through London headed by a ceremonial carriage (*rath*). This carries the images of Jagannath (Lord of the Universe) and of his brother, Baldev and sister, Subhadra. The London Rathayatra is modelled on the celebration at Puri, in the Indian state of Orissa, where hundreds of thousands of devotees worship God in this form as they did in the days of Chaitanya.[15]

In Britain, with the prior agreement of the Metropolitan Police, the Rathayatra takes place on a Saturday in July. From the Hindu Temple in Coventry a full coach leaves each year for the Rathayatra amid triumphal cries of 'Rathayatra *ki jay*' ('long live Rathayatra'). Everyone is in festive mood, singing hymns to Krishna and sharing out tasty home made sweets and savouries. In 1986, at about noon, the coach reached Marble Arch where a crowd was gathering around the *rath*, a brightly painted wooden vehicle surmounted by a framework covered with scarlet and yellow cloth in the shape of a North Indian temple. This could be raised and lowered during the procession by a devotee cranking it up and down from inside, so avoiding collision with overhanging branches. Jagannath, Baldev and Subhadra were the deities enthroned. Devotees, mainly male Westerners clad in *dhoti* and with their heads shaven except for a knotted tuft of hair on the crown, rode on the *rath* which was festooned with garlands of French marigolds and traditional temple hangings (*toran*). Throughout the procession the *mahamantra*, '*Hare Krishna Hare Krishna Krishna Krishna Hare Hare, Hare Rama Hare Rama Rama Rama Hare Hare*' was sung, amplified from the *rath*. A crowd of adults and children, and infants in baby buggies, moved slowly along a route lined by police to Battersea Park, arriving there at about four pm. A lifesize image of Prabhupada in a velvet chair was borne aloft in front of the procession and a small portable shrine, containing Jagannath, Baldev and Subhadra was pulled along. The *rath* itself was pulled by dozens of people holding the two ropes. Ritu and Deepak were glad to join in this symbolic act of service to God. In Deepak's words:

People pull the *rath* as a way of bringing good luck and fortune to their family. That's why there are a lot of people pulling it.

In Battersea Park there was a pavilion tent where the deities from the *rath* had been set up in a shrine on stage. Prabhupada's figure was also installed and appeared to be presiding over the crowd. Celebrities spoke on religious themes and copies of ISKCON's *The Great Classics of India* were displayed on stage. The *gurukula* (school) children performed a play with the message that Krishna is the supreme personality of godhead. Long queues formed for the vegetarian food (*prashadam*). The mood was happy and relaxed. To quote Deepak: 'You have a nice day. They put on plays about Krishna and they give chips and ice creams as well'.

When it was time to leave the park the Coventry children clambered on board the coach wearing garlands from the *rath*. Deepak carried his *dholki* (drum) to accompany singing on the homeward journey.

For Ritu and Deepak, Krishna Consciousness was not just a matter of occasional celebrations or contact with Bhaktivedanta Manor. Their evening worship at home followed a liturgical pattern which was distinctive of ISKCON. The light was not circled during the singing of '*om jay...*', as happens more generally in Hindu worship, but before it. Deepak and Ritu played an active part, singing, playing *tabla* and harmonium, and circling the lamp in front of the upstairs shrine. They could point out the differences between this and the form of *arati* used in the temple. This was not just because of involvement but also because of semi-formal teaching during the weekly *kirtan*.

Since 1988 this congregational hymn singing has taken place on Sunday afternoons in the Shri Shri Radha Krishna Community Centre, the ISKCON temple in Coventry. But throughout the research period *kirtan* was held in private homes on Saturday evenings, often in Ritu and Deepak's parents' or uncle's house. A shrine would be set up on a low table against the living room wall. On it were pictures of Prabhupada and of Krishna. Men sat facing this on one side of the room, women on the other. For half an hour everyone sang *bhajans*, especially the *mahamantra*, accompanied by Deepak on the *dholki* (drum). Small boys danced to this, their arms over their heads and their orange bags of meditation beads swaying at the right wrist. A homily for the adults followed during which children went upstairs. On one occasion a devotee from outside Coventry addressed the adults. The children rejoined their parents, and more *bhajans* were followed by *arati* and *prashadam*, a full scale vegetarian meal, eaten seated on the floor.

ISKCON provided extra content and a firmer framework for the lives of Ritu's and Deepak's family than more general community involvement. It represented a further commitment over and above their involvement in worship at the Hindu temple and their calendar of work, school, family engagements and life cycle rites. The distinctive emphasis of ISKCON, clearly expounded (often in English), afforded Deepak and Ritu a way of understanding and articulating Hinduism in general. Commitment to ISKCON brought them close to other families, both Gujarati and Punjabi, who shared a similar commitment.

☐ Sathya Sai Baba

His red cassock and halo of fuzzy black hair make the living South Indian *guru*, Sathya Sai Baba instantly recognisable.[16] Probably the majority of Hindus in Coventry have heard his name and seen his picture although only a few have reordered their lives in strict accordance with his teachings. Some are mildly sceptical about devotees' claims for his divine status and miraculous powers. Like ISKCON, Sathya Sai Baba, a charismatic and controversial figure, has a high profile. This is partly because of his reputation for performing supernatural acts, materialising such things as holy ash and Swiss wrist watches. His movement also has a high level of organisation, best exemplified in Britain by the Bal Vikas classes for children which are described in more detail in chapter ten. Although in Coventry his followers are all Gujarati, Sathya Sai Baba, like ISKCON, has indigenous followers in many Western countries as well as followers who are Hindus from diverse regional backgrounds. Also like ISKCON the Sathya Sai Baba organisation is a twentieth century phenomenon which can only be understood by taking a historical view of Hindu tradition (Jackson and Killingley 1988: 183). Like ISKCON, but for different reasons, Sathya Sai Baba is also censured by some Hindus.

In accordance with his teaching the followers of Sathya Sai Baba have no public place of worship in Coventry. Anita's home is recognised by the Sai Council of Great Britain as a Centre (Rodway nd). Every Thursday evening during our field work, the living room of her family's terraced house filled with friends singing *bhajans* in praise of Sathya Sai Baba. Every Sunday afternoon people gathered at her aunt's, and on Monday evenings a 'Sai Study Circle' met at Anita's to share Sathya Sai Baba's teachings.

These teachings, like those of the *gurus* of ISKCON and Pushtimarg, include strict vegetarianism. Followers not only display pictures of Sathya Sai Baba in their homes but set up a domestic shrine in which his picture, framed and garlanded, is the focus for worship. As noted in chapter seven, daily worship takes a distinctive form. Anita's day begins with the *suprabhatam* (morning prayer) and closes with the rite of *arati* in which the hymn '*om jai jagadisha hare, Swami Sathya Sai hare*' is sung to a quickening tempo and is followed by distribution of powdery ash (*vibhuti*) as *prashad* (Bhajanavali 1983:171).

For Sathya Sai Baba's followers Hindu concepts, words and actions assume the mould characteristic of the movement. The annual calendar is enriched with additional days of celebration. Major festivals such as Mahashivaratri and the birthdays of Rama and Krishna receive a new emphasis, since for devotees Sathya Sai Baba is a present day *avatar* (literally 'descent' ie incarnation) of Shiva, Vishnu and Mataji. He is God, the recipient of all prayers, whether they are addressed to Jesus, Allah or God by any other name. The story of Sathya Sai Baba and his movement is available elsewhere.[17] What follows is the briefest of summaries.

Sathya Sai Baba was born in 1926 in Puttaparthi in the South Indian state of Andhra Pradesh. He was given the name Satyanarayan Raju. In 1940 he declared himself to be the incarnation of a popular Maharashtrian saint, Shirdi Sai Baba, who had died in 1918. This was widely accepted, as was his subsequent claim in 1963 to be the incarnation of Shiva-Shakti (the divine creative power in both male and female form).

Sathya Sai Baba preaches that God is *nirguna*, beyond attributes. What appears as reality is in fact *maya* (illusory), but through *bhakti* (devotion) people can realise what is true. Love and God are one. Devotees are to sing *bhajans* together and to perform *seva* (service) to the community. Anita took this seriously. Her repertoire of *bhajans* in English, Gujarati, Hindi and Sanskrit was extensive. Her commitment to social service was evident at school where, for example, she organised a sponsored 'stay awake' to raise money for charity.

Sathya Sai Baba was usually referred to not by his full name but by the one word 'Baba', a title expressing love and respect. It was important to the children that unlike 'other gods Sathya Sai Baba is still alive' and could even be visited. Accounts of his miracles made an impact on the children, none of whom evinced any disbelief. One ten year old Gujarati boy had seen Baba in his headquarters in South India. He felt that miracles were a necessary means of convincing sceptics of Baba's powers.

> I met him before and I even spoke to him. I was wondering, 'Why doesn't he show them something like Jesus' miracles? Why doesn't he do a miracle?' And I mean really people see it, not just no-one's there. He does something and then people come and say, 'Oh, look at that'.

In June 1985, at an audience of devotees from Great Britain, Baba materialised a *lingam*, a small phallus-shaped symbol of Shiva, from his mouth. This miracle, which is now performed annually on Mahashivaratri, was described by a twelve year old girl. Two words in her account may need explanation. Shankar is a name for Shiva and *shivling* is another term for *lingam*:

> They told us that Baba, every year I think it is, gets a Shankar, a Shiv Shankar, out of his mouth, and if he doesn't then something happens to him. It comes through his body, up to his mouth, you know, *shivling*. He's got to get that out of his mouth every year. If he doesn't get it out I don't know but something happens. The world will be destroyed, something like that.

Each week a leading British devotee poured water over the *lingam* that had been materialised in 1985 and gave some to the sick, as instructed by Baba. The ten year old boy, quoted above, explained:

> This man had this *lingam* from Baba. It's kind of round like this. It's long with a kind of round thing at the end of it, and the man, when he poured water over it, he gave it to the sick people, they became better.

Anita's family kept some of this sacred water in a plastic two-litre squash bottle near the shrine downstairs. They had some more in their upstairs *mandir*. Anita was accustomed to people, often complete strangers, some not Indian, knocking on the door and asking for some of their water as they had heard that it could cure the sick. The family kept adding tap water to it so that it never ran out before someone arrived with some more from London. The water, Anita emphasised, always remained cold (see chapter five).

According to Anita, Baba also healed the sick through other people. She remembered that while she was staying at Prasanthi Nilayam in 1985:

> We were sleeping one night and someone knocked and said, 'We need O negative blood'. Someone was dying. There was not time to test. Only the blood of two people was needed. She didn't die. It was three in the night. Swami was in Prasanthi and we were outside in the village. He doesn't come and heal you like that. He helped by giving two people.

In conversation Anita articulated clearly her belief in Sathya Sai Baba. He is believed, as an incarnation of both Shiva and Shakti, to be both male and female. She explained that in Telugu, his mother tongue, 'Sai' is goddess, 'Sathya' is truth. She drew attention to a colour print of Sathya Sai Baba standing with a white cloth tying his hair back. This, she explained, was a way of showing him as mother.[19]

Anita regarded Baba's actions as imbued with deeper meaning. For example as he chewed betel nut he was really chewing people's *karma*, their bad deeds, so, through his grace, diminishing their *karmic* debt.

Anita would refer to particular points which she felt distinguished Baba's teaching from Hinduism generally. For example on the question of whether marriage should be with someone from the same caste she said, 'Baba's thing — you don't believe in caste or creed or colour'. Children's love for Baba was sustained by the *gurus* who taught them efficiently and affectionately in weekly Bal Vikas classes (see chapter ten).

The *gurus* organised summer camps and festival celebrations in which children participated with hymns, dancing and drama. Bhavesh, Hitesh and Anita were fully involved in these classes and in the organised religious programmes. They would speak readily about Baba and their enjoyment of religious activities.

For Anita, involvement in the Sathya Sai Baba movement brought meaning to everything and added content to an already extremely active routine. Her life was already full with school and family activities including housework. She participated enthusiastically in sport and Indian dance, music and events organised by the temple and the *samaj* (the organisation for members of her caste). Daily worship of Baba and weekly attendance at Bal Vikas left little time to spare. Her year was further punctuated with Sai celebrations. Some coincided with major Hindu festivals such as Divali, Mahashivaratri and Janmashtami. Christmas was observed as a religious festival too (see chapter six). Other celebrations were specific to Sai devotees — notably Easwaramma Day, the anniversary of Sathya Sai Baba's mother's death, and November 23rd, Sathya Sai Baba's birthday. Below is listed a selection from the many events in Coventry organised by Sathya Sai Baba's devotees during our fieldwork. In all these Anita participated and the descriptions are hers.

November 1985 — 24 hours of singing *bhajans* for peace at Anita's house:

> I am going to write about the 24 hours of *bhajans* (Glory to God) for peace throughout the world. It started at 6 pm on Saturday 8th November and finished at 6 pm on Sunday 9th November. At 6 o'clock not many people came, but soon many people started coming. Some even stayed overnight. It was a very good experience for the people who were doing it the first time.

November 1985 — Celebration of Sathya Sai Baba's birthday in Wellingborough:

> On the 22nd November we went to Wellingborough for the celebration of Baba's Birthday. It was a very good experience. I loved it. There were all different types of performances going on — cultural dances, folk dances, classical dance dramas, and speeches by members of the UK

council. We had lunch there and we also brought a few books back for us to read here. There was this large cake made for Baba's Birthday. It was enough for everyone to have some and we are going to celebrate Baba's Birthday here on the actual day.

November 1985 —Sathya Sai Baba's birthday, celebration at Anita's house:

Today I am writing about Baba's Birthday celebration in my house. Yesterday it all started at 7.30 pm. We sang lots of *bhajans*, in Hindi, Sanskrit, Gujarati and English. We also prepared a cradle for him (to) lie in and the house was lit up with *divas*, candles and Christmas lights. Near the end we all started singing Happy Birthday. We blew out the candles on the cake that my mother had made and cut a piece out for Baba. At the end of the 'party' I had to do all the clearing up.

August 1986—Janmashtami (Gokulashtami) involving a Bal Vikas programme in a hired church hall:

On the 16th of August we had a programme in St Peter's Hall. It was in aid of Lord Krishna's birthday, Gokulashtami. It started at 4 pm. We had songs, prayers, dance, speeches, talks, stories, music, instruments and many, many, many other things. My friend and I done a dance as we usually (do) but it went really well for once. There was lots and lots of people and everyone enjoyed themselves. After the show we had refreshment, *ghanthia* (crunchy Gujarati savouries), squash, coffee, tea, fruit, biscuits and after all that we only had one hour left to get ready because at half past seven we were to have *bhajans* until 12 am in the morning —5 hours —it was really really good fun.

On the *garbi* (central shrine) during Navaratri, Sai devotees have symbols —including the cross and crescent —for the world's major religious traditions. This, like the badge of the movement, stresses the point which Anita made that Sathya Sai Baba's followers acknowledge all religions, not just Hinduism. However, the ritual idiom and religious language of the devotees are unquestionably Hindu in their derivation. Indeed the claim to 'acknowledge all religions' is a deeply Hindu claim.

☐ Conclusion

The three examples of Pushtimarg, ISKCON and Sathya Sai Baba illustrate the impact on children of Hinduism as expressed in three vigorous *sampradayas* in Britain. In each case there are strict dietary rules, a specific devotional focus and a sense of solidarity with other devotees. In no case did the children perceive their tradition as separate from the rest of Hindu society.

Anita's enjoyment of the Sai devotees' celebrations was evident. Deepak and Ritu were similarly enthusiastic about ISKCON's activities. This enthusiasm will be an important factor in the continued existence and vitality of both the *sampradaya*, and Hinduism as a whole, in the coming decades.

How easily children could verbalise the content of a *sampradaya* and its meaning for their lives depended considerably on whether or not adults conversed with them in English about their *gurus'* teaching and the practices required of followers. Films viewed on video also increased their exposure to and grasp of a particular tradition. Supplementary classes contributed significantly to the children's understanding. These aspects of cultural transmission, informal and formal, are the subject of the next two chapters.

Notes

1. Swallow (1982:123) outlines the factors involved.

2. A detailed account of the emergence of the Arya Samaj is provided by Jones (1976).

3. The Brahmakumaris are briefly described by Knott (1986a:193-194).

4. Much has been published on the Swaminarayan tradition. See for example Williams (1984).

5. For an account of devotion to Jalaram by Gujaratis of the Lohana caste in Britain see Michaelson (1987:43-45). See also Jackson and Nesbitt (1990:45).

6. The Valmikis are the subject of Nesbitt (1990 a and b and 1991).

7. Hundreds of people go to the Balaknath temple in Coventry because of the founder's reputation for curing disorders. For background information on the cult of Baba Balaknath see Sharma (1970). More has been published on Radhasoami. See, for example, Juergensmeyer (1988).

8. See Michaelson (1987:36).

9. See Pocock (1973:108 ff). Barz (1976) provides details of the life of Vallabhacharya.

10. In translation this commences:

    With heart filled with joy, I bow down before Sri Yamunaji who is the bestower of all spiritual achievements.

11. The literature on ISKCON is large and growing. See Knot (1986c) for an outsider's sympathetic account. See also Carey (1987).

12. For example Bala Books (1978a).

13. To the best of our knowledge no Valmikis or Ravidasis have become involved in ISKCON, but only Punjabi Hindus from higher castes.

14. The research period coincided with controversy over the right of Bhaktivedanta Manor to continue functioning as a place of worship open to the public. Consequently ISKCON regularly came to the notice of the media.

15. Jackson and Nesbitt (1990:13) has a picture of Coventry children participating in Rathayatra.

16. For a picture of Sathya Sai Baba and of devotees' worship in Coventry see Jackson and Nesbitt (1990:30-31).

17. Of the published material on Sathya Sai Baba the following deserve particular mention. Bowen (1988), Haraldsson (1987), Knott (1986a: 164-167) Swallow (1982), Taylor (1987) and White (1972) are scholars' accounts. Gokak (1975) and Murphet (1971) are the work of devotees.

18.
For scholars' references to this phenomenon see Bowen (1988:188-19, Haraldsson (1987:239-40), Swallow(1981:15ff) and Taylor (1987:126).

19. Both Anita and her father denied that Sathya Sai Baba ever wore a *sari*, as stated by Brooke (1982:197). See Haraldsson (1987:107) for accounts of Sathya Sai Baba's male and female sides.

CHAPTER 9

Cultural Transmission: the Arts

Hindu children in Britain encounter and absorb elements of Hindu tradition at home and outside. Devotional practice, fasting, life cycle rites and festivals — all channels of cultural transmission — have been discussed already. Formal nurturing of religion in supplementary classes and teaching about Hinduism in maintained schools will be examined in the next chapter. Here we look at the part played by the arts — storytelling, iconography, drama, dance and music — in the transmission of Hindu tradition in Britain. These are all inextricably bound up together but in this chapter we attempt to look at them separately. They are also inseparable factors in the popularity of Indian movies. These are widely viewed on domestic video cassette recorders, and so we look in some detail at the phenomenon of Indian film in the lives of Britain's Hindu children.

☐ Stories

As the Hindu tradition is alive it is constantly developing and combining with non-Hindu culture. Both appear in imaginative interplay. Children often cannot understand the traditional stories when these are read in Hindi, Gujarati or Punjabi, so they do not know the stories which are read, for example, in association with performing a *vrat* (vow). But they readily pick up stories from films. Children are most familiar with those stories which are channelled by a number of different media, at school as well as at home. Not surprisingly 'Rama and Sita' is the most widely known Hindu story.

Both adults and children also make up their own stories with clear borrowings from older tradition. Sarita made up a story about the goddess Bhuvaneshvari Ma in which the goddess behaved like a fairy godmother. All that humans had to do was to follow her instructions. This is a recurrent pattern for the *katha* (story) told at the time of a *vrat*. Some adults made up their own stories, weaving familiar Hindu characters into new tales for their children. A Punjabi girl recalled:

When my daddy was here, when we were quite small, he used to make up these stories like ... these two — one was a girl and one was a boy — they had a dog. They went in the forest and this monster and a witch came, and then Krishna came and made the witch scared, and things like that. Once they were in a train and the ghost came and strangled two boys and girls, and then Krishna came along, and then he quickly got them out and fighted the dragon and things like that.

During the 1985 Bal Vikas Summer Camp participants saw the following story in a puppet show presented by children from the Leicester group of devotees of Sathya Sai Baba.

Shiva and Parvati were dancing on a holy mountain as it was the festival of Shivratri. People were praying to Shiva and Parvati and they asked him if heaven would be big enough for all these people to go there. Shiva said there would never be too many.

Next Shiva and Parvati visited a school in Coventry where they saw two boys talking and girls playing hide and seek and arguing. Seema was pushing Jane. Shiva and Parvati then visited Mr. Patel's house. Here Shilpa was saying that she had too much homework to help her mum, but Shiva and Parvati saw that in fact she was reading comics.

Shiva and Parvati turned into an old man and woman. When Parvati fell over, Shiva asked a boy who was playing nearby to help her, but he refused. But another boy came to their rescue. He gave them the shopping which he had got for his mother and wondered if she would be angry with him. Then he realised that the old couple had disappeared and in their place stood Shiva and Parvati. They announced that the boy had made them happy by speaking the truth and showing kindness, so he would go to heaven.

The puppet show ended with the words:'So child, if you want to go to heaven, you must speak the truth.' Once again the gods proved themselves at home in the children's twentieth century world and, on this occasion, they emphasised a strongly moral message.

☐ Iconography

The traditional art of puppetry, once so popular in India, has declined there and is also a rarity for Hindu children in Britain. But Hindu culture makes a visual impact in a host of ways. For example, in their homes and temples, on wedding invitation cards and trade calendars Hindu children see symbols and visual images which are unfamiliar to other children. They may not be able to put a name to them, but they accept them and can often recall them in detail whereas the non-Hindu is more likely at first to react with puzzlement or distaste to brightly coloured pictures of many-limbed deities and may well associate the *swastika* with the National Front. Iconography will be discussed under the headings 'symbols', 'pictures' and 'images'.

☐ Symbols

Of symbols distinctive of Hinduism, the *om* and the *swastika* are the ones which are most frequently encountered. In chapter seven we noted the significance of the syllable *om* in prayer. As a visual symbol it is equally rich in attributed meaning.[1] It looks like the Arabic numeral 3 with a 'tail' surmounted by an arc and a dot.

Children constantly see the *om* in home and the temple. There is one on the pendulum of the clock in Arun's living room. Deepak mentioned the *om* on the red pennant outside the Ram Mandir. The *arati* light which Anita daily circled in front of Sathya Sai Baba's picture in evening worship was *om*-shaped. *Om* was one of the symbols marked in red on Bhavesh's doorstep by his mother at Divali. Jyoti mentioned a *rakhi* decorated with an *om* and Mridula referred to the red *om* on the coconut carried by a bride's young female relative when she ceremonially met the bridegroom. *Om* is marked in red on the glass which fronts Hitesh and Nina's family shrine. Not surprisingly Sunil chose to fill a page of his notebook with a beautifully shaded *om* sign edged with more diminutive *om*s and when Bhavini drew a picture of the Shree Krishna Temple from memory she added a large *om* to the gable.

The *om*, ingeniously recreated in many media, is a recurrent motif of religious celebration. During Navaratri Gujarati women compete, usually on the eighth night (*atami*), each making the most beautiful design she can on the *thali* (round tray) which she will rotate during the *arati* hymn. This happens, for instance, in Leicester, in the Soni community to which Arun belongs. The design is often an *om*, carefully worked in *kanku* (red powder) or in desiccated coconut, dyed with food colouring agents. (See Jackson and Nesbitt 1990:39 for a photograph of an *om* design, worked in rice, lentils and glitter, for the ceremony marking the conclusion of a *vrat*.)

When the Goddess Randal Ma was worshipped in Bhavini's home, her mother decorated a *thali* in this way. When Arun's mother concluded her fast to the god Dharamraja, an *om*, surrounded by other motifs, was painstakingly created by Arun's *mama* (maternal uncle) for the concluding ceremony from lentils and beans of different colours, enlivened with particles of glitter, on the *bajath* (low table) on which the deity would be installed.[2]

The *swastika* (*sathiyo* in Gujarati) is equally familiar to Hindu children as a visual religious symbol.[3] Unlike the *om* it has no corresponding sound value. It too is a favourite motif for *rakhis* (amulets given at Raksha Bandhan) and on greeting cards, and for decorating *thalis* for *arati* and thresholds for the festival of Divali. A *swastika* balances the *om* on the glass sliding doors of Hitesh's family shrine.

At Arun's *mundan* (head shaving ceremony), as his mother recalled, he sat on a stool over a *swastika* which had been made in moong beans (*mag*) on the carpet. As is usual among Gujaratis, once his hair had been removed, his mother made a *swastika* with moistened *kanku* on his bare scalp.[4] At a *simant* ceremony, children could see that the white blouse sleeve of the pregnant woman had been marked in red with a *swastika*. Coconuts for use in *puja* are similarly marked, with a dot in each of the quarters of the *swastika*. After the Dharamaja *vrat* Arun's mother gave the Brahmin priest who officiated at the concluding *puja* a small postage stamp-sized silver square stamped with a *swastika*. This was one of the items essential to the ritual, and Arun saw a *swastika* marked by his mother by the sink in the kitchen on the day of Shitala Satam.

☐ Pictures

Distinctive Hindu symbols are incorporated into many of the vividly coloured religious pictures which enliven the children's environment. Not only in the domestic shrine but elsewhere in their homes, often prominently displayed on the walls of the living room, are pictures of deities and saints. Some are trade calendars advertising a local retailer. Sometimes pictures have been painted or embroidered by girls or adult members of the family. Most often the pictures are chromolithographs, brightly coloured representations of a god or goddess, full-face, staring straight into the viewer's eyes.[5]

Although the Indian film industry has influenced the criteria for the deity's physical attractiveness and for the backdrop of lush, mountain scenery, nevertheless the posture, accoutrements and composition of the pictures adhere to traditional norms. For example Krishna is most usually represented as a plump infant with tell-tale traces of white butter round his lips, as a young flute-playing cow-herd beside his consort, Radha, or as Arjuna's charioteer on the battlefield of Kurukshetra in North India.

Each child who was interviewed recognised a number of religious pictures. In conversation the children often referred to deities not by name but by describing their salient visual characteristics. They spoke of Shiva in terms such as 'the god of snakes' because popular lithographs show his neck encircled by a cobra. The goddess Ambe Ma was usually referred to as the 'goddess on a tiger', since she is shown, with her six arms outstretched, seated side-saddle on a roaring tiger. The children's periphrasis echoes 'Sheranwali Ma', the epithet most frequently used by Punjabis. This means 'the mother on the tiger'.

In temples where there is no regular priest in attendance, there are pictures but no statues. Pictures of the deities do not require the daily rituals — such as offerings of food (*naivedya*) — necessitated by a duly installed statue. But the pictures frequently bear marks of respect — a garland hung from the top of the frame or a red cloth draped around the frame or a red mark applied to the glass over the subject's forehead. So children's awareness of the content of a picture is bound up with a sense of love and honour, and of behaviour appropriate to worship. What is necessary for family routine is not factual knowledge but appropriate behaviour. This the children demonstrated in their unselfconscious mirroring of adult procedure. So, for example, they would stand facing a picture and say '*jay*' with hands pressed together. They would circle a lighted lamp or incense stick clockwise in front of the picture or know that a calendar with a deity's picture on it must not be thrown away in the usual manner but treated with more respect.

☐ Images

In some homes, in addition to pictorial representations, there are three dimensional images (*murtis*) of deities — usually a small statue in the shrine. Some of the Coventry homes which we visited had a room set aside as a temple but in none of these had marble statues been ritually installed. In some British Hindu households, however, this is the case and outsiders will then visit the shrine for a *darshan* (glimpse of the deity) and at least one member of the household attends to the *murti* (statue) with the detailed daily worship which takes place in the temples established for public worship.

Most Hindu children visit a public temple — even if only occasionally — and there they not only see pictures but also marble statues, richly clad and decorated with jewellery and flowers. In front of these *murtis* any visiting devotees pause, show their respect by prostrating themselves or by pressing their hands together in salutation. They make an offering and pray.

Children learn that, by comparison with pictures, there is something more powerful about a statue which has been installed ceremonially in the temple (see Jackson and Nesbitt 1990:48-49 for an account of a *murti pratishtha* ceremony).

Some *murtis* are believed to be so powerful that they can only be open to public gaze for a few minutes at a time. When a coach party from Coventry — including Anita — visited the temple of Srinathji in Leytonstone everyone was told to have only a very brief *darshan*. A few minutes after people had entered, prostrated themselves before Srinathji, or otherwise paid their respects, they had to vacate the room and the curtains were again drawn over the image. A Punjabi girl related that there was a temple in India where:

> I heard that they have sort of big deities, and I heard that there's this lady who was staring at him and God came out and he was running away with her and everybody was running after him. And they put him back and now they only let you see them for five minutes. I think it's Krishna ... a long time ago. Once my aunty was staring at him and one lady said 'Don't look like that, otherwise he's going to follow you and we don't want him to go with you'.

However *murtis* are not remote or frightening, and at a Bal Vikas summer camp Anita, Bhavesh and dozens of other children watched while a *guru* from Wolverhampton, aided by four boys, demonstrated how to make figures of Shiva and Krishna from plaster of Paris in a latex mould.

☐ Dressing up

On occasions when they perform a dance or enact a tableau at a festival, children dress up as gods and goddesses. At the camp, mentioned above, a boy was picked from the audience to show the others what is involved in dressing as Krishna. His finery included a *mukat* (crown) topped with a peacock feather, one of the distinguishing features of Lord Krishna. Sometimes a girl dresses up as Krishna, as Ritu did for instance, in a drama in the temple. Similarly a boy may represent Sita as Bhavesh did in a Bal Vikas programme. Hindu children's experience differs in this respect from their Muslim peers, for no pictures or statues or dramatic representations of Muhammad or Allah are allowed. Although Sikhs have pictures of the Gurus and children are encouraged to draw them, they have no statues and no one is allowed to impersonate the Gurus.[6] The degree to which visual and dramatic presentation mutually reinforce each other is probably unique to Hinduism. For Hindu children the points of access to their heritage are more diverse than in Sikhism or Islam.

☐ Indian Films

The scope for human representation of deities enriches the formal nurturing of children in their tradition. It has also proved a rich seam for the Indian film industry to quarry.

In many cases it is from Indian movies, through the songs, dances and colourful festivals, that children gain familiarity both with a deity's visual representation and with mythological stories. Before embarking on the research we had assumed that children were learning traditional stories from parents and grandparents. In fact this means of cultural transmission has clearly been overtaken by the Hindi movie, available on video cassette for home viewing. In cases where film was reinforced by other channels of cultural transmission — such as a school assembly, a festival celebration, a parent's account or by reading a library book — the children's grasp of a story was surest. This was clearly the case with the story of Rama and Sita, which has come to be associated in many local schools with the festival of Divali. Because video figures so prominently, its place in the lives of Hindu children is now looked at in some detail.

One philological point is of interest. Both *veda* (the most ancient Hindu texts) and *video* share common Proto-Indo European linguistic roots. *Video* is the Latin verb 'I see'. This in turn is derived from the stock from which sprang the Sanskrit *veda* and the classical Greek *oida* 'I know'. With this linguistic link in mind one scholar's recent assessment is particularly apt:

> film has ... been hailed as a fifth Veda — the medium accessible to all castes and featuring entertainment and diversion which the gods requested in Bharata's *Natyasastra*. (Pfeiderer and Lutze 1985, quoted in Haggard 1988).

The impact of video technology on the cultural life of South Asians in Britain is apparent from studies made since 1978 when video cassette recorders (VCRs) came on the market.[7]

As Holm remarks, in relation to the use of video:

> Indian culture, with its frequent religious references has become a much more intensive experience for the children, and is making them much more conscious of their identity as Indians and Hindus. (Holm 1986)

There is no doubt that home video viewing is of significance in the lives of Hindu children in Coventry. All but one of the families who were followed closely in the research project owned a video recorder. All the children mentioned watching video and it was clear from conversation and from observation in their homes and in other Hindu households that video was significant in the following ways. It took up a considerable amount of their

135

time. It increased their exposure to aspects of South Asian culture and to certain Indian languages. The children regarded video very positively, and were receptive to what it showed. Both the time spent and the content of their viewing differentiated them from their non-Asian peers.

The use to which the VCR is put continues to differentiate South Asian families from others. Although it is used for time shift recording of television programmes and for English films as in non-Asian homes, it is chiefly used to provide a cultural alternative:

> the domestic video has come to perform an educational function for children which draws away from the model based on the lifestyle and values of white culture and adds to their repertoire of potential behaviour which reflects some of the Asian values. (Sharma 1983:39)

Popular films in Indian languages — usually Bombay Urdu/Hindi — are often enjoyed by all the family. From frequent viewing children acquire an understanding of Hindi, although this is the mother-tongue of relatively few Hindu children in Britain. They enter a shared escapist world of song and heroic feats in which the villain always loses. The films introduce children from very diverse backgrounds to the same pan-Indian culture of the movies (Pfeiderer and Lutze 1985).

Arun's diary account of the movie, *Durga Maa*, shows how familiar Hindu themes — in this case the intervention of a deity in human form — are reworked as the plot of modern films:

> On Monday we saw a film called *Durga Maa*. It was about a little girl. There was this couple who had an eight year old girl called Durga. There was a villain, and his friend killed the girl by pushing her over a cliff. When her parents found out that their daughter had been killed, they went to Durga Maa's temple. They prayed and told Durga Maa to bring their daughter back, so goddess Durga became a little girl but her parents didn't know that she was a goddess. When Durga was saying about things that was really going to happen, her parents thought that she was dreaming. One day in a temple a priest didn't come to read the story of Durga Maa, so the girl stood up and sang a song of Durga. In the end she gave a *darshan* as Durga and made that little girl alive. Her parents became glad and did an *arti*. Then the film ends.

With the closure of 'Asian' cinemas in Britain the social dimension of film viewing, the opportunity for South Asians of different religions, classes and ethnic backgrounds to gather together, has disappeared. The film is now viewed at home, and so is a form of recreation shared with relatives and reinforcing family ties.

The use of video to record family events such as marriages confirms this tendency. Families relive events by replaying the video and share in family events in India which they were unable to attend (Larson 1988b).

In addition to Hindi movies and family events, many children also see videos of a third category. These films are commercially available and are exclusively religious in content. They include videos of the life stories of gods and *gurus* (eg Sathya Sai Baba) and recordings of major religious events such as a celebrated spiritual leader's preaching and singing on a visit to Britain (see chapter eight). Some videos are specific to a particular religious movement. Thus Deepak had seen videos of the worship of Jagannath in Puri and of the life of Chaitanya, both of which are important to members of the International Society for Krishna Consciousness. In Mridula's home her grandmother had a video of a *saptah* (seven-day reading of the *Bhagavat Purana*) in Leicester, at which the Pushtimargis' spiritual leader, Sri Indira Betiji, was present. Anita's father had a collection of videos relating to Sathya Sai Baba which included ones of his life, of his fiftieth and sixtieth birthdays and of a Bal Vikas camp and a Conference on Human Values. All these Anita had watched.

In all these ways video is playing a formative, central role in the transmission of tradition. As it is modern technology children react positively to video and are predisposed to the material which it records and relays. It seems likely that because of video children are more able to reconcile Hindu mythology with contemporary, secular society than they would otherwise be. On many occasions children referred to a film when they were describing a god or some other aspect of their religion.

Often the films in question were not primarily religious but, whatever the style of the film, religious characters were presented according to traditional iconography. To quote a young teacher at the Shree Sanatan Mandir, Leicester:

> Our Asians are very religiously minded. Even when they make the films they try not to depict anything in a false way. For instance recently I saw a film about Jesus in a very comical manner on television. We wouldn't think of doing that. There is a film in Hindi out, called 'Yehi hai Zindagi', which means 'This is Life', in which this person in his dream receives *darshans* and things like that of Lord Narayana. But that form of Lord Nayarana is still with four arms.

On the subject of gods in films Anita wrote:

> I watch many many different religious films like *Mahabharat, Ramayan, Krishna Leela, Jai Maha Kali* and many many more. These films help me learn more about the gods and all the different goddesses. I enjoy

watching these films. It's very good to show all ages. Even young children, even though they cannot understand, at least they can see the pictures on the TV.

On another occasion Anita remarked:

Everything you watch on TV's got a moral. All Indian films have got something to do with God.

When the names of gods and goddesses cropped up in conversation the children mentioned seeing them on video. Krishna stealing butter, Krishna conquering the snake, Sheranwali Ma, Vishnu and other gods were all familiar from films seen at home on video. Some of the children had seen the 'Divali Story' (the story of Rama and Sita) and celebration of Divali. For children in Britain films often provide their most vivid experience of the Holi festival (Gillespie 1989a:237). So, for example, when he was asked about Holi, one Gujarati boy said that he knew from a video what Holi celebrations in India involved. As he spoke he mimed squirting from a syringe:

pumps, bike pumps. They (put) paint inside, little grains of paint, and as you go like that it all comes over. (Here) we don't do anything.

Video technology and aspects of Hindu culture interact in numerous ways in children's lives. Bhavini's mother was the female singer in a Gujarati group. At a charity performance during October 1987 the songs, including the opening prayer in classical style, were all taken from popular movies seen on video.

This programme of live songs was then, in its turn, recorded on video for future viewing. Many of the songs and dances performed at the Gujarati Education Society's parents' evening were from films. Children had learned the dances from watching the stars on the video and then improvising on this basis. So had the adults who coached them. Video cassettes can be played and replayed whereas in the days of cinema this was impossible.

☐ Radio and Audio Cassettes

Audio tapes of songs, devotional and otherwise, and radio programmes — particularly from Radio Leicester — of Indian song requests are also a means of cultural transmission. Punjabi children enjoy listening to *bhangra* tapes as well as to tapes of Western groups. Mridula's favourite tapes were of Jagjit and Chitra Singh, Pankaj Udas and Anup Jalota.[8] The children's parents too derived great pleasure from their tape recordings of film songs and devotional singing.[9]

Sometimes parents' and children's preferences differ! A Gujarati girl commented on the conflict of interest when her mother wanted to listen to tapes of the celebrated Gujarati preacher and singer, Morari Bapu reciting the *Ramayana* from memory:

> It's like at home we've got tapes of the whole thing all the way through and that's all my mum listens to, and I have to listen to it because she doesn't let us do the TV while it's on. If that's on nothing else is.

In fact in this case the saturation possible through modern technology had diminished the girl's interest in Morari Bapu's live recitations of the *Ramayana*:

> I find it boring. Everyone else is sitting there listening to it (ie on cassette), and when the summer holiday comes we have to go to the actual thing, and when you go to that thing all you're doing is sitting there. You get so tired and sleepy.

Like video recordings, however, audio cassettes played a useful part in encouraging children to present dramas on traditional themes. On the evening of Janmashtami (Lord Krishna's birthday) the congregation in the Ram Mandir saw teenagers mime the story of Dhanna and Thakurji. On tape were the words of the dialogue and appropriate hymns. The tape recording enabled the children to present the story without having to learn their lines.

Sometimes this technique was used in larger scale dramatic productions. Anita, Sarita, Arun and Mridula's grandmother were all in the audience for *Sur Shyam Matwala*, a dance drama presented by Bharatiya Vidya Bhavan (London) to raise funds for the Shree Krishna Temple Building fund. They saw a London cast, including children as young as five years old, performing a dance drama of the life of the poet Surdas. Slides projected on to a screen at the back of the stage set the scenes and sometimes combined with silhouettes, reminiscent of shadow puppetry, as dancers moved behind the screen. The lyrics and dialogue had been pre-recorded by professional performers in India.

Although pre-recorded soundtrack added to the ease and professionalism of such performances in which children took part, often children presented a drama without such backing. This might be a hastily rehearsed scene prepared during the ISKCON *kirtan* (see chapter eight) or it might be more carefully rehearsed for a larger audience. Sometimes the play — above all the story of Rama and Sita — could be rehearsed in school, often with a parent assisting the teacher concerned. Bal Vikas children performed plays not only from Hindu tradition, but also from the Christian repertoire, such as a nativity play or a 20th century version of the story of the Good Samaritan. Bal Vikas pupils also produced dramatic sketches illustrating 'human values', one act plays with such themes as honesty or love.

On occasion children from Bhaktivedanta Manor, the British base for ISKCON, performed in Coventry. They enacted scenes from Krishna's life for Janmashtami in 1986. They also acted plays with an unambiguously ISKCON message annually in Battersea Park on the day of the Rathayatra.[10] Dramatic performances are integral to the activity of Hindu supplementary classes and, for a much wider young Hindu public, they provide an attractive contact point with their religious inheritance.

☐ Music: Vocal and Instrumental

Several of the children who were interviewed had outstanding musical aptitude. During their interviews and with no musical cues to help them, some children sang *bhajans* (devotional songs). Others knew only an opening line. Allowing for the differing memory capacity of different children, our observations suggest that the children who were most familiar with words and music learned them in supplementary classes, sang or played them during community worship and frequently, if not daily, during domestic worship. Of the children who learned to sing *bhajans* at festivals and cultural events few had more than a very general idea of what the words meant. Ritu would pick up words and melody quickly from her mother or the priest and her excellent Hindi pronunciation gave no clue that she did not altogether understand the meaning of the words. She would note the words down in the Roman alphabet as they sounded to her to help her to memorise them.

Music is a vital part of Hindu tradition — vital both in the sense of being an integral part and in the sense that it is very much alive in Britain. Since it is alive it is changing — particularly in the instruments which are used and, as we have already noted, in some of the ways in which it is learned. Of their own accord Hindu children are playing Indian film tunes and devotional music on their recorders and violins.

Sarita described in her diary a Divali show which had been put on by the Prajapati *Samaj* in which children were allowed to perform any act of their choice.

> My cousin taught me and some other children a piece to play. I played the violin and so did another cousin of mine. A boy called Nilesh played the harmonium. We played a piece from a film called *Dosti*. Right at the end of the show the men presented us (all who took part in the show) with a £5 Boots voucher.

It is nothing new for Indian music to be played on instruments from elsewhere. Probably the instrument most widely used by Indians for accompaniment of the voice is the harmonium, a keyboard which is played with one hand while the other operates a bellows to regulate the supply of air. This

140

instrument was first introduced to India by European missionaries in the nineteenth century, but was soon adapted for use in playing Indian music.

Coventry Hindu children who showed musical aptitude were encouraged to play a leading role in community worship. Not only did Ritu and Deepak accompany daily worship at home on harmonium and *dholak* or *dholki* (drum) respectively, but in the Ram Mandir, whenever he was present, Deepak accompanied the singing and Ritu, like her mother, sang solo on occasion. Anita was competent both on harmonium and *tabla* and she and her elder sister often led the singing of their fellow Sai devotees who gathered in their home each week.

☐ Formal Teaching

Although music, like the Hindu tradition as a whole, is to some extent imbibed unconsciously without formal teaching, some children have music lessons. In Coventry there is less provision than there is in London where Vidya Vihar, Bharatiya Vidya Bhavan and other Hindu or Indian centres were running a wide range of classes (see chapter ten). Deepak was receiving *tabla* lessons and the priest at the Ram Mandir began to teach Ritu to play the harmonium. When he returned to India she continued on her own, practising lines learned by ear. The Bal Vikas *gurus* encouraged musical ability in their pupils and where possible provided instruction.

In maintained schools it is still rare for a teacher to have any appreciation of, let alone competence in, any aspect of Indian music. But, increasingly, music teachers are showing interest, and some in-service sessions on Indian music have been organised. An introductory book by Leela Floyd on Indian music was in use in Mridula's school. Her guitar teacher there showed her how to play some Indian film song tunes on the guitar, and some Indian music had been introduced. Bhavini recognised the *vina* (a sitar-like stringed instrument) in a picture of the goddess Saraswati because she had heard '*vina* and *sitar*' in 'Time and Tune' at school.

The *sitar*, whose notes still introduce virtually every BBC radio programme on India, is almost as foreign to the Hindu children of Coventry as it is to their non-Hindu peers, although the *vina* is visually familiar to some of them from pictures of Saraswati and from *slokas* which describe her.

Here, for example, as transliterated by devotees, is a *sloka* which children were learning in a Bal Vikas class:

Poorna chandra shami kanti
Dudhasa vastra ujada
Haath ma chabhati veena

The English translation is:

She is as bright as the light of the full moon,
Her clothing is as white as milk,
In her hand is the *vina*.

☐ Percussion

Percussion instruments, which maintain the *tal* (rhythm) are important to Indian music. Ashish listed the instruments used for percussion:

I played the *tabla* and drum — *dholki*. There's *tabla*, cymbals and you can clap your hands.

With or without percussion instruments people love to clap their hands to accentuate the rhythm of *bhajans*, and Gujaratis clap when dancing the *garbo* (see below). By cymbals Ashish meant the *manjira*. Many children called this 'Indian bells', the name by which it is known in British schools. There children learn to hold them up by the tape linking the two cymbals together and then clink them together in a horizontal plane. This is a far cry from their use in Hindu worship where they are struck together like cymbals, often extremely fast and with great verve.

The uninhibited enjoyment of rhythmic percussion begins early, spontaneously and informally. During *bhajan* singing Deepak's little brother would sit on his father's lap and delight in playing the *manjira*. No one objected. A father will sometimes hold his child's hands in his to encourage him, feeling that the infant's keenness to play shows a predisposition towards God.

When taught percussion systematically, as Bal Vikas pupils are, the children learn to count, clapping on each number marked with an X in a printed sequence (see Floyd 1980). In Bal Vikas classes Anita, Bhavesh and the other pupils learned clapping patterns to enrich their rendering of a *bhajan*. Commencing with 1 2 3 4 5 6 7 8 as a simple clapping rhythm they progressed to other patterns, played on the *manjira*.

Both Deepak and Anita would accompany congregational singing, Deepak on *dholki* (a convex-sided wooden drum) or *tabla* (a pair of tuned drums played with the fingers and palms of the hands), Anita on *tabla* or harmonium.[11] In his private lessons Deepak had learned a few of the many *tals* (rhythm sequences). In his words:

You never finish learning. There's no ending. People are still making *tals*. *Tintal* is 16 beats da din din da da din din da da din din etc. *Japtal* is 10 beats; *rupkatal* is 9 or 7, *ek tal* is 12 beats; *karva* is 8, 12, 4; *dadra* is 6.

He explained further, demonstrating *tin* and *ta*, the notes which he struck with his right hand on the black circle and whitish outer area of the *tabla* face. He had to strike the *tin* with his fourth finger, with his middle finger in the air.

With his index finger he struck the *ta* while he played the metal '*tabla*' with the *ge*, the two middle fingers of his left hand (see note 11).

In Bal Vikas classes children learned to sing the scale — sa re ga ma pa dha ni sa — to a harmonium accompaniment. They practised patterns such as: sa re sa re ga ga ga re ga re ma ma etc.

☐ Music Groups

The children did not associate Indian music only with religious occasions and sentiments. As mentioned above, Bhavini's mother was the female singer in a newly formed group which played for social functions in Coventry and further afield. The group had invested in a sound system and synthesizer. The songs were mainly from Hindi films, but the group also sang *garbo* and *ras* during the Navaratri festival.

A Valmiki Hindu Punjabi boy said that it was as a result of the development of modern *bhangra* that he was proud to identify with his Indian heritage. *Bhangra* is a jubilant Punjabi folk dance. A Westernised style of this *bhangra* music is played at weddings and other celebrations and has caught the interest of young Punjabis in Britain. To the loud and extremely rhythmic music adults and children dance uninhibitedly with thrusting arm movements (Banerji and Baumann 1990; Baumann 1990). This boy played in a *bhangra* group. None of the instruments was traditional — he played electronic keyboard — but the words were in Punjabi, bought from songwriters. Thanks to *bhangra* he now relates positively to his Indian background.

☐ Dance

As we have noted, some children learn 'film dances' by imitating the song and dance sequences in popular movies. Film dances — like film songs — combine classical Indian, regional and Western styles. Copying these does not require the discipline of classical dance training. In Coventry relatively few children have formal teaching in the classical dances of India, such as Bharat Natyam. Dance thrives, however, in its more popular forms — *bhangra* and *ras garba*. For many non-Hindus, their initial contact with Hindu culture is an invitation to witness and to join in the dancing on the nine nights of Navaratri (see chapter six). At this time Gujarati families flock to temple premises and hired halls to dance *garbo* and *ras*. These are both circle dances. Babies are carried round. Older children participate with their mothers and grandmothers. Boys and men usually take part only in the *ras*, the stick dances, but with their fathers and grandfathers they sit watching the *garbo* dances. The *garbo* (plural *garba*) is a clapping dance in honour of the goddess. For the *ras*, which is associated with Krishna, sticks are used. At its simplest two concentric circles of dancers dance, one going clockwise and the other going anti-clockwise, each person holding a stick in the right hand. Each dancer must strike the stick of the person facing him or her on the appropriate beat. Music is live and usually electronically amplified. 'Disco *dandian*', a style more similar in tempo and volume to the loudest Western discotheque music, is popular with teenagers. Nevertheless, however much the music may change, the religious focus of Navaratri remains in the centre of the dancers like the hub of a wheel. This is the *garbi*, a shrine — usually with six sides — hung with pictures of the goddess, and decorated with lights. The apex of this six-sided structure is surmounted by a *garbo*, a small pot. Towards the end of each evening *arati* is performed by the participants who all stand facing this shrine.

Ras garba, as the dances are often called collectively, is not restricted to Navaratri. On Sharad Punam (the night of the full moon), five days later, Gujaratis dance again, and when Pustimargis gather to worship each week the *bhajans* are followed by *ras* dancing. This is appropriate as their devotion is directed to Krishna who, in Hindu mythology, danced with his beloved *gopis*, the cow-herd girls, in Vrindaban.

Many children and teenagers cannot understand, let alone translate, the words although they speak enthusiastically of the dancing. The girls wear their best clothes for the dancing on the nine nights of Navaratri. Their dress is usually Indian in style, but not always Gujarati; Punjabi suits are growing in popularity — almost exclusively with unmarried girls. Small girls are often dressed in traditional Gujarati finery — the *chaniyo choli* which is called *ghaghra pulka* in the Kathiawari dialect of Gujarati.

The happy circles of dancers during Navaratri, three or even four generations together, leave a powerful impression of the hold and flexibility of Hindu tradition. Music and spectacle, youth and age, devotion and entertainment all combine and the outsider is made welcome.

☐ Conclusion

Our more recent research among non-Asian Christian children in Coventry shows a higher level of weekly, out of school participation with children of their own age in uniformed organisations, such as Girl Guides, in music classes and sports teams. They also spend time with their pets and, in some cases, following individual hobbies. Much of their cultural experience is broken up into regular, measured doses.

By contrast, like their non-Hindu Asian contemporaries, Hindu children spend most of their evenings and weekends with their relatives. In the home the television or video is usually on. Social functions are attended by all members of the family, from babies to grandparents, however late into the night they continue.

So far British Hindu children's exposure to the music, dance, drama and iconography of their tradition is largely informal. However, as chapter ten shows, formalisation, though involving a minority of children, is well under way.

Notes

1. Arun's mother provided one interpretation of its form. The three connected arcs which constitute the major part of the emblem represent the trinity of Brahma, Vishnu and Mahesh (Shiva). The *tika* (ie dot over the vowel) is Mataji, the goddess. (With this statement compare e.g. Bryant (1983:114) 'The sacred face of Ganesa ... represents the *om*'.)

2. The *om* sign is a key motif in funerals also. Arun's mother commented that in crematoria in Britain an *om* is now available. This is put up in the chapel for Hindu funerals. With her mother's dying gift of money she had bought a golden *om* in her memory. Another Gujarati woman described a 'bedspread' of flowers which she had made the previous year for her father's coffin. In the centre she had worked an *om* — 'peace', as she explained.

3. See Majmudar (1965 :291) for further details of *sathiyo*. *Swastika* is the Sanskrit word for 'health bringing' and so is a propitious sign.

4. Crooke (1926 :34) similarly lists incidence of the *swastika* including 'on the shaven heads of children on the marriage day in Gujarat'.

5. As Blurton (1988) explains the devotee can enjoy a *darshan* of the deity by looking into his or her eyes. Blurton's article is a useful account of contemporary popular religious iconography in India.

6. Occasionally statues are to be found — eg outside the gurdwara at Mehtiana Sahib, district Jagraon, Punjab there are statues of the *panj pyare* (the five first Sikhs to be initiated by the tenth Guru) and other Sikh heroes. But such statues are not used in worship. The cinematographic convention is to show a bright light in lieu of any of the Gurus.

7. See particularly Gillespie (1989a and b); Helweg (1986); Holm (1986); Larson (1988a); Nesbitt (1980 :118); Sharma (1983); Singh (1986); and for the impact of video on young Hindus in Trinidad see Vertovec (1987).

8. Arun's mother learned to sing new *bhajan*s by hearing cassette recordings of professional singers such as Anup Jalota.

9. As *bhajan*s are often set to film songs the two genres merge. Printed booklets of *bhajans*, of the type used by the priest at the Ram Mandir, often indicate the film song to which a hymn is to be sung.

10. For example in 1987 they gave a dramatic presentation of human life as a 'Journey to Blissville', which they enacted as a railway journey enlivened by references to aptly named stations such as Gravesend.

11. Strictly speaking *tabla* is the name of one of the drums, the wooden one. The second of the pair is called *baia* (left) and is made from metal. See Shepherd and Sahai (1192) for an introduction to *tabla* playing.

CHAPTER 10

Formal Teaching

☐ Introduction

The *yagnopavita* (sacred thread) ceremony is a reminder of an earlier, idealised period when high caste boys left home to spend several years studying sacred texts with a *guru* before they undertook the responsibilities of adult life. Their sisters and the children of lower castes learned appropriate domestic duties and occupational skills within the extended family largely by imitation of their elders. In contemporary India, however, most children attend state schools in which the teaching of any particular religion is forbidden. They 'learn' their family's traditional religious attitudes and practices simply from growing up in this environment. In the evenings or at weekends they do not attend classes on their religious tradition. They are more likely, if parents can afford it, to be preparing for their examinations in civics or physics, English and Maths in paid 'tuition' sessions. Despite these priorities, however, and although India is officially secular and religious education is not on the curriculum of state schools:

> Children hear stories from the *Ramayana* and the *Mahabharata* at school because the two great epics are an integral part of Indian culture (Holm 1983:116).

Between the ethos of home and school there is less of a difference than there is between the homes and school of many Hindu children in Britain. Even in the prestigious English medium Christian educational foundations in India there is a sense of shared home culture. Hindu teaching in schools in India is confined to a limited number of establishments in the private sector (Holm *op cit*).

147

☐ Supplementary Classes

In East Africa pupils such as Arun's mother attended schools in which many Asian norms prevailed and Gujarati was taught. In Britain, however, out of mounting concern that their children are losing touch with tradition, Hindus have set up additional classes to teach them about Hindu religion and to make children literate in an Indian language. As described below there have also been moves to establish Hindu day schools. The establishment of Hindu classes parallels similar moves in North America (Williams 1988:236). As these classes are provided by organisations or individuals outside school hours they can be called supplementary classes. Of the Coventry children who were the subject of our case studies all had experience of such classes except for Sunil, Jyoti and Sanjay who attended Indian language classes in their schools. Bhavini, Anita, Sarita and Mridula attended Gujarati classes run by Gujarati Hindus in a local community college. Arun went to a class taught by a friend of his mother in another school. Anita, Hitesh, Nina and Bhavesh attended Bal Vikas (child development) classes run in two different venues by the Sathya Sai Baba organisation. While Deepak usually stayed with the adults in the ISKCON *kirtan* (devotional singing session) his sister Ritu joined other children in a class which was held during the homily.

Although it is probably still true that in comparison with Muslims, a smaller proportion of Hindu children attend supplementary classes (Anwar 1976), a growing number are enrolled in a widening range of classes. Our research is not comprehensive, and the pattern is a changing one, so our observations do not allow us to estimate the percentage of Hindu children who participate. Nor do they allow us to draw other conclusions of a quantitative nature. On the basis of participant observation over a two year period in Coventry it is, however, possible to say that from their attendance at supplementary classes the children involved gain both information and assurance in their religious tradition.

Children's attitudes varied. Bhavini found the Gujarati classes boring and preferred to spend her Sunday mornings in other ways. The Bal Vikas classes were popular and children frequently mentioned Bal Vikas with enthusiasm.

☐ Hindu Classes Nationwide

The supplementary classes attended by Hindu children in Coventry are best viewed against the background of the ethnic and sectarian balance of the local Hindu population and in the context of Hindu supplementary provision nationwide.

In 1984 we visited ten supplementary classes.[1] These were run by Hindu groups which differed in their Indian region of origin, caste composition, sectarian emphases, general level of formal education and their migration history. Six of the organisations were predominantly or exclusively Gujarati. Five were partly or predominantly Punjabi. Despite the fact that none of the groups was of Tamil, Bengali or of any other ethnic background, the differences in ambiance and teaching content were striking.

The conscious aims of the organisers of Hindu supplementary classes varied, but overlapped. Some emphasised the teaching of mother tongue or Hindi while others stressed religious instruction. In practice it proved impossible to separate the two. The teaching of an Indian language was regarded by many adults as vital for the preservation of Hindu tradition. Language classes run by Indian Volunteers for Community Service, the Gujarati Education Society and the Vishwa Hindu Parishad all included religious material such as stories from the *Mahabharata* and *Ramayana* epics, and the lives of historical personalities such as Mahatma Gandhi and the Buddha, and in all these classes the proceedings opened with a prayer, albeit in some cases a non-scriptural, non-sectarian prayer acceptable to different religious communities.

Studies of Asian language classes have been published, Nagra (1981/2) reporting the range available in Coventry, and Logan (1989b) describing a Gujarati class in London. However, neither writer examined the part which such classes played in the religious nurture of Hindu children. Classes with a specifically religious purpose have received little scholarly attention (Jackson and Nesbitt 1986), one notable exception being Dwyer's study of formal nurture in Leicestershire (1988).

This chapter provides an overview of a lively, ever-changing range of provision for Hindu children. Supplementary classes were taking place in private homes, temple premises, schools and community centres. Some of the teachers were paid, many were voluntary. In most cases organisers and teachers had struggles, at least initially, with inadequate resources and facilities. Their dedication and enthusiasm were significant factors in their pupils' experience of their tradition.

Most of the organisations encouraged children to engage in expressive activities of a religious character. Dramatic activities included the performance of the Prahlada story for the Holi festival while traditional Gujarati *garba* and *ras* dances were performed for Navaratri. *Bhajans* (devotional songs) featured prominently in two classes. Reasons cited for the use of the expressive arts were that they sustained interest, built up children's confidence, familiarised them with their culture and were the most effective way of teaching. Prayers, dances, *bhajans* and dramas were prepared for performance at parents' evenings and other cultural occasions through which some organisations hoped to recruit more pupils.

From conversation and observation certain common elements emerged —
particularly, in nearly every case, the concern that children should be competent in their mother tongue or Hindi. (Those Hindus whose mother tongue
is Punjabi regard Hindi as having a greater affinity than Punjabi with Sanskrit
tradition and also respect it as the national language of India.) Most of the
classes included some teaching from the two great Indian epics, the *Mahabharata* and *Ramayana*. Furthermore, teachers hoped to instil moral qualities
such as respect for others. This meant addressing others and referring to them
by the relationship words appropriate to them. Among other qualities teachers
aimed to foster were self-discipline and enhanced self-esteem through the
children's knowledge of their culture.

By attending Hindu supplementary classes children gained a conscious
cultural identity as part of a peer group whose 'ethnicity', religion and mother
tongue they shared. Much of what they learned was via a 'hidden curriculum',
reinforcing nurture at home. Such concepts as *karma* (the cosmic law of cause
and effect) and *dharma* (appropriate behaviour) were implicit without being
named. The traditional dress and demeanour of adults, and the Indian style
of the language primers, contributed to the children's sense of cultural
identity. The sacred pictures and images in the temples where some classes
were held, powerfully conveyed Hindu concepts of deity. In the Vishwa
Hindu Kendra water flowing from Shiva's backdrop of mountain peaks
vividly represented the birth of the Ganga — a fine visual aid to learning.

All the classes observed were autonomous but they were related to classes
elsewhere sometimes organisationally, sometimes through the literature used
or through their devotional orientation or through a combination of these
features. Thus in classes teaching Gujarati language the same series of books
published in India was used.

Most communities were running classes in circumstances that were difficult in terms of accommodation and finance. Attendance at all classes was
erratic because almost all the families' Hindu cultural activities — marriages
in particular — had to be packed into weekends. Much depended upon one
local individual's vision and determination. In some cases inadequate,
cramped accommodation was giving way to new venues. In temples there
were no facilities such as desks and chairs but a rich devotional context. In
local authority buildings the audio visual impact of temple images, pictures
and the activities of worship were lacking. New books and materials were
being acquired, but none of these had been prepared with the needs of British
Hindu children in mind.

☐ The Diversity of Classes

Classes were run by temples catering for a general Hindu clientele — such as the Shree Sanatan Mandir, Leicester and by religious movements with a strongly sectarian emphasis in their teaching. Dwyer (1988) provides a detailed comparision between classes run by organisations of these two types. The following examples, three from 1984, and one from 1987, provide comparative material for examining the Coventry scene. Leicester's Shree Sanatan Mandir is a former Nonconformist church, colourfully refurbished with *murtis* (images) including those of Radha, Krishna and Shiva and framed pictures including Sant Jalaram, Guru Nanak and Sathya Sai Baba. Here seventy Gujarati children sang prayers together on Sunday morning before dividing into mixed groups, according to age. They sang *bhajans* antiphonally from specially prepared folders of hymns to Rama, Krishna, Vishnu and Hanuman typed in Gujarati transliterated into Roman script. Sanskrit verses had been printed in Roman capitals followed by an English translation. The teachers, mostly aged about twenty, had experience both of life in Africa or India and of education in Britain.

The Arya Samaj, Ealing had a deliberate policy of encouraging the active participation of children and young people in programmes aimed at the whole community or in worship. During the research visit a teenage girl made a speech from the platform defending vegetarianism. On other occasions children sometimes conducted the *havan*, the ceremony consisting of chanting Sanskrit verses around a fire to which libations of clarified butter *(ghi)* and fragrant substances *(samagri)* are made. Here the teachers were from a generation of Punjabis whose formal education had all taken place in India.

At 10 am, after Sunday morning worship in the crowded Shree Kutch Satsang (Bhuj) Swaminarayan Temple, a three storey building in Bolton, some two hundred children sang a hymn together in the main temple before dispersing to nine groups according to sex and age. The focal pictures of Swaminarayan (Sahajanand Swami, founder of the movement), garlanded with threaded dahlia and African marigold heads, had been covered by gauze curtains and the screens that usually divided men from women in the congregation had been pushed aside. The devotees were Leva Kanbi Patel by caste, mainly artisans and textile workers from Bhuj in Cutch, the area of Gujarat nearest to the Pakistan border. Girls over thirteen had to wear *saris*. For two hours the children sat in their groups cross-legged, clustered in front of a teacher of the same sex, chanting the Gujarati alphabet or words in loud unison or writing in their exercise books. After two hours they reassembled to sing *bhajans* accompanied by vigorous clapping. In all the *bhajans* the name 'Swaminarayan' recurred frequently and each ended with a loud 'Swaminarayan *ki jay*' (Glory to Swaminarayan). An elderly gentleman next explained in Gujarati a page of *shikshapatri* (Swaminarayan's teaching) elaborating Swaminarayan's injunctions to wash, apply a *tika* (spot of vermilion powder) to their foreheads and greet others with '*Jay Swaminarayan*' (Victory to Swaminarayan) each morning. At nearly 1 pm they left, each with a cardamom-flavoured milk sweet. The teachers, all educated in India, were ill at ease in English.

A new departure in the provision of formal Hindu nurture in Britain was marked by the opening in 1985 of *Vidya Vihar*, an Independent Saturday School. Since the research period it has closed. Run by the Academy of Vedic Heritage it offered courses in Indian music, dance, languages and religious teachings. In December 1987 there were over 220 children who were taught by 28 staff members. Children arrived at 10 am at Nower Hill High School, North Harrow and left at 4.30 pm. Pupils ranged in age from under fives who stayed for half a day to fourteen year olds. Most were Gujarati Hindus and most lived in the Harrow/Pinner area of London. Some travelled as much as twenty-five miles. Regular attendance was expected throughout the year which ran from January to December with holidays. Children had to follow the full curriculum and were expected to do homework.

To quote from an information sheet (1985):

> The curriculum is so designed to provide a balanced programme of education in order to enhance the child's progress in physical, mental and cultural growth. During the day children are expected to participate in Vedic prayer, slokas, Yoga, Sanskrit, Games, GUJARATI or HINDI, Culture Course, fine arts such as Harmonium, Vocal, Sitar, Tabla, Bharat Natyam and Kathak.

The day began with corporate prayer (from Dave 1987). The children were then divided according to age and level. At the end of the year (December) they were examined in each subject. In their Culture Course children aged 6-8 years answered a multiple choice printed question paper and oral questions — put to them in turn individually by the teacher such as:

> What did Hanuman mistake for a fruit when he was a baby?
> Why did Dhruva go to the forest for meditation?
> Where does the River Ganga flow from?

During the year Vidya Vihar celebrated a number of occasions such as Gandhi Jayanti, Christmas and the anniversary of its founding.

As a uniform, children wore a tracksuit emblazoned with the Vidya Vihar logo. A few wore grey though most preferred the scarlet alternative. They brought a vegetarian packed lunch, which they ate after saying a prayer. In its scale, curricular range and insistence on details such as uniform, Vidya

Vihar offered a more complex educational supplement than the organisations functioning in 1984.

In 1990 Hindu College, London, was established with the aim of promoting Indian languages, the arts and 'Hindu *dharma*'. In the coming decade such institutions may provide metropolitan Hindus with a greater range of classes than has been previously available.[2]

☐ Coventry: Gujarati Classes

The largest scale Hindu supplementary provision in Coventry is the Gujarati school run on Sunday mornings in a local community college. This began in 1976 with classes run in the Shree Krishna Temple. Sarita's maternal grandfather was appointed headmaster.

In 1982 the Gujarati Education Society was set up and the school was run by a committee. About 300 children were listed during the research period but competing claims on their time, such as weddings, reduced attendance. Children ranged from complete beginners in the written language to 'O' level candidates. Termly and annual examinations included questions on religion for classes three to six. Textbooks used by some teachers were produced in English by an Arya Samajist organisation in South Africa and reflected that group's radical views on caste and the use of images, contrasting with the children's family experience.

The classes lasted from 8.45 — 12.45 on Sunday mornings of the LEA term. Pupils of all classes assembled for corporate prayers before dispersal to different classrooms. Teachers ranged from teenagers who had grown up in this country to grandparents with no educational experience in Britain but with a much deeper knowledge of Gujarati lore and language. For the annual parents' evenings, children prepared dances, songs and prayers performed to an enthusiastic audience.

When homework allowed, Arun attended the much smaller Gujarati classes held on Wednesday evenings in another local school and community college where the teacher was his mother's Brahmin friend. The book he used was *Gujarati Vachanmala*, (literally 'garland of words') which is used in schools in Gujarat. It begins with pictures of a boy with his hands in the position of prayerful greeting, saying '*Jay*' — a traditional Hindu greeting showing respect to the gods for example. Through rituals such as this one, Hindu cultural norms are reinforced. The teacher's methods were also traditional. For example she would write the Gujarati for 'k' on the blackboard and then add the different vowel signs and ask the pupils to pronounce each (as described in Logan 1989b).

153

☐ Coventry: Hindi Classes

In mid 1987 about thirty Punjabi Hindu pupils from infants to teenagers, were attending a Friday evening Hindi class. Primers printed in India were in use and beginners were also given photocopied alphabet sheets. Classes took place not in the prayer hall of the temple but in rooms near the kitchen on the lower floor of the house where the priest resides. Each week lessons began and ended with a prayer. For festivals the children would prepare an item to present in the congregation. So, for Divali in 1986 they sang a song. For Ramanavami in 1987 they presented *slokas* from the *Ramayana* with a translation in contemporary Hindi.

As British Punjabi Hindu children usually learn to read and write Hindi rather than Punjabi, they are acquiring a community identity in line with the division in Indian Punjab. There, for a century, the language issue has fuelled intercommunal political controversy and resulted in the subtraction of Haryana and Himachal Pradesh from Punjab. Hindi and Sanskrit share the *Devanagri* script whereas Punjabi, their mother tongue, is written in *Gurmukhi*. This probably leads Punjabi Hindus to believe that Hindi is also closer to Sanskrit in its grammar and vocabulary than are Punjabi or for that matter other North Indian languages. This discrepancy between mother tongue and the language of literacy and worship distinguishes Punjabi Hindu children from other Hindu communities and puts them on a par with Punjabi Muslims who learn to read and write not Punjabi but Urdu and Arabic. It also marks a boundary between the Sikh and Hindu children although their shared spoken language is Punjabi.

☐ Sectarian Classes in Coventry

i. ISKCON

Of the Hindu religious movements two in Coventry were providing teaching for children. These were ISKCON, the International Society for Krishna Consciousness, and the Sathya Sai Baba organisation. The children who attended these were confident in articulating information about Hinduism, how to perform *arati*, or why meat should be avoided. One could argue that the experience of growing up in a family committed to a *sampradaya* or religious movement is of itself bound to increase children's understanding of Hinduism and their capacity to speak about it. If relatives spend time explaining in the children's terms this may be true. But parents and grandparents often feel ill equipped to answer children's questions, saying that in their day no one asked such questions. In the classes children learned largely in English the teachings of ISKCON or Sathya Sai Baba and these provided a key to the religious activity they witnessed elsewhere. In many cases parents had adopted their own practices in India or Africa without this specific sectarian emphasis. So through the classes and experience unique to their generation children were learning about Hinduism both by a more formal means and with a more sectarian emphasis than their elders had experienced.

Whereas the Bal Vikas classes — attended by children of Sathya Sai Baba's followers — were graded and arranged so as not to coincide with devotional gatherings, the ISKCON class was much smaller and more informal, being held while older relatives were listening to a religious lecture downstairs during the weekly *kirtan*. Both Bal Vikas and ISKCON classes were conducted in private houses.

The ISKCON classes began for practical reasons. When a group of Punjabi and Gujarati Hindus began holding weekly ISKCON *kirtans* the participants' concentration on the *katha* (religious lecture) was disturbed by children playing and crying. Hence an adult would go upstairs with the children. Rather than simply withdraw them it was decided to provide them with an alternative religious activity. At first the responsibility fell mainly to a recently qualified infant school teacher, educated in Kenya and Britain. While the children, about ten in number, were upstairs the younger ones enjoyed colouring in duplicated outline drawings from books published by ISKCON such as *The Krishna Colouring Book No. 1 Childhood Pastimes and Friends*.[3] One of these shows Krishna's mother Yashoda churning butter. She faces the vertical churning stick which stands in the pot while infant Krishna tugs at her *sari*. The teacher would tell the children a story (their favourite being *Agha the Terrible Demon*) and rehearse small dramas. She gave the children exercise books for writing on religious topics. When the homily was over the children came downstairs and proudly held up their colouring sheets, read what they had written or acted the play.

Dramas which the children acted reflected and reinforced the emphasis of ISKCON's distinctive tradition. One was the story of the infant Nimai (ie Chaitanya) who was sitting, decorated with jewels, in his parents' courtyard, when two thieves came to steal him away. Unable to resist Nimai's influence they went round in what proved to be a circle so that he ended up in his parents' courtyard safe and sound and the thieves ran away.[4] Other dramas included the story of Krishna moving Govardhan Hill, the story of Rama and Sita (for Divali) and the story of Narsinghadev, the man-lion incarnation of Lord Vishnu.

As well as performing dramas for their parents, the children would also show them what they had written in their exercise books. One day the children were encouraged to write what they would say if their school teacher asked them what they believed. Ritu wrote:

If our teacher asked about our God I would say our God is Krishna and he made the world. Then the teacher would say, 'Who is the son (of) God?' and I would say, 'Jesus is' and would also say, 'We don't believe in Jesus because he was made for English people'.

Her friend wrote:

If my teacher did not understand, then I would give her a *Bhagavad Gita*.

Previously children had written 'why we need a Guru'. On one page Ritu drew a picture of a robed figure holding a long pole and wrote below this 'Gurudeva Swami Das'. Facing this she explained Gurudeva's relationship to Swami Prabhupada, the founder of ISKCON.

If we didn't have a Guru we wouldn't know about Krishna. Before Prabhupada died he chose Gurudeva to take his place. So that's why we need a Guru. If we didn't have a Guru we wouldn't know about Krishna.

The tone and content of the teaching which Ritu and her friends received indicates consciousness of a wider, non-ISKCON and non-Hindu world in which children would hear other truth claims.

☐ Bal Vikas

During the same period the Sathya Sai Baba organisation was running two Bal Vikas groups in private homes. *Bal* means child, *vikas* means development or (a *guru's* translation) 'blossoming'. Bal Vikas is the title of the classes run by devotees of Sathya Sai Baba. Sathya Sai Baba emphasises the five values of peace, love, non-violence, right conduct and truth. To instil these in children as widely as possible the Sri Sathya Bal Vikas Trust was set up. This programme is now called 'Education in Human Values' and as such was accepted by the Government of India for implementation in its primary schools (Taylor 1984 and 1987). Under Sathya Sai Baba's auspices, colleges in India, now affiliated to universities, have been set up with the intention of influencing the teaching of morals and values to students.

The UK programme was introduced through the Education in Human Values Society, founded by a member of the Sai Council in Great Britain. In 1984 and 1985 this organised an In-Service Teacher Training Course on Human Values in Multi-Ethnic Education in conjunction with ILEA (see Taylor 1984 and 1987). The impact of EHV on state schooling is small, its main thrust being the many supplementary classes currently run in Britain. In 1985 *Education in Human Values Journal* was launched. In this the principles of the philosophy are set out with examples of their application in practice. Teachers are urged to introduce children to the key values through

156

'silent sitting' (meditation), prayer, group singing, stories and group activities (Jumsai 1985). In 'silent sitting' children are helped to sit cross-legged in silence with their minds focused on what is beautiful — a flower or religious image.

> When we teach a child to sit silently two things are achieved directly. One is that it enables the process of intuition to develop. If intuition is awakened and the capability to draw upon it, the level of intellectual perfection will be higher than that of a child who does not have this ... The second thing is that the voice of the eternal, the voice of divinity can be heard, the voice of peace. (Jumsai 1985:18)

Prayer is equated in Bal Vikas literature with 'quotation'. Children are given words such as 'try and try again until the goal is reached' to think about and remember. Prayer also involves making a petition to God. Group singing is emphasised as a means to greater personal equilibrium and social harmony. Equally important as a teaching method is the telling of enjoyable, memorable stories with an inspiring message which the children understand. Stories heard during fieldwork included one about the former Indian President, Sri Rajendra Prasad, losing his temper and one about Mahatma Gandhi on the subject of avoiding wastefulness. Lastly teachers endeavour to make children more aware of the five human values through guiding them in such group activities as role play, attitude tests and motivation games.

From their locations Coventry's two Bal Vikas groups were referred to as Bal Vikas Hillfields and Bal Vikas Holbrooks. Both groups were graded according to age and met weekly in the houses of followers of Sathya Sai Baba. Children from six upwards attended, although Anita said she had begun when she was less that six. The children were encouraged to wear white. The girls wore skirts or Punjabi suits until they were old enough to wear a white *sari*, like the female *gurus*. Boys and girls were taught in the same room but sat separately.

The children seemed enthusiastic about the Bal Vikas sessions which they attended. In each venue classes, graded by age, met for hour long sessions. Young people of sixteen and over met for discussion on Sunday mornings. The younger children's classes sustained their interest well, as the following account of provision for the six to nine year olds illustrates.

The hour long lessons were flexible within a clear framework which the children happily accepted. As the register was called by the *guru* each child in turn responded '*Jay* Sai Ram'. The major part of the lesson consisted of varied group activities — chanting Sanskrit *slokas*, singing *bhajans*, learning the words, meaning and basic melody and rhythm, writing out prayers, listening to stories, discussing behaviour. Children were given the English translation of prayers and hymns and were expected to learn these. Their favourite *bhajans* were in English, sung in the same musical style as *bhajans* in Indian languages. An example is:

We bow to you O my lord.
We your children pray to you for grace and forgiveness.
We your children pray to you for peace and happiness.

The moral points raised by stories would be considered, and children were encouraged to look critically at their own conduct. On their 108-bead rosaries they might spend part of the lesson repeating '*Om* Sai Ram'.

Each class ended with a brief period of 'silent sitting', begun and ended by intoning '*om*'. The children would sit crosslegged (as they did for the rest of the class), with their eyes shut. Their hands were upturned on their knees or else they put their palms together fingers pointing upwards. They were told to think of God in whatever form they wished. After chanting four times '*Om lokha samastha sukinu parvantu*' (O Lord bestow happiness on everyone) they intoned '*Om shanti shanti shanti hi*' (peace, peace, peace), then stood for the *arati*. They sang the version acclaiming Sathya Sai Baba. A child was asked to circle the lamp, and then to sprinkle water clockwise around a *thali* (metal tray) after placing it on the floor in front of the focus of worship (the couch on which Satya Sai Baba's pictures were displayed).

Then the holy ash (*vibhuti*) was distributed while the children sang the appropriate prayer. Sometimes a child spooned a little from a small bowl into each child's right palm. The children would mark their brow with the tip of a fourth finger of the right hand and then swallow the residue. Alternatively the children in turn put the tip of their fourth finger into the small bowl of ash as it was brought round. They then marked their own foreheads and licked the residue from their finger. Throughout the distribution of *vibhuti* the children remained standing facing towards the couch. Finally they would pay their respects to Baba. One by one the boys prostrated themselves, lying full length on the floor facing toward the couch. One by one the girls knelt with their heads on the floor.

After paying homage to Baba each stood, hands together in prayer, and all together said 'Sai Ram'. As the children left they received *prashad* — fruit and Indian sweets.

☐ Camps

Particularly popular with all concerned were the summer camps organised regionally by the Bal Vikas *gurus*. The Bal Vikas Summer Camps 1985 and 1986 in which Anita was fully involved ran from Saturday morning until Sunday afternoon in a local church annexe. Children stayed overnight and met children from the other Bal Vikas classes in the Midlands. Anita's elder sister was one of the many *sevadars* (servers) who ensured that the camp ran smoothly. Activities were devotional, physical, creative and informative.

In 1985 campers saw a puppet show and in 1986 a demonstration of statue making. Both years the subjects of health and hygiene were included in the programme. Competitive games were clearly popular. In 1985 Bal Vikas Challenge was played by teams, each of which was drawn from all the Centres represented at the Camp. Each team remained out of the room until its turn came. Then each had to answer the same questions. These included:

Name Rama's Guru.
What is the Christians' holy book?
What instrument does Sarasvati play?

In 1986 boys and girls, whose names had been picked out at random, competed, three at a time, in a fun quiz. Questions were of three sorts, namely role play, matching words on a blackboard and, lastly describing what one would do in a particular situation such as seeing a notice on the grass saying 'Five pounds fine for anyone walking on the grass' with a five pound note lying near it. Matching words included matching the words, 'service', 'intelligence', 'non-violence' to their Hindi equivalents *'seva'*, *'buddhi'*, *'ahimsa'*, and matching words for appropriate qualities with the names of the celebrities Mahatma Gandhi, Bob Geldof, Mother Teresa and Vivekananda.

Other Hindu organisations also ran youth camps. One is the Hindu Swayam Sevak Sangh or Hindu Self Help Union. This originated in India and was established in Britain in 1966. Its published aims are to 'advance Hindu religion' and to build up character and self-discipline. National Youth Camps are an important part of its outreach. In August 1984 such a camp was held in the University of Bradford and involved, among many other elements, a prizegiving for winners of a national essay writing competition.[5]

On a camp site near Southampton the Acadamy of Vedic Heritage (Vidya Vihar) ran an annual Character Building camp (*Jeevan Ghadtar Shibir*) for its students. During a four day programme, which included prayer and outdoor pursuits in the New Forest, the organisation hoped to:

introduce new members to aims and objectives of the Vedic Heritage and to create a sense of unity amongst youngsters and provide disciplined atmosphere and a chance to uplift and build one's character (Vidya Vihar 1987).

Camps, games and competitions were undoubtedly popular with participants, but it is only a minority of Hindu children who experience these. Anita filled an exercise book with puzzles and quizzes designed for younger Bal Vikas pupils. Ritu and Deepak had enjoyed trying out Swans and Crows, *Bhatta-haris* and other 'Krishna Conscious Games' (Jyotirmayi dasi 1981:5,9). In June 1987 Ritu entered a competition organised in Birmingham for children under twelve years of age. Pupils in the Gujarati School were also encouraged to submit entries. Each entrant had to colour in a picture of Krishna and write twelve sentences in English about him. The picture showed Krishna as *makkhan chor* (the butter thief).

Examinations are also an incentive to the small number of children who take them. In December 1986 Sarita was one of seven local children who sat an examination on the *Bhagavad Gita* set by the National Council of Hindu Temples.

☐ Hindu Schools

In Europe the largest Hindu communities live in the Netherlands and the UK. Consequently it is in these countries that the question of Hindu schools has been raised and initiatives have been taken.[6] However, like the vast majority of Hindu children, those in Coventry in our study attended local maintained schools (one moved to an independent school) and their parents evinced no desire for full time Hindu schooling. There is evidence that some Hindu communities are opposed to the establishment of separate schools on the grounds of their potential racial and cultural divisiveness. A questionnaire which we sent in 1983 to Hindu organisations and associations in different parts of England included the following question:

> What are your organisation's views about the setting up of schools for religious minorities (eg Muslims, Hindus and Sikhs) *within* the state education system?

Of the forty two replies which we received, eleven (some with various reservations and conditions) supported the establishment of such schools, six failed to respond or were unclear in their response, while twenty five were opposed to the idea.

The following statements were among the negative responses:

> We are totally against it because it hinders integration and the consequence would be another Northern Ireland type of situation.

> We do not support the idea because it will not help integration, but on the other hand, will promote separation.

> An exclusively denominational school would appear to be racial in character — the very thing we would like to avoid.

One of the most radical steps taken so far by a Hindu organisation was an attempt to establish a Hindu Voluntary Aided school within the state education system (Kanitkar 1979). This vision of a Hindu aided school was never realised for the Steering Committee failed to get the full support of Hindu communities and of the Local Education Authority in London and the project was abandoned in 1981.

Despite recent political moves to gain voluntary aided or grant maintained status for New Independent Christian schools and Muslim schools, Hindu communities, on the whole, have remained critical of separate schooling, being concerned both to maintain high academic standards and to avoid racial divisiveness.

At the time of the field work few independent schools in Britain could be classified in any way as Hindu. Two London schools were founded in 1975 by the School of Economic Science (Bigger 1987). Pupils study Sanskrit, and bow to the Supreme Spirit, *Paramatman* before and after each lesson. Schools more tenuously linked with Hindu tradition are the Theosophist schools, Rudolph Steiner schools, Dartington (which was founded by Rabindranath Tagore) and the Small School in Devon founded by Satish Kumar. Brockwood Park School near Winchester, founded in 1969, is one of seven Krishnamurti schools worldwide (Hunter 1989). Since 1981 the followers of 'Oshe' (Rajneesh) have provided schooling first in Suffolk, then in Devon. In 1979 a more unambiguously Hindu school was opened by Western adherents to another minority movement. This was Chaitanya College set up by ISKCON at Severn Stoke, Hereford and Worcester. This has now closed. The ISKCON school at Bhaktivedanta Manor in Hertfordshire, one of thirty ISKCON schools worldwide, has also existed since 1979. The school day starts at 4.30am in the temple for pupils, who numbered less than forty at the time of our research.

1992 saw the opening of an independent Hindu school on a larger scale, the Swaminarayan School, Neasden, London. Although the school had in Spring 1993 about a hundred pupils on roll, it has the space to cater for as many as a thousand if numbers increase. In March 1993 all staff were Hindu. Of the pupils, approximately a third were from a Swaminarayan background. Religious teaching was predominantly 'Hinduistic' and only vegetarian foods containing no eggs, onions or garlic were permitted.[7]

☐ The Impact of Maintained Schools

The ways in which 'Hinduism' has been constructed and presented in Religious Education literature are discussed in Jackson (1987). There is no research on the teaching of Hindu tradition in the classroom, however, so we are including a few children's responses, even though they are anecdotal, in addition to the discussion in chapter six of the role of the maintained school in teaching about Hindu festivals. Our impression was that, in the main, children's self-esteem was raised through teachers taking an interest in their religious tradition. Some children were, however, critical of or embarrassed by tokenism or by teachers who had done little to check important matters of detail such as the pronunciation of names and technical terms or who did not consult members of Hindu communities over religious and cultural practice. Mridula, for example, had attended two secondary schools in which a high percentage of the pupils were of South Asian origin with Hindus strongly represented. She made a number of critical comments and felt that teachers should be better briefed if they were going to cover material from religious or cultural traditions other than their own. To cite one example which she gave: at Navaratri (1986) the second years had performed two dances. A group of girls wore *saris* but they had not been provided with appropriate music or dances and only one of them was a Gujarati girl and so knew what to do. The others wore Punjabi-style garments. The girls proceeded to dance to a love song and Mridula remarked that children who 'understood' (ie others of South Asian origin) '...took the micky out of us. They weren't the right dances. You never dance *garbo* to love songs'.

By way of a contrast, there were examples of children who responded positively to what RE teachers presented as Hindu belief. A Punjabi girl had learned about reincarnation in Hinduism in RE:

> When I heard it at school I believed in it. It had a great effect on me because it was my own religion and I thought that it was true.

Both examples illustrate that sometimes there are differences of emphasis or inconsistencies in children's experience of their tradition in the home and community and in its representation in schools. This is partly explicable by the fact that so much religious education literature presents 'Hinduism' as a discrete religion having key characteristics in parallel with Western religions (hence the emphasis on beliefs such as reincarnation). This tendency to structure the tradition is also part of children's experience as insiders, however, as some of those responsible for formal nurture try to find ways of presenting religious teaching to Hindu young people, or seek to contribute ideas to educational bodies on what from Hindu tradition should be covered in RE (see chapter eleven). The gap that can exist between a school's understanding and that of a child is illustrated in one Punjabi Hindu girl's discovery of a Hindu identity:

> I just found out that I'm Hindu; well my mum told me because this teacher said; 'Are you a Hindu?' and I said, 'I don't know', so she said,

162

'Go and ask your Mum and tell me'. And when I came back, when I told her the other day she said, 'OK' and she wanted to know about Divali; that you celebrate Divali if you're a Hindu.

☐ The Present and Future

With regard to the formal transmission of Hindu culture, there have been some significant developments since we completed our research. Five annual youth festivals have been organised by the National Council of Hindu Temples (UK) for young Hindus in the twelve to seventeen and eighteen to twenty six age ranges and have been attended by young people mainly from the Midlands, Greater London and the North of England.[8] The second was held in Manchester in 1990, the third at the University of Aston in 1991, the fourth in Leicester in 1992 and the fifth in 1993 in Bristol. Festival programmes have included sports and traditional Indian games, classical dance, drama and music, workshops on topics such as racism, vegetarianism, ecology from a Hindu perspective and Hindu religion, dramas dealing with Hindu values and fun activities such as *bhangra* pop and a *ras garba* marathon. These events are reported in *Hindu Today*, the quarterly newsletter of the NCHT, which also includes a supplement *Hindu Youth Today*, largely written by young Hindus and incorporating reviews of the youth festivals. The festivals show a great concern for the educational and spiritual needs of Hindu young people. In line with the views expressed generally in NCHT publications, a unitary view of Hinduism is presented and the festivals represent part of the Council's attempts to offer a national organisational structure for Hindu bodies.

☐ Conclusion

Camps, competitions and examinations are, like supplementary classes, a pointer to the future in which relatively small numbers of Hindu children will be involved in increasingly formalised enculturation.

In Britain to date, however, Hindu society has not appropriated a Christian mould to the extent of the Hindus described by Vertovec (1987; 1988) in Trinidad who teach a Hindu creed in English. Although Hindus in cities such as Coventry are far less scattered than Hindus in North America they are responding to a similar perceived need for a distinctively Hindu dimension of their children's otherwise largely Western educational experience. Classes vary greatly in ethos and content.

As suggested in Dwyer's comparative study in Leicester religious classes run by *sampradayas* may be more 'successful' in terms of religious nurture than non-sectarian religious classes (1988). Certainly our observations of the classes in Coventry run by ISKCON, and more especially, by devotees of Sathya Sai Baba, lend support to Dwyer's conclusions which were based upon the Swaminarayan temple in Leicester. However the non-sectarian classes in Coventry have a specific focus on language teaching and so are not strictly comparable.

Community leaders, such as those involved in Coventry's Gujarati Education Society, point to a need for financial help and support. They are not impressed with arguments for separate voluntary aided or grant maintained Hindu schools, which they see as potentially divisive and unlikely to be able to support a strong, academic and professionally oriented curriculum. The one attempt in 1979 to establish a Hindu voluntary aided school faltered for just these reasons (Jackson 1985). Meanwhile the representation of aspects of Hindu tradition in children's day schools and the quality of its presentation are also factors contributing to their experience and construction of 'Hinduism'.

Notes

1. The organisations are listed in chapter two. In each case a forty five minute interview was tape recorded, usually with a person who had completed the questionnaire, and wherever possible at least part of a lesson with each group of children was observed, and the literature used in teaching was noted. In 1987 a visit was paid to Vidya Vihar, Harrow.

2. The establishment of this college was announced in *Asian Times* 14th August 1990, *India Mail* 22nd August 1990, *India Weekly* 31st August 1990, and *New Life* 10th August 1990. The reports point out that the college had not yet acquired premises.

3. The books which the teacher used were Govinda dasi (nd); Bala Books Inc (1977, 1978a, 1978b, 1978c, 1981) and comic-style books in the Amar Chitra series. This includes many stories from Indian mythology and history.

4. This story, which is based on *Caitanya Caritamrita* by Sri Krishnadas Kaviraj, appears in Bhakticaru Swami (1984:5).

5. Entries could be written in 'Hindi, English or Mother Tongue'. For 10-13 year olds the subject was 'My Mother'. For 14-17 year olds the subjects were 'My ideal hero', 'My favourite Hindu festival', 'Hindu family tradition' and 'Hindu Swayamsevak Sangh'. For 18-21 year old entrants the topics were: 'Hindu philosophy', 'Hindus in UK', 'Hinduism as I understand' and 'Any prominent Hindu epic'.

6. The development of Hindu day schools in Britain differs significantly from that in the Netherlands, the only European county with a comparable Hindu population. Hindus of North Indian ancestry from the former Dutch colony of Surinam live mainly in the cities of Amsterdam, Rotterdam, Utrecht and the Hague. In 1988, 1989 and 1990 Hindu schools were opened in the Hague, Amsterdam and Rotterdam respectively (Shri Saraswati Basisschool 1990 and nd). The Goverment pays on the same basis as in standard state schools and the curriculum is standard with the addition of Hindi and '*Dharma*'.

7. We are grateful to Paul Hancock, the headmaster, for these details.

8. Over thirty temples and societies in Britain are affiliated to the National Council of Hindu Temples. The Council tends to give a unified view of Hinduism and to develop organisational structures.

CHAPTER 11

Conclusions and Reflections

What conclusions are we able to draw from our studies? The first point to make is that we can draw only tentative conclusions from the data in our possession. Our principal studies are of groups of children mainly in one city at a particular time. Further our methods are interpretive and, though informed by literature of ethnography and religious studies, provide only a basis for forming general impressions about trends in theory. Nevertheless, some reflections might be valuable to others working in related areas and to members of diaspora Hindu communities. In speculating about possible future trends (especially in the educational sphere) we do refer to some developments which have taken place more recently than those described in our Coventry research.

☐ Perceptions of Change in Hindu Tradition

We have raised earlier the issue of representation, especially about the various uses of the term 'Hinduism' and the problems associated with conceiving of the tradition as a religion. There is a consequent problem of characterising change within the tradition, exacerbated by attempting to do it in the case of diaspora communities. Theoretical frameworks are needed in order to describe and account for change. One such model is provided by Timothy Fitzgerald (writing from within the field of religious studies) who makes the analytical distinction in Hindu tradition between *dharma* 1 and *dharma* 2 (Fitzgerald 1990). The former is an ideology of hierarchy, typified by the matrix of purity and pollution and most evident to the observer in the

167

institution of caste (1990:112). In the *dharma* 1 sense, Hinduism is not a 'religion', a phenomenon which can be uprooted from its social setting and transplanted elswhere. In Fitzgerald's words:

...it is, analytically speaking, the centre of gravity, the context within which the other phenomena, the sectarian soteriologies, the potential religions for export, are rooted (113).

Dharma 2, on the other hand, is conceived as systems of personal salvation, and is associated with 'sectarianism'. Unlike *dharma* 1, it is 'other worldly', and inclines towards individualism and egalitarianism rather than hierarchy. In *dharma* 1, correct ritual action is crucial in the fulfilment and maintenance of cosmic order. In *dharma* 2, however, ideas of 'faith' and 'commitment' are central. Typically, the authority figure is the ascetic, in contrast with the Brahmin who figures so importantly in *dharma* 1. Caste is a key concept in *dharma* 1, whereas in *dharma* 2, caste is in various senses opposed 'rather in the sense that the other-worldly renounces the this-worldly'.

Fitzgerald is drawing attention to the particular significance of sectarian movements in the Hindu tradition, and is aware that his distinction is schematic since, in the field, it would be extremely difficult or impossible to isolate sects from their *dharma* 1 context, in India at least. This is where his analysis is relevant for discussions of 'Hinduism' in the diaspora. Since *dharma* 2 sects are not essentially related to a particular society and have universal soteriological claims, they might be especially significant in being reproducible in alien cultural contexts. Fitzgerald remarks:

Hopefully this framework may...provide a view on the important questions about continuity and discontinuity, not only within the sub-continent of India itself, but between Hinduism in India and Hinduism in Britain, for example (115).

Fitzgerald's discussion is especially helpful in countering the 'world religions' view of Hinduism as a discrete religion and in drawing attention to the *sampradaya* as especially significant in the development of the Hindu tradition outside India. Our findings show the vibrancy of the 'sects' among many migrants and their children, as well as the appeal of some of them to people of non-Indian origin. In terms of caste, Fitzgerald's remarks are also pertinent. Caste seems no longer to be fundamentally an indicator on the scale of ritual purity and pollution and no children we interviewed perceived caste in this way. For the young people we studied, caste helped to shape their outlook and self-image but featured very little in their religious understanding. Bhavesh's perception that Brahmins are vegetarian and pray more than other Hindus is one of the few examples. Some Valmiki children were aware of stigma associated with their background, but they did not know why it was felt. By Gujarati parents, their *samaj* (caste association) tended to be perceived as a club or friendly society, while Sarita used the words 'community' and 'religion' to explain the term *samaj*.

As a general explanation of change, however, Fitzgerald's framework is an oversimplification, at least as far as our data are concerned. Some of the ritual features of the tradition, for example, turn out to be remarkably resilient in the diaspora situation. The practice of *vrats* remains important in the domestic sphere, as do *puja*, certain life cycle rituals and the customs associated with the festival of *Raksha Bandhan*. This last ceremony reinforces certain family roles and values, as do a whole range of interactions and expectations in domestic life. In the public sphere, communal prayer in an Indian language retains its significance, and children are aware that the utterance of the sacred words is of more importance than comprehending their meaning. Festivals too are an opportunity for cultural affirmation, and certain distinct Indian regional traditions may be maintained. *Sampradayas* are not perceived as entirely free-standing 'sects' by young people, but as a part of the wider Hindu tradition.

Yet associated with most of these examples there is evidence of change. *Vrats* are still practised by some children, but young people tend to be unfamiliar with the associated stories (*kathas*), usually available only in Indian vernacular versions. Public prayer might be in an Indian language, but private prayer tends to be in English and to have formal features in common with Christian petitionary prayer. Festivals might retain certain Indian regional or even local features, but there are significant adaptations to do with climate, calendar and a variety of other factors. Children might perceive their family's *sampradaya* to be part of the Hindu tradition, but their knowledge of their 'sect' depends partly on adults' interactions with them on the subject in English. The continuities and discontinuities with India are complex and on-going, as are the processes resulting from acculturation. Nevertheless Fitzgerald raises the fundamental point of a possible shift in the character of Hindu consciousness in non-Indian contexts. Although his model does not correspond to the complexities in the field, his basic point is suggestive and we will return to it later.

☐ Change through Multiple Influences

More fruitful, in terms of discussing the complexities of change is the list of factors suggested by Kim Knott (1986b; 1991). In pointing out the need for continuous research to chart the ways in which South Asian religions in Britain are adapting to life in non-Asian cultural settings, Knott draws attention to five factors which need to be considered in relation to the content of religious tradition, namely: home traditions; host traditions; the nature of the migration process; the nature of the migrant group; and the nature of the host response. We will consider Knott's categories in relation to the transmission of Hindu culture within the families we studied.

In terms of our data, home traditions include the maintenance of mother tongue and dialect together with practices associated with a particular locality or region in Gujarat or Punjab, or with a particular religious movement or caste. These are traditions perpetuated mainly, though by no means exclusively, within the domestic domain. In this respect women play an especially important part in the transmission of religious practice (McDonald 1987; Logan 1988b). Also there is children's contact with India, indirectly through visits by influential spiritual teachers and Hindi videos, and directly through visits from and to relatives. Less direct is the influence of institutional groups in India, such as the Vishwa Hindu Parishad, founded in 1964 and cultivating a broad definition of Hinduism intended to transcend internal differences and standardise doctrine and ritual, and now having branches in Britain.

Host traditions include elements of popular culture, such as pop music or soap operas ('Neighbours' was watched regularly by most of the children), the English educational system, rituals and practices associated with special events such as marriage or Christmas and perhaps most of all the underlying values associated with individualism and personal autonomy and Western perceptions of what counts as a 'religion'.

The character of the migration process and the nature of the migrant group are factors which draw attention to the origins and varied experiences of British Hindu families. These are not simply a matter of family history, but had consequences for patterns of settlement and for present networks of relationships. Children are not only aware of aspects of the family's migration history, but interact with relatives in Britain or in other countries who have lived through parallel experiences. Children are also very likely to have direct or indirect experience of India by way of relatives who never left the sub-continent or who returned at some stage. Arun's perceptions of being Hindu, for example, are influenced by his parents and by relatives in Coventry, Leicester and London (some of whom were born and spent their formative years in Kenya or Aden), by his relations in different parts of Canada and the USA, and by his family members in Bombay who also own property and are patrons of two temples in the family's ancestral village in the Saurashtran peninsula of Gujarat. These networks provide more than personal contacts and influences; they are channels of cultural influence through video, fashion and music.

The nature of the host response is also a factor influencing the organic development of Hindu tradition. Fortunately experiences of overt racism were mentioned by only a few of the children, Bhavini and two boys. Perhaps significantly all these children lived in the south of the city, a more prosperous area into which South Asian families are moving from the city's northern suburbs, and where they are heavily outnumbered by non-Asian pupils in school, some of whose parents probably resent the presence of Asian famlies in their neighbourhood. This is the background for Bhavini's explanation that she and her one friend, a Sikh, had no other friends. For Bhavini, being Hindu was associated with being brown, which in turn was associated with being racially abused. For an alternative finding with regard to young Sikhs in Coventry see Sohal (1989:6).

There are influences too from those in the dominant society who respond positively to Hindu culture. Religious education in schools can be one such influence. Although we found evidence that sympathetic discussion of Hindu tradition in schools raised self-esteem among Hindu pupils, some treatments were tokenistic and the conceptions of the tradition embodied in many textbooks, and often adopted by teachers, were inherited from an Orientalist scholarly tradition which perceived 'Hinduism' as 'a religion' to be analysed primarily in terms of a set of beliefs. The juxtaposition of children with perceptions of their cultural background based on home and community experience and teachers having a 'world religion' conception of Hinduism can lead to misunderstandings (Jackson 1987). British educational structures have also influenced Hindu supplementary and independent education and are now influencing the ways in which some Hindu writers hope to see Hinduism presented in maintained school curricula (see below).

As Knott points out, it is the interaction of these factors which results in the fluid, organic nature of British Hindu tradition. Our picture of that tradition needs to be revised constantly and to be compared with developments in other diaspora situations as well as with developments in India.

New trends are appearing and particular attention needs to be given to the emergence of new institutional groups which are having an effect on children's perceptions of 'Hinduism', either through their impact on formal nurture and youth activities or through their potential influence on the curricula of maintained schools. Further, we must take care to remind ourselves of the shifting nature of each of the factors. Since our research was conducted, the shape of the map of Eastern Europe has changed, with a consequent resurgence of nationalisms and racism, while events in India, following the destruction of the Babari mosque in Ayodhya, have had some repercussions in Britain. To predict the directions of change in any detail would be an uncertain and risky enterprise.

With regard to institutional developments in Britain, there is a major change from the pattern of cultural transmission in India in what we have called formal 'nurture'. This is a significant moulder of Hindu identity, though for a limited number of children who attend supplementary classes. In this context children's experiences differ according to the representations of the tradition offered by the groups organising the classes. The orientation may be clearly 'sectarian', as it is for children attending Bal Vikas classes run by the Sathya Sai Baba movement or instruction provided by members of the International Society for Krishna Consciousness. More 'mainstream' classes offered in supplementary schools (often organised by temples and teaching language as well as culture) may offer a view of Hindu tradition reflecting the tendency in some organisations to evolve a unitary view of 'Hinduism' with a particular content of religious and moral teaching and advocating particular key texts. As noted in chapter ten, Hindu supplementary schools are a phenomenon of the diaspora and not of the Indian cultural scene, so their potential for reinforcing certain institutional views of the tradition should not be underestimated, even though a minority of young Hindus currently attends them.

☐ Ethnicity and Religion

Also relevant to the issue of religious transmission and change for 'migrant' groups in diaspora situations is the relationship between religion and ethnicity. Early 'primordial' views of ethnicity define it in terms of 'givens' such as common language, culture and kinship patterns (eg Geertz 1963). One problem with this view is that it does not register the organic and evolving nature of any of the stated categories. It also does not acknowledge internal diversity, a notion that is particularly significant when one is thinking in terms of 'migrant' groups. Gujaratis may be Hindu, Jain or Muslim, or from some other religious background. Different subsets of 'Gujarati Hindus', to take one example, will have completely different migration histories, speak different dialects, have different (or no) 'sectarian' allegiances etc. Further, their sense of group identity may change over time and in relation to other groups. And within the category 'Gujarati Hindu', there are caste associations (institutions often formed in East Africa, and often having ancestral origins in one part of Gujarat) and other non-caste based institutional groups of various kinds pursuing their own religio-political or social agendas which may be different from those of, say, a mother perpetuating domestic rituals or a grandmother attending her *satsang* group.

The 'situationist' view of ethnicity, as exemplified in the work of Frederick Barth (1969) seems at first sight to take these factors into account. In Barth's analysis ethnicity becomes a process, a feature of social organisation. The ethnic identity of a group can change or evolve through its interactions with and responses to other groups. Of particular interest is the formation and maintenance of ethnic 'boundaries' and the interactions which take place across them. Ascriptions by both insiders and outsiders influence the shifting nature of an ethnic group, as do factors concerned with inequalities of power. Individuals belong to different kinds of groups related to gender, age and class, as well as being influenced by some of the factors referred to above such as 'home traditions' and migration history. All of these and other factors can influence the reshaping of ethnic identity.

Though the situational view of ethnicity represents an important advance on the primordial view in terms of interpreting the religious and cultural lives of migrants and their descendents, it nevertheless still tends to allow an understanding of culture that involves closure. As a model it still does not fully allow for the variety that exists within groupings. For example, are Gujarati Hindus an ethnic group or a sub-ethnic group?[1] And if they are a sub-ethnic group, what are Kathiawari Gujarati Hindus from a particular caste, with part of a family history in Kenya and part in Aden? Unless qualified, even the situational view can be made consistent with the representation of British young people with a Hindu background as being a 'halfway generation' or 'between two cultures' or with the portrayal in education, the social services and elswhere of an apparently monolithic 'Hindu community'.

Some writers feel that even the situationist view of ethnicity with its use of terms such as 'group', 'boundary' and 'maintenance' still potentially 'locks' individuals into particular identities and fails to reflect the varied political and ideological agendas on the ground. Donald and Rattansi, for example, draw attention to the limitations in some multicultural accounts of ethnicity which concentrated on shared descent, preferring to emphasise 'individual agency' in relation to 'cultural authority' in their consideration of the concept of culture (1992:4).

Our position is to take a flexible stance in a debate complicated by a degree of terminological confusion.[2] The view we take in this book is to regard the term 'ethnicity' as still connoting some sense of 'shared peoplehood', distinguishable from but often closely related to 'religion', while acknowledging that ethnicity can never be fixed or static. A sense of shared descent is a necessary but not a sufficient condition of common ethnicity. At the same time we acknowledge the internal variety of ethnic groups and that the 'level' at which someone expresses a sense of shared peoplehood, or is perceived to express it, may vary situationally. With reference to the Hindu tradition in Britain, ethnic distinctions may be drawn along the lines of linguistic and broadly cultural origins in India. In this sense it is intelligible to distinguish between Gujarati and Punjabi ethnicities. In other contexts ethnicity may be perceived more narrowly (as in the case of Gujarati Hindus born in East Africa in distinction from Indian-born Gujaratis or the case of Cutchis as distinct from Kathiawaris), or more broadly (as when, institutionally, 'Hinduism' as reshaped by Hindus from different linguistic and cultural backgrounds is perceived as being ethnically Indian). It is also important to remember that perceptions of ethnicity can vary situationally, as in the case of children we interviewed who saw themselves as 'Indian' when in England, but were more ambivalent about their ethnic identity when recalling visits to India. Rather than abandoning a useful term in favour of a matrix such as 'individual agency' and 'cultural authority', we prefer to keep using the term when there appears to be no better alternative, but using it flexibly with meanings that should be apparent according to context. One should also recall that the classification system which includes terms such as 'religion' and 'ethnicity' is a device of Western academics. Some of the children we interviewed did not distinguish between 'religion' and 'ethnic' characteristics, such as language.

The basic issue is that of the relationship between individuals and groups. The young people who were the subjects of our case studies all saw themselves as members of various 'ascribed' and 'achieved' membership groups (Harré 1983) as well as individuals. 'Ascribed' groups include family, gender, caste and 'religion' in the general sense of 'being Hindu', while peer group and being a member of a school are examples of 'achieved' groups.

In some situations children referred to symbols marking the boundary between being Hindu and belonging to a different religious membership group. For example the relatively free attitudes towards dress and haircutting experienced in their Hindu backgrounds were distinguished from those perceived to be experienced, respectively, by Muslims and Sikhs. Punjabi Hindus' valuing of Hindi as a language associated with Hindu tradition, in clear distinction from the Punjabi Muslim advocacy of Urdu, was another case of boundary location. We also came across examples of children making no clear distinction between religion and language. In their perception it was the particular mix of custom, practice and language that marked the boundary between one group (which the outsider might designate as 'Gujarati Hindu', for example) and another. Valmiki and Ravidasi children were a challenge to Western academic modes of religious classification, although they sometimes had a clear sense of identification with Hindu or Sikh tradition.

☐ Multiple Cultural Competence

While acknowledging that some practices may reinforce boundaries, our studies suggest that the situation is not clear cut and is becoming less so. Rather than being individuals with a fixed sense of belonging to this group or that, or feeling comfortable in only one type of cultural situation, it became clear that, in general, the children we were studying could move unselfconsciously from one milieu to another. With one possible exception, the children who were the subjects of case studies did not show the stresses of living 'between two cultures', but exhibited 'multiple cultural competence'.[3] Adults, especially 'outsider' adults, do not necessarily recognize this capacity. Too easily teachers, for example, assume that a child who mixes happily at school with non-Asian peers and who competently accomplishes the tasks set is 'Westernised' and has little if anything to do with Hindu culture. All too readily non-Asians who see evidence of children engaged in, say, temple activities assume that they are alien, not fully British. The reality is that the nine year old girl who has the lead part in the Pied Piper at school, or who enjoys football, is the same child who sits in her summer shorts at home informally practising a Punjabi folk song or a Hindi film song and who, in Punjabi suit, performs in an Indian cultural programme.

Different children formed different complexes of partial identifications with members of their own ethnic groups and other groups. With the possible exception of Bhavini, the children who were subjects of our case studies did not appear to be experiencing acculturative stress, though the degree to which they exhibited multiple cultural competence varied from one individual to another. With regard to many aspects of their lives, it was the children who were most proficient in a Western mode who were also most skilled in its Indian counterpart. Those children who were most fluent in English were often the most proficient in Gujarati, Punjabi or Hindi. Those with skill in singing devotional Hindu songs or playing Indian instruments could play Western insruments in Western style with equal ease .

It is important to treat ethnicity as flexible and to understand it as only one factor in a person's sense of identity. As both Donald and Rattansi and Cantwell Smith recognise in their different ways, one needs to recognise the uniqueness of each individual in relation to cultural authority or 'tradition'. One also needs to acknowledge the ways in which individuals are influenced by and identify with different kinds of reference and membership groups, some of which themselves change situationally. This is well understood by identity theorists from the social psychology field who have devised complex frameworks for analysing the relationship between individual identity and various types of group or social identity (eg Tajfel 1978; Weinreich 1986,1989).[4]

Weinreich offers a sophisticated methodology for analysing identity structure. In the context of our ethnographic studies, we can only share observations based on sustained field work. Combining insights from Wilfred Cantwell Smith's work in Religious Studies with that of anthropologists (eg Geertz 1973; 1983) and social psychologists interested in the relationship between individuals and groups (eg Tajfel 1974; 1978a; 1978b; 1981) we construct a matrix in which the most generalised 'whole' is the religious tradition which, although inevitably constructed in different ways by different insiders and outsiders, is a reference point for individuals and groups. Then there are 'membership groups' of many kinds (some of them having an 'ethnic' character), each evolving situationally in relation to other groups. Then there is the individual, deeply influenced through the membership of groups and identifiable as part of the wider tradition, and yet being personally unique. It is this personal synthesis and expression of religious belief and feeling that Cantwell Smith calls 'faith' (1978:156-7). The interpretation of a religious world view involves examining the relationship between individuals and groups, using the wider tradition as a general reference point.

This analytical matrix can be illustrated by reference to Anita, one of the children who was the subject of a case study. As noted in chapter two, Anita's parents are of Gujarati Hindu ancestry (her mother was born in South Africa) and migrated to Britain in 1962. They became devotees of Sathya Sai Baba in 1972. Anita herself was born in Coventry. During the fieldwork period, she was nearly twelve years old and was in the first year at a Coventry comprehensive school.

At school Anita wore the same style of school uniform as any other girl in her class. Her spoken English showed no signs of being her second language. Her favourite school subjects were the sciences and she participated enthusiastically in school sports. She was at ease with her peer group and she had high academic aspirations.

At home among her family, Anita mainly spoke Gujarati. Like the rest of her family Anita was a devotee of Sathya Sai Baba and talked with considerable knowledge, understanding and feeling about his teaching, his miracles and his values. She described in detail a visit to Sathya Sai Baba's headquarters at Puttaparthi in South India in order to have his *darshan* ('sight') and to receive his blessing. Like most of our interviewees, Anita regarded herself as a 'foreigner' and distinguished herself from 'the India people' while in India, but described herself as 'Indian' when in Britain. She felt no inner conflict in making these situationally different identifications.

In the evenings, Anita and her family sang *bhajans* (devotional songs) before the shrine to Sathya Sai Baba, situated at one end of the living room. On at least one evening per week they were joined by other families, with Anita — dressed in the white clothes worn by Sathya Sai Baba's devotees — often leading the worship, playing *tabl*a and harmonium, and performing the *arati* ceremony. She attended Bal Vikas ('child development') classes run by Sai devotees, and once a year attended a youth camp. In the classes she learned 'silent sitting', a meditation technique, and explored the movement's central values of truth (*satya*), righteous conduct (*dharma*), peace (*shanti*), love (*prem*) and non-violence (*ahimsa*). She also received instruction on food, health and hygiene, especially the importance of a vegetarian diet and the principle of *jutha* (see chapter five), her *guru* emphasising that when serving food the spoon must never touch people's plates.

Although Anita perceived the Sathya Sai Baba movement as transcending 'Hinduism', she was conscious of her Hindu heritage and of being Gujarati. She preferred Gujarati style vegetarian food and Gujarati is her mother tongue. She had attended the supplementary school (run by members of the predominantly Gujarati Shree Krishna Temple) where she learned to read and write the Gujarati language and heard about aspects of Hindu religion and culture. She had, for example, performed a dance — a stylised version of the *arati* ritual — at an open evening of the school, held mainly for parents. She was one of 250 (predominantly Gujarati) Hindus who took part in a pilgrimage to five *mandirs* (temples) in England one day in 1987 and she attended events associated with the Shree Krishna temple in Coventry such as the Bhumi Pujan, a ceremony of 'purification of the earth' at the site on which the new temple was to be built. She was also aware of the Matiya Patel (or Matiya Patidar) caste to which she and her family belonged.

At an individual level, Anita interpreted aspects of the Hindu tradition in a very personal way and her developed personal spirituality is evident, although the influence of the Sathya Sai Baba movement can be detected in some of her judgements.

> When I perform *arati* I think of it as giving my mind peace and rest, instead of always asking 'God give me this' or 'God give me that'. If I do it at the end of the day I say 'Thank you God for such a good day'. I don't perform *vrats* (making vows, often accompanied by keeping a fast) because I think that means you're always asking God for something. I think he's given you enough — food, clothing and so on.

She had strong personal views on the *samaj* (caste association) to which her family belonged:

> *Samaj* is really nothing. It's just a few people getting together to try and rule over all the people who are the same sort of caste. I personally don't like the *samaj* thing.

Anita held views about equal opportunities for girls and women that show the generational difference between her and her grandfather (with whom she could discuss such issues freely) and the influence of current thinking in the wider society (see chapter four). She did not, however, find such views a threat to her Hindu identity.

Anita moved skilfully from one cultural situation to another, exhibiting no obvious tensions and participating energetically in the life of the different groups in which she was involved. She had internalized language, knowledge, skills and values from the world of school as well as from various member-ship groups through being part of a particular family and religious movement. In a sense the 'conversation' between different world views took place in her own personal and social life.

Using an analytical matrix of 'faith', 'membership group' and 'tradition', this thumb nail sketch gives just a hint of some of the dimensions of Anita's life in the late 1980s. Only further research would show whether in later adolescence she had experienced conflicts with her family or with peers or teachers, had had her basically optimistic perspective altered negatively through experiences of racism or had come to reinterpret her religious feelings or to modify or question any of her religious allegiances. What is clear is that during the research period, Anita could employ skills enabling her to move from one cultural context to another with apparent ease. She seemed as comfortable with the language of school, peer group and academic subjects as she was with the concepts of the Sathya Sai Baba movement's Education in Human Values course or with the rituals associated with public prayer.

☐ Hinduism as an Ethnic Religion

The transmission of Hindu tradition in the cases of the families we studied involves a complex interplay of influences, which vary in strength according to which membership groups children and their families belong and the variety and intensity of their experiences within these groups. It is through the interpretation of changes resulting from these influences that we can begin to form a sense of how the tradition might continue to develop in Britain. This relates to the point about a possible shift in the character of Hindu conscious-ness in non-Indian contexts related to Fitzgerald's distinction between *dharma* 1 and *dharma* 2. An increase in the popularity of some of the Hindu 'sectarian' movements in Coventry has been evident since we began research on Hindu communities in the late 1970s. The involvement in religious movements of some of the families featured in the present study provided extra content and a firmer framework, supplementing their more general involvement in Hindu life, and giving children a way of understanding and articulating 'Hinduism' than might otherwise have been gained. This is consistent with Fitzgerald's view that Hindu tradition in the *dharma* 2 sense is likely to be perpetuated in diaspora settings and with Williams' observa-tions in the United States that allegiance to religious leaders 'around whom sectarian groups form' is becoming a more important marker of religious identity for American Hindu children than the maintenance of mother tongue (1988:283).

Yet domestic traditions continue to be of great importance in the British situation, and, despite some adaptations, many of them continue to be perpetuated. For younger people, however, they no longer seem part of a total world view or way of life. For many, the *sattvik* nature of food, for example, is a matter relevant to the performance of a ritual within the tradition and not to the whole of life. It might be important for some of the children we studied to eat vegetarian food, but its precise type seems to be less important outside the ritual context, especially when socializing with non-Hindu Westerners. Similarly, festivals retain their vibrancy, sense of fun and their connection with spiritual values, but they have become 'special events', and, for the young at least, do not highlight an annual cycle of time that is part of a distinctly Hindu world view. Visits to India retain their importance, and pilgrimages to traditional sites of spiritual importance are still a feature of practice for some Hindus in Britain. But pilgrimage sites are now beginning to be established in Britain (Jackson and Killingley 1988:147) and features of the traditional pilgrimage can be found in the visit to five temples in Britain in which Anita was involved. Temple worship is well established in Britain, but various adaptations of practice and use and reinterpretations of tradition are taking place (Knott 1987), although changes relate specifically to the nature and migration history of the main Hindu population visiting the temples and are not simply to be explained in terms of accommodation to life in Britain (Vertovec 1992c).

These shifts are consistent with the institutionalisation of cultural transmission through supplementary education. The strategies adopted for strengthening a sense of Hindu identity in this context are more akin to Sunday school and Western youth organisations than to the experience of the children's parents or contemporaries in India. So diaspora communities are adopting the structures of the dominant society and, in the struggle to ensure that their tradition survives and is regenerated, it is compared with the other 'religions' in society and recategorised accordingly (cf Tajfel 1978b). 'Hinduism' becomes more of a chosen pursuit, a rich subject for organised children's classes, camps and festivals, rather than a total way of life.

This is analogous to the sociological paradox of detribalization and retribalisation noted in Nigeria by Cohen. As Hindus in Britain adjust to a new social reality they are 'developing new customs under traditional symbols' (Cohen 1969:1). Orans observed a similar process at work among the people in a North Indian city (1965). Supplementary classes, undoubtedly an effective means of stengthening Hindu children's sense of group identity and empowering them to articulate their tradition, are arguably an appropriation of alien social structures.

☐ Parental Views

What parents felt was important for their children to know about Hindu tradition was related both to nurture in the domestic context and to formal nurture in supplementary education. Most parents referred to language, to family values, and to vegetarianism.

Language, whether Gujarati or Hindi (in the case of Punjabis), was regarded as essential to a Hindu lifestyle, to understanding devotional and liturgical material and for communication with other relatives, especially grandparents. While language classes teach their pupils an elementary literacy, oral language is primarily passed on in the home. So too with the other two strands of Hindu tradition which emerged prominently from our research, namely the expression of the values underpinning family life and the emphasis on vegetarianism. These were evident in both formal and informal nurture.

Elders' concern to instil moral qualities, such as respect for others, was general, regardless of people's regional or sectarian background. Hindu children, like others of South Asian origin, are brought up with a strong sense of family responsibilities implicit in particular relationships. The role of brother or sister, son or daughter, maternal uncle or paternal aunt involve particular duties and privileges. Children also learn by seeing older relatives performing certain obligations because of the specific relationship in which they stand. Children learn these and other roles through observation of the event, of its replay on video, and by their own involvement and enjoyment. It seems likely that the potential clash between the view of the individual as a highly autonomous decision-making agent assumed in many areas of Western life, and the Hindu conceptions of family honour, wider responsibility and a more corporate sense of identity can lead to conflict, and may engender accommodation and change.

Diet, and more specifically vegetarianism, was the third issue to emerge clearly from adults' conversation about their concerns and from children's accounts of their tradition. Many mentioned this as the most distinctive feature of Hinduism, and the avoidance of beef was a recurring theme. What Hindus eat and their ideas about food are a significant strand in Hindu tradition. The range of reasons which children gave for avoiding beef or non-vegetarian food illustrates the complex of interlocking criteria for their behaviour and assumptions, though the influence of religious movements such as Sathya Sai Baba and especially the International Society For Krishna Consciousness was often evident in their explanations. Discussion of the importance of vegetarianism was also a feature of workshops at the Youth Festivals organised by the National Council of Hindu Temples. Perhaps vegetarianism will emerge as a symbol of British 'Hinduism' that distinguishes it from other traditions.[5] What was striking from the field work was not so much the prevalence of vegetarianism in practice (as many Hindu parents and children were not vegetarian in all situations) as the recurrence of the theme in conversation about Hindu tradition.

☐ Religious Education

We have already noted in chapters six and ten the influence on children of conceptions of 'Hinduism' derived from religious education in maintained schools. Through changes resulting from the implementation of the 1988 Education Reform Act possibilities for British Hindus to be involved in the representation of their tradition in maintained schools have emerged. There is now a mechanism whereby the interests of Hindus in Britain and of religious education in county schools are able to meet. The 1988 Education Reform Act, in principle, allows a Hindu presence on Agreed Syllabus Conferences and on Local Education Authority Standing Advisory Councils for Religious Education. In Coventry there was Hindu representation on the Conference which produced the 1992 Agreed Syllabus and there are Hindu members of the Coventry SACRE. In some areas of the country British Hindus are now in a position to influence the conceptualization and presentation of Hindu tradition in schools.

Nationally a group of Hindus from different backgrounds has (in 1992 and 1993) provided material for the National Curriculum Council, to be used in advisory guidelines written for use by local Agreed Syllabus Conferences. The nature of these contributions inevitably is influenced by the perceptions of Hindu tradition held by those portraying 'Hinduism' on such committees.

An article for a professional magazine associated with the Coventry SACRE written by two Hindu contributors mentions the role of school RE in helping Hindu pupils to maintain a cultural identity and emphasises co-operation between schools and Hindu communities in order, in the perception of the writers, 'to be sympathetic to children caught in the crossfire of dual cultural adherences'. It also advocates negotiations over content in order to:

> ... ensure that the school does not teach a 'different type' of Hinduism and further confuse the child with a conflict of factual accuracy between parent and school. (Chaudhary and Naik 1992:14)

The type of Hindu teaching advocated, however, is neither the evolving regional and local traditions that might be practised in the home nor 'sectarian' teaching, but rather a generalised Hinduism influenced by *sanatana dharma*, and also partly shaped by being distinguished from other 'Asian or Ethnic' religious groupings such as 'Sikhism, Buddhism (and) Islam'(15). 'Hinduism' is portrayed as a religion with 'specific...religious doctrines, orientations (and) cultural aspects' to be studied through story and texts such as the *Mahabharata* and *Ramayana*, 'much in the same way the Bible is studied in traditional RE classrooms'.

☐ Conclusion

Taking together the shifts of consciousness as exemplified in children's interpretations of domestic devotional practice, the concerns of parents, the development of supplementary education and the involvement of British Hindus in the definition of 'Hinduism' for a wider educational audience, there appears to be a trend towards the representation of Hinduism as an 'ecumenical' religion (Williams 1988:4) or as an 'ethnic' phenomenon (Burghart 1987; Vertovec 1992b), that is a 'religion' whose content is formulated both in distinction from and under the influence of 'others' and whose members are perceived as a single community by both insiders and outsiders. It seems likely that 'Hinduism', for the children we studied, is becoming a more discrete area of experience, one which can be deliberately avoided or which can be visited, for cultural enrichment or fellowship with co-religionists, rather than being a total way of life. Increasingly, consciousness of religion as a subject for discussion and comparison has profound implications for the individual's perception of his or her relationship with it. 'Hinduism' can now, it seems, be appropriated to special events and locations in a way unthinkable when the *dharma* of each caste determined the Hindu's place and function in society. Nevertheless, the British manifestation of Hindu tradition is as valid as any other and shows no signs of ossification or decline. British Hindu children may be helping to reshape it, but they are still very much part of it.

☐ Notes and References

1. Verity Saifullah Khan, writing in the situational ethnicity tradition of Barth, employs the term 'sub-ethnic identity' to account for diversity within ethnic groups (1982:113).

2. There is a good deal of terminological confusion in the literature on ethnicity. Many writers, even those who support situational views of ethnicity, still commonly use the term as if they are referring to a state, along the lines of 'a shared sense of peoplehood' (Dashefsky 1972). Ethnicity is regarded as parallel to religion, both being aspects of individual, group or social identity, though different writers express different views on the relationship between the two. For Dashefsky, for example, they are barely distinguishable and he refers to religio-ethnic groups (1972:239). Others regard the two concepts as separate but related, so that religious differences may divide ethnic groups while the coextensiveness of religion and ethnicity might act as a binding force where each reinforces the other (Francis 1976). Think of the relationship between Sikhism and 'Punjabiness' for example. In relation to Islam in Britain, the religion acts as a regulating agency on all aspects of life (including ethnicity), but ethnicity also has an impact on religion (Anwar 1980). For Hans Mol, the two concepts are interrelated, but are different qualitatively, with religion acting as a conservative force, a 'harnesser of social change', and as 'sacralizer of identity', whether ethnic or some other feature of identity (1979:34-35).

   The confusion occurs when some writers with a situationist view of ethnicity refer to it as a *process* (eg Barth 1969). The active, 'verbal' element implied by the term process seems odd when applied to a noun grammatically without an active element. One might say that ethnicity, like religion, is in a constant state of change. This is different from calling either religion or ethnicity a process. The coining of an alternative term, such as 'ethnic re-formation' might have removed some of the confusion.

3. We are grateful to Steven Vertovec for suggesting this term to us.

4. Tajfel's theory of social identity (1974; 1978a; 1978b; 1981) provides a linked set of concepts allowing a consideration of an individual's acquisition of identity within a particular culture and a particular social structure. One key concept is *categorisation*, the human tendency to generate meaning by classification and to exaggerate differences between members of the same category. Tajfel emphasises that individuals are members of many categories; no-one's social identity (to introduce a second key concept) can adequately be described in terms of one social category such as ethnicity. A third key concept in Tajfel's theory is that of *social comparison*. Individuals frequently compare their own membership groups with other membership groups, thereby developing mechanisms for maintaining (or adopting) their positively valued distinctiveness. The cognitive processes of social categorisation and social comparison provide a psychological basis for social identity, though the 'content' of that identity, as it were, is determined by sociological factors.

Weinreich, while recognizing the value of Tajfel's work, points out the dangers of single theories attempting to give an explanation for all the socio-psychological processes of identity maintenance. He uses methods and procedures related to several theoretical perspectives, in particular Erikson's psychodynamic approach to identity (employing, for example, Erikson's concept of identity diffusion and Hauser's concept of identity foreclosure) and George Kelly's personal construct theory which attempts to explain how the self is constructed and reconstructed through the organisation and reorganisation of bipolar categories related to value systems and used by individuals to give meaning to the world (Weinreich 1986; 1989). Weinreich's metatheoretical approach provides, for example, a means to distinguish the different kinds of pressure which might result in a person's feeling adrift and in a confused state about self or with a foreclosed sense of self that rules out any consideration of change or development. A report of the application of Weinreich's approach in a study of Pakistani Muslim and Greek Cypriot adolescents is Kelly (1989).

5. This has not always happened in diaspora Hindu communities. The Hindu community in the Netherlands, for example, is mainly Surinamese in background and does not have a strong tradition of vegetarianism.

APPENDIX

Field Research Methods

The general methodology employed in this research is outlined in chapter two. Here we give a more detailed account of the research methods.

☐ Ethical and Practical Issues

Research of this kind raises numerous ethical questions. For example we had to decide how far we were justified in intruding into private homes for private family occasions. Confidentiality had to be respected during and after the period of fieldwork, and individual identity had to be protected when material was made public, but not at the cost of distorting the data.

It was also realised that relationships sincerely entered into by Hindus with the researchers were for the latter, in part at least, a means to an end. We knew that after the field work period all relationships could not easily be sustained. This factor had to be balanced carefully against any inter-cultural under-standing to which the research was dedicated. We also had to decide to what extent to observe and be known to observe rules of behaviour expected or respected by religious Hindus.

There were also practical difficulties posed by the demands of participant observation. In Britain most religious events, apart from the daytime *satsangs* mainly attended by older women, take place in the evening or, primarily, at weekends. On a Saturday evening it was difficult to decide which of the many possible venues to visit. There was also the stress factor mentioned by Pocock for researchers moving repeatedly from one culture to another (Pocock 1976:341).

☐ Working with Children

Careful thought was given to the best means of gaining information from children, and as the research continued, these became clearer. The richest data resulted from using different techniques in combination. Naturally each child is unique and each research context differs, minutely or substantially, from every other. After over three years of investigation, however, it is possible to report which methods have proved their worth, and to argue for a strategy which may be adapted to other research in which children provide data.

The value and necessity of preliminary exploration cannot be over-emphasised. Familiarity with the ethnographic literature was vital in providing a wider context, for clarifying factors in a community's immigration, settlement, ritual practice or belief system. Coventry's Hindus could be better understood thanks to literature on previous generations in India or on earlier diaspora communities (eg East Africa) and contemporaries in India and other parts of Britain and the world. Researchers elsewhere alerted us to points which might otherwise have escaped our attention. Criticial examination of their methods was useful in avoiding pitfalls. Ongoing scrutiny of social scientific theory and discussions of field work technique enabled more confident decision-making in the field. The exchange of ideas and experiences with contemporary researchers was also challenging and supportive.

The value of this exploration of relevant research was all the greater because it continued during the period of research contact with children. This was true too of participant observation in the child's domain. Children felt confident in articulating their experience as fully as possible because they knew that a researcher had been present at the event under discussion. The need for this was perceived at the outset, but its full justification and indispensibility only became apparent subsequently, when interviews with children were under way.

Thus, participant observation was necessary for an informed selection of children who would be the source of future data. It was necessary for deciding the cues (verbal questions, visual stimulus material, etc) to be used in eliciting information, and it was vital for understanding children's statements (non-English words used, gesture accompanying verbal description). Finally it proved essential to being accepted and trusted by children's families.

Before asking people to impart information it is reasonable to explain why one is questioning them and to what use their answers will be put.[1] Where children were concerned, parental approval was necessary. The researchers explained to children that they worked in a department of the University where teachers were trained and that any information collected would be used to help teachers to understand more about the lives of Hindu pupils. Where, during fieldwork, children and their older relatives accepted the researchers

186

and felt that they understood the research objectives, this contributed to the ease with which information continued to be elicited from the children.

For this research most data was verbal statements made by children and material written by them. When, during participant observation, children responded to questions and other verbal cues from peers, teachers or other adults, the exchange was noted but this was not exploited as a major source of data. (Eavesdropping in school was a technique used by Larson 1988). An advantage of data obtained in this way is that the cues are neither influenced nor dictated by the researcher. One disadvantage is that a great deal of time is required for acquiring a volume of information from children, which could be achieved more quickly through interviewing them. It may also be more difficult to organise and analyse the data than it is with data from, say, parallel interviews.

Most data were deliberately collected during conversation between the researcher and child on an individual basis. This consisted of informal chats (the topics to be addressed had not been decided in advance); semi-structured interviews (conversation steered in order to get answers to questions decided in advance) and, finally, structured interviews. These entailed questioning children on the basis of an interview schedule and tape recording the conversation. Although children were encouraged to sing and draw as ways of demonstrating what they knew, most information, of course, was verbal, as were most stimuli. This may seem unjustified, given the fact that cultural experience derives from all five senses of taste, smell, touch, hearing and sight. Collecting children's responses to non-verbal stimuli would have been beneficial and so the use of recordings of devotional music as cues for children's response was considered. However our 'focused interviews' used only visual stimuli.

☐ The Focused Interview

This was one of the most valuable techniques we used and it developed during the fieldwork periods. In this outline the term 'focused interview' refers to the use of visual stimuli to elicit information from children. The process developed as we realised how much children could relate when commenting on photographs in their family album or on video films of weddings and other rituals. On occasion children were shown colour transparencies and invited to describe what they depicted. In many cases these were slides which had been taken during fieldwork showing the child and/or family participating in cultural events such as a life cycle ritual, a festival or an outing. Sometimes the slides were deliberately chosen to show events and activities in which the child in question had not participated or was known not to participate. For example, a Gujarati child might be asked to comment on a picture of a Punjabi occasion such as Lohri or Karwa Chauth. A child whose family members were not involved in ISKCON or the Sathya Sai Baba movement, would comment on a slide of an event characteristic of one of these movements.

By chance, one of the most instructive interviews occurred when slides taken at Bhaktivedanta Manor (ISKCON's British headquarters) came out light-damaged. Children who were familiar with the shrine proceeded to identify what was missing and what clues there were to the identity of the missing images.[2]

Another valuable means of gaining information from children was the diary. Children were given notebooks or folders and encouraged to write and draw. They were free to write about hobbies and any aspect of their lives, but knew that the researchers were especially interested in their religion. For some children difficulty in writing was an obstacle, but in every case the diaries afforded information on which subsequent oral questions were based.

Throughout the research period certain principles of procedure held good. Research techniques had to be disciplined yet flexible, responsive to the unexpected and to any insights arising from constant review of the situation. However unequal or contrived the relationship between a researcher and a Hindu family might be, the principle of reciprocity was maintained. Care was taken, for example, to offer copies of research photographs to families concerned, and to give practical help or advice when this was requested, regardless of whether it was connected with the research.

☐ Venue

The nature of the venue affected the data because it affected both interviewer and interviewee. For example, in a Hindu child's living room there were religious pictures on the wall which influenced the content of the exchange. A school classroom might contain no visual links with the children's life out of school.

The venue also implied a certain relationship between the researcher and the child and the child's significant elders. If the location was a school then the researcher first obtained permission from the Director of Education, the headteacher and the child's parents. The child viewed the researcher as on a level with or sanctioned by teachers. In the context of a temple, supplementary class or community event, researchers, as outsiders from another cultural base and less familiar than the child with the dominant language and devotional procedure, felt relatively powerless. Here the child was on familiar territory and had the power to act as interpreter and gatekeeper. When contact occurred in the child's home, the relationship of mutual trust and respect and the balance of power differed again. Here the degree of sympathy and support

188

felt by the child's parents and other senior relatives played a vital part in the degree of ease which researchers felt.

One factor in deciding suitable venues was the likely degree of privacy. On the one occasion, when the child's school teacher sat in on an interview, very little information was forthcoming. Children and interviewer often felt inhibited by the presence of others. For example the interviewer was conscious that parents might misunderstand or dislike some questions. The child was sensitive to looking ignorant or silly in the eyes of peers or siblings.

Where parents expressed the wish to listen in on an interview conducted in their house it seemed most politic and conducive to a trusting relationship to accept this warmly. If a parent intervened or commented later on a child's answer, this too was treated as useful data. If a discussion arose among the family (eg on caste), this was valuable for insights into the varying perceptions within one household and for noting such factors as age and generation in the thinking of Hindus. At least as informative as their answers to interview questions were children's interactions with siblings, visitors and older relatives. One could note their tone of voice, language medium, use of relationship words and honorifics.

Timing was another key factor. Visits were made when most convenient to the family concerned. Favourite television programmes (especially the TV soap *Neighbours*) often proved a more pressing concern for children than homework. The family's private calendar — marriages, visits to India and so forth — combined with Hindu festivals and school holidays, placed constraints on the visiting schedule. The timing of a visit also affected the quantity and quality of children's accounts, of a festival for instance (Bullivant 1978:159). Care was taken not to make visits too frequently or to continue interviews when children were tired.

☐ Communication

Our research depended heavily upon conversations with each Hindu child. Every child spoke English readily, not only with people who did not know the child's mother tongue, but also as a matter of course with some relatives, and particularly with peers and friends, including those with the same mother tongue. Every conversation was different in content and context, and the children varied in chronological age and linguistic competence both in one or more Indian languages and in English. Nevertheless four broad factors required consideration in all cases.

Firstly there there was difficulty for every individual in verbalising feelings and values, areas of experience which one cannot fully articulate to oneself. Secondly, the level of conceptual development varies from one child to another. Some of the younger children were more articulate than older children. Age was not a decisive factor (Logan 1989a). Thirdly, all the children were exposed to at least two Indian languages plus English. The Punjabi children were growing up hearing Punjabi, Hindi and — in ritual contexts — Sanskrit. The Gujaratis heard Hindi and Sanskrit in addition to Gujarati. Often their family's Gujarati included Swahili words, although children did not realise this (Logan 1989a). It was particularly in the culinary and the 'religious' aspects of their lives that children were immersed in Indian language.

Regardless of their relative proficiency in English and their family's mother tongue, the children found it easiest to express themselves, as did older English-speaking relatives, in English sentences studded with Indic nouns. In some cases this was because they did not know the English equivalent. More often it was because no equivalent existed. This is the fourth factor. It is not easy to express culturally specific concepts, actions or ideas in a language shaped by a culture in which these play no part. This is a hard task even for adult scholars of the languages and cultures involved. It is in the 'religious' detail of their lives that these children's cultural experience is particularly unlike that of their non-Asian peers.

The difficulty facing children who attempt to describe religious activities to an outsider (such as a researcher or a teacher) is real and complex even when the child is uninhibited and the outsider is, and is perceived to be, receptive. Indeed, unless the latter is already familiar with what the child is endeavouring to describe, many essentials of Hindu worship are hard to visualise or identify. For example, in Hindu acts of worship one integral detail is the application of a paste to the forehead of those participating. Images and holy pictures are reverently marked in the same way. Thus on pictures of Sathya Sai Baba, devotees mark the centre of his forehead with sandalwood paste. Red powder (*kumkum/kanku*) moistened with water is widely used though not felt to be appropriate for widows. It is usual to reciprocate when someone imprints a *chandlo/tika* on one's forehead. The paste is usually applied with the tip of the fourth finger of the right hand and dry grains of uncooked rice are often added to the red mark. Understandably children have difficulty explaining in English as these attempts suggest:

A sort of red thing that you put on your head and it's got rice in it.

It's sort of red and you've got to put it like this and there's some sort of long thing... it's *chokha*...

Although this girl denied that *chokha* meant rice, her subsequent reference to kedgeree made it clear that her problem was more one of 'English as a second language' than anything else.

These factors, particularly children's difficulty in explaining certain concepts and terms from Indian languages in English, have contributed significantly to some people's conclusion that Hindu children are drifting away from their tradition. When one adds the further consideration that a child may feel ill at ease, threatened or afraid of the mockery of non-Hindus within earshot, it is easy to see why many children appear ignorant of their culture. The material in this book provides plenty of evidence to challenge the notion that children are uninvolved or uninterested in Hindu tradition.

Notes

1. The principle of giving the subjects' informed consent is enshrined in the BSA Code of Practice and in the Association of Social Anthropologists of the Commonwealth *Ethical Guidelines for Good Practice*, (1987).

2. For the study on Valmiki and Ravidasi children, as the fieldwork period was short, we decided to give each child a focused interview in which she or he was shown twenty five pictures and encouraged to comment. These were devotional pictures of the type found in homes and places of worship. They were chosen on the basis of background reading and fieldwork, to represent a wide range of Punjabi Hindu devotion. Thus 'great tradition' Hindu deities, Sikh Gurus, contemporary religious leaders, caste-specific deities and Indian pictures representing Islam, Christianity and Buddhism were included. These were obtained for the most part from a local Gujarati retailer who supplies local South Asians with religious pictures. A wealth of data resulted from this method.

BIBLIOGRAPHY

Adiraja dasa (1984) *The Hare Krishna Book of Vegetarian Cooking,* Letchmore Heath, Bhaktivedanta Book Trust.

Anon. (1983) *Bhajanavali,* Hong Kong, Santhi Nilayam, Sai Baba Center of Hong Kong.

Anwar, M. (1976) 'Young Asians between Two Cultures', *New Society, 38, December 16th, pp 563-565.*

Anwar, M. (1980) 'Religious Identity in Plural Societies: the Case of Britain', *Journal of the Institute of Muslim Minority Affairs,* 2:2/3:1, 110-121.

Anwar, M. (1990) 'The Participation of Asians in the British Political System' in Clarke, C., Peach, C. and Vertovec, S. (eds) *South Asians Overseas: Migration and Ethnicity,* Cambridge, Cambridge University Press, pp 297-315.

Association of Social Anthropologists of the Commonwealth (1987) *Ethical Guidelines for Good Practice.* London, Association of Social Anthropologists of the Commonwealth.

Bahree, P. (1984) *The Hindu World.* London, Macdonald.

Bala Books Inc. (1977) *Agha the Terrible Demon;* (1978a) *Rama Colouring Book;* (1978b) *Krishna and the Demons;* (1978c) *The Krishna Colouring Book No. 1 Childhood Pastimes and Friends;* (1981a) *Sakshi Gopal a Witness for the Wedding;* (1981b) *Krishna, Master of All Mystics;* (1982) *ABC Colouring Book No. 4,* New York, Bala Books Inc.

Banerji, Sabita and Baumann, Gerd (1990) 'Bhangra 1984-8: Fusion and Professionalisation: a Genre of South Asian Dance Music', in Oliver, P., (ed), *Black Music in Britain: Essays on the Afro-Asian Contribution to Popular Music,* Open University, pp 137-152.

Barot, Rohit (1981) *The Social Organisation of a Swaminarayan Sect in Britain,* unpublished PhD thesis, University of London, School of Oriental and African Studies.

Barth, F. (ed) (1969) *Ethnic Groups and Boundaries,* London, Allen and Unwin.

Barton, Stephen (1986) *The Bengali Muslims of Bradford : A Study of their Observance of Islam with Special Reference to the Functions of the Mosque and the Work of the Imams*, Monograph Series, Community Religions Project, University of Leeds.

Basham, A. L. (1967) *The Wonder That Was India*, London, Sidgdwick and Jackson.

Barz, R. (1976) *The Bhakti Sect of Vallabhacarya*, Faridabad, Thomson Press.

Baumann, Gerd (1990) 'The Re-Invention of Bhangra: Social Change and Aesthetic Shifts in a Punjabi Music in Britain', *The World of Music, Journal of the International Institute for Comparative Music Studies and Documentation* (Berlin) 32, 2, pp 81-97.

Bennett, Olivia (1987) *Holi: Hindu Festival of Spring*, London, Hamish Hamilton.

Beteille, A. and Madan, T.N. (eds) (1975) *Encounter and Experience: Personal Accounts of Fieldwork*, Honolulu, University Press of Hawaii.

Bhakticaru Swami (1984) *The Childhood Pastimes of Lord Chaitanya*, Calcutta, Bhaktivedanta Book Trust.

Bhattacharya, A. (1957) 'Traditional Literature Associated with Religious Ceremonies', *Bulletin of the Ramakrishna Institute of Culture*, February, pp 35-40.

Bigger, Hugh D. (1987) *Hindu Nurture: The Historical Tradition and the British Reality*, unpublished MA dissertation, University of Lancaster.

Blackman, Winifred (1925) 'Rosaries' in Hastings, J. (ed) *Encyclopaedia of Religion and Ethics* 10, pp 847-856.

Blurton, T.R. (1988) 'Tradition and Modernism: Contemporary Indian Religious Prints', *South Asia Research* 8, 1, May, pp 47-70.

Bott, E. (1971) *Family and Social Network*, London, Tavistock.

Bowen, David, (ed) (1981) *Hinduism in England*, Bradford, Bradford College.

Bowen, David (1988) *The Sathya Sai Baba Community in Bradford: Its Origin and Development, Religious Beliefs and Practices*, University of Leeds.

Brand, M. (1979) *Santosi Mata: A New Hindu Goddess*, unpublished BA dissertation, Canberra, Australian National University.

Bridger, P. (1969), *A Hindu Family in Britain*, Exeter, Religious Education Press.

Briggs, G.W. (nd) *The Chamars*, Calcutta, Association Press (YMCA), Oxford University Press.

British Sociological Association (1989) 'Code of Practice', *Network, Newsletter of the British Sociological Association*, No. 43, pp 4-5.

Brook, Tal (1982) *Avatar of Night: The Hidden Side of Sai Baba*, Tarang (Sangam).

Bryant, M.T. (1988) *A Way to God: A Study of Some of the Beliefs and Practices of Hindus in Leicester and Leicestershire*, unpublished MPhil thesis, University of Leicester.

Bullivant, Brian M. (1978) *The Way of Tradition: Life in an Orthodox Jewish School*, Hawthorn, Australian Council for Educational Research.

Burgess, Robert (1984) *In the Field: An Introduction to Field Research*, London, Allen and Unwin.

Burgess, Robert (ed) (1985) *Field Methods in the Study of Education*, Lewes, Falmer.

Burghart, Richard (ed) (1987) *Hinduism in Great Britain: Religion in an Alien Cultural Milieu*, London, Tavistock.

Bushnell, Horace (1967) *Christian Nurture*, New Haven, Yale University.

Campbell, J. and Little, V. (eds) (1989) *Humanities in the Primary School*, Lewes, Falmer.

Carey, Sean (1987) 'The Indianisation of the Hare Krishna Movement in Britain' in Burghart, R. (ed), *Hinduism in Great Britain*, pp 81-99.

Chaudhary, A. and Naik, D. (1992) 'Multi-Faith Education: The Hindu View', *Broadly Christian*, April, pp 14-15.

Chaudhry, Sanjeev (1985) 'Introduction to Methodology of EHV', *Education in Human Values Journal*, 2, pp 27-39.

Clarke, Colin, Peach, Ceri and Vertovec, Steven (eds) (1990) *South Asians Overseas: Migration and Ethnicity*, Cambridge, Cambridge University Press.

Clifford, J. and Marcus, G. (eds) (1986) *Writing Culture: The Poetics and Politics of Ethnography*, Berkeley, University of California Press.

Cohen, A. (1969) *Customs and Politics in Urban Africa: A Study of Hausa Immigrants in Yoruba Towns*, London, Routledge.

Cole, W.O. and Sambhi, P.S. (1986) *Baisakhi*, Exeter, Arnold-Wheaton.

Commission for Racial Equality (1985) *Ethnic Minorities in Britain*, London, Commission for Racial Equality.

Courtright, Paul (1987) 'The Elephant God and his Daughters: The Vitality of Myth in Contemporary India', *The World and I* 2, 7, July, pp 568-579.

Crooke, William (1926) *Religion and Folklore of Northern India*, Oxford, Oxford University Press.

Dashefsky, A (1972) 'And the Search Goes On: Religio-ethnic Identity and Identification', *Sociological Analysis*, 33, 4, pp239-245.

Dave, Jagdish, J. (ed and trans) (1987) *Prarthana Pothi*, Harrow, Academy of Vedic Heritage.

DES (Department of Education and Science) (1988) *Report by HM Inspectors at Chaitanya College, International Society for Krishna Consciousness,* Severn, Stoke, Hereford and Worcester.

Desai, R. (1963) *Indian Immigrants in Britain*, Oxford, Oxford University Press.

Donald, J. and Rattansi, A. (eds) (1992) *Race, Culture and Difference*, London, Sage.

Dosanjh, T.S. (1969) 'Punjabi Immigrant Children', University of Nottingham, Institute of Education, *Educational Papers* No. 10.

Dunn, Peter (1987) 'The Village Where Yellow is Less than Mellow', *Independent*, August 17th.

Drury, Beatrice (1990) 'Blackness: A Situational Identity', unpublished paper for conference on New Issues in Black Politics, University of Warwick.

Dwyer, Johanna (1988) *Formal Religious Nurture in Two Hindu Temples in Leicester,* unpublished PhD thesis, University of Leicester.

Dumont, L. (1970) *Homo Hierarchicus:The Caste System and its Implications,* London, Paladin.

Epstein, A.L. (ed) (1967) *The Craft of Social Anthropology,* London, Tavistock.

Erricker, C. and Barnett, V. (eds) (1988), *World Religions in Education: Women in Religion,* London, Commission for Racial Equality.

Ewan, J. (1977), *Understanding Your Hindu Neighbour,* London, Lutterworth.

Fitzgerald, T. (1990) 'Hinduism and the 'World Religion' Fallacy', *Religion,* 20, pp 101-18.

Floyd, Leela, (1980), *Indian Music,* Oxford, Oxford University Press.

Forward Planning Division (1989) *Unitary Development Plan Monitoring Report: Ethnic Minority Statistical Digest,* Coventry City Council, Department of Economic Development and Planning.

Francis, E. K. (1976) *Interethnic Relations,* New York, Elsevier.

Francis, Leslie,J. (1984) *Teenagers and the Church:A Profile of Church-Going Youth in the 1980s,* London, Collins.

Francis, Leslie, J. (1987) *Religion in the Primary School* London, Collins.

Freilich, Morris, (ed) (1970) *Marginal Natives: Anthropologists at Work,* New York, Harper and Row.

Geertz, Clifford (1973) *The Interpretation of Cultures,* New York, Basic Books.

Geertz, Clifford (1983) *Local Knowledge,* New York, Basic Books.

Gillespie, Marie (1989a) 'Technology and Tradition: Audio-visual Culture Among South Asian Families in West London', *Cultural Studies,* 3, 2, pp 226-239.

Gillespie, Marie (1989b) *The Audio-Visual Culture of the South Asian Community in West London (Southall),* unpublished thesis for MA in Film and Television for Education, Institute of Education, University of London.

Glinert, Lewis (1985) *Aspects of British Judaism,* University of London, School of Oriental and African Studies.

Gokak, V. (1975) *Bhagavan Sri Sathya Sai Baba: The Man and the Avatar, an Interpretation,* New Delhi, Abhinav.

Gonda, J. (1986) *Vedic Ritual,* Leiden, Brill.

Gopalan, G. (1978) 'Vrat: Ceremonial Vows of Women in Gujarat, India', *Asian Folklore Studies,* 31, I, pp 101-129.

Govinda dasi (nd) *Jagannatha Activity Book,* Los Angeles, Bhaktivedenta Book Trust.

Haggard, Stephen (1988) 'Mass Media and the Visual Arts in Twentieth Century South Asia: Indian Film Posters 1947-Present', *South Asia Research,* 8, 1 May, pp 71-88.

Haraldsson, Erlendur (1987) *'Miracles are My Visiting Cards': An Investigative Report on the Psychic Phenomena Associated with Sathya Sai Baba,* London, Century.

Harré, R (1983) 'Identity Projects', in Breakwell, G (ed), *Threatened Identities,* Chichester, John Wiley.

Helweg, Arthur W. (1986a) *Sikhs in England*, Delhi, Oxford University Press (2nd edn).

Helweg, Arthur W. (1986b) 'The Indian Diaspora: Influence on International Relations' in Sheffer, Gabriel (ed) *Modern Diasporas in International Politics*, London, Croom Helm, pp 103-129.

Helweg, Arthur W. and Helweg, Usha M. (1990) *An Immigrant Success Story: East Indians in America*, London, Hurst.

Hershman, Paul (1974) 'Hair, Sex and Dirt', *Man*, (NS), 9, pp 274-298.

Hershman, Paul (1977) 'Virgin and Mother' in Lewis, L.M. (ed) *Symbols and Sentiments*, London, Academic Press.

Hindu Swayam Sevak Sangh (nd) 'A Decade in Brent', London, Hindu Swayam Sevak Sangh.

Hoens, D.J. (1979) 'Mantra and Other Constituents of Tantric Practice' in Gupta, Sanjukta, Hoens, Dirk Jan and Goudriaan, Teun (eds) *Hindu Tantrism*, pp 90-117.

Holm, Jean (1984) 'Growing up in Hinduism', *British Journal of Religious Education*, Summer, pp 116-120.

Holm, Jean (1986) 'Religious Nurture Within an Alien Culture: A Study of Hindu Children and Their Families in Cambridge, England', unpublished paper, International Seminar on Religious Education and Values, Dublin.

Howell, C. (1975) *Discovering the Goddess: An Analysis of the Vrat Katha*, unpublished MA thesis, University of Virginia.

Hull, John, M. (1984) *Studies in Religion and Education*, Lewes, Falmer Press.

Hunter, Alan (1989) *Seeds of Truth: J. Krishnamurti as Religious Teacher and Educator*, unpublished PhD thesis, University of Leeds.

ISKCON Board of Education (1990) *ISKCON Education Journal*, 11, Winter.

Jackson, Robert (1976) 'Holi in North India and in an English City: Some Adaptations and Anomalies', *New Community*, 5, 3, Autumn, pp 203-210.

Jackson, Robert (1981a) 'The Shree Krishna Temple and the Gujarati Hindu Community in Coventry' in Bowen, David (ed) *Hinduism in England*, Bradford College, pp 61-83.

Jackson, Robert (1981b) 'The Place of Hinduism in Religious Education' in Bowen, David (ed) *Hinduism in England*, Bradford College, pp 110-117.

Jackson, Robert (1985) 'Hinduism in Britain: Religious Nurture and Religious Education', *British Journal of Religious Education*, 7, 2, pp 68-75.

Jackson, Robert (1986) 'Hindu Festivals' in Brown, A. (ed) *Festivals in World Religions*, London, Longman, pp. 104-139.

Jackson, Robert (1987) 'Changing Conceptions of Hinduism in Timetabled Religion' in Burghart, R. (ed) *Hinduism in Great Britain: Religion in an Alien Cultural Milieu*, London, Tavistock, pp 201-223.

Jackson, Robert (1989a) *Religions through Festivals: Hinduism*, London, Longman.

Jackson, Robert (1989b) 'Religious Education: From Ethnographic Research to Curriculum Development' in Campbell, J. and Little, V. (eds) *Humanities in the Primary School*, Lewes, Falmer, pp 171-191.

Jackson, Robert (1993) 'Religious Education and the Arts of Interpretation', in Starkings, D. (ed) *Religion and the Arts in Education:Dimensions of Spirituality,* London, Hodder and Stoughton.

Jackson, Robert and Killingley, Dermot (1988) *Approaches to Hinduism*, London, John Murray.

Jackson, Robert and Killingley, Dermot (1991) *Moral Issues in the Hindu Tradition,* Stoke on Trent, Trentham Books.

Jackson, Robert and Nesbitt, Eleanor M. (1986) 'Sketches of Formal Hindu Nurture', *World Religions in Education,* Journal of the Shap Working Party, pp 25-29.

Jackson, Robert and Nesbitt, Eleanor M. (1989) 'British Hindu Children and Their Traditional Festivals' in Wood, A. (ed) *Religions and Education,* London, BFSS National RE Centre, pp 75-78.

Jackson, Robert and Nesbitt, Eleanor M. (1990) *Listening to Hindus,* London, Unwin Hyman.

Jackson, Robert and Nesbitt, Eleanor, (1992) 'Christian and Hindu Children: Their Perceptions of Each Other's Religious Traditions', *Journal of Empirical Theology,* 1992, 5, 2, pp39-62.

Jackson, Robert and Nesbitt, Eleanor M. (forthcoming) 'Authority and Values in the Experience of British Hindu Children' in Gates, B.E. (ed) *Freedom and Authority in Religions and Religious Education,* London, Cassell.

Jaffrey, M. (1985) *Seasons of Splendour,* London, Pavilion.

James, Alan G. (1974) *Sikh Children in Britain,* Oxford, Oxford University Press.

James, Alan G. (1982) 'What's Wrong with Multicultural Education?', *New Community,* 10, 2, Winter, pp 225-232.

Jones, K.W. (1970) *Arya Dharm: Hindu Consciousness in Nineteenth Century Punjab,* Berkeley, University of California Press.

Juergensmeyer, M. (1982) *Religion as Social Vision: The Movement against Untouchability in 20th Century Punjab,* Berkeley, University of California.

Juergensmeyer, M. (1988) 'Radhasoami and the Notions of Sikh Orthodoxy and Heterodoxy' in O'Connell, J.T. et al (eds) *Sikh History and Religion in the Twentieth Century,* University of Toronto, Centre for South Asian Studies.

Jumsai, Art-Ong (1985) 'Exposition of the Basic Human Values', *Education in Human Values Journal,* 2, pp 9-26.

Jyotirmayi dasi et al (1981) *The Book of Krishna Conscious Games: Popular Games Adapted for Devotee Children,* New York, Bala Books.

Kakar, Sudhir (1981) *The Inner World: A Psycholanalytic Study of Childhood and Society in India,* Delhi, Oxford University Press, (2nd edn).

Kanitkar, Helen (1972) *The Social Organisation of Indian Students in the London Area,* unpublished PhD thesis, University of London, School of Oriental and African Studies.

Kanitkar, Helen and Jackson, Robert (1982) *Hindus in Britain,* University of London, School of Oriental and African Studies.

Kanitkar, Hemant, (V.P.) (1979) 'A School for Hindus?', *New Community*, 7, 2, Summer, pp 178-183.

Kanitkar, Hemant, (V.P.) (1984) *Hindu Festivals and Sacraments*, New Barnet, V.P. Kanitkar.

Kanitkar, Hemant, (V.P.) (1987) *We are Hindus*, Edinburgh, The Saint Andrew Press.

Kasturi, N. (1961-86) *Sathyam Swayam Sundaram: The Life of Bhagavan Sri Sathya Sai Baba*, four parts, Prasanthi Nilayam.

Kelly, A. J. D. (1989) 'Ethnic Identification, Association and Redefinition: Muslim Pakistanis and Greek Cypriots in Britain' In Liebkind, K. (ed) *New Identities in Europe: Immigrant Ancestry and the Ethnic Identity of Youth*, London, Gower, pp. 77-115.

Kelly, Elinor (1990) 'Transcontinental Families - Gujarat and Lancashire: A Comparative Study of Social Policy' in Clarke, C., Peach, C. and Vertovec, S. (eds) *South Asians Overseas: Migration and Ethnicity*, Cambridge, Cambridge University Press, pp 251-267.

Khare, R.S. (1976) *The Hindu Hearth and Home*, Delhi, Vikas.

King, Ursula (1978) 'True and Perfect Religion: Bankim Chandra Chatterjee's Reinterpretation of Hinduism', *Religion*, 7, pp 127-148.

Knott, Kim (1981) 'Statistical Analysis of South Asians in the UK by Religion and Ethnicity', *Community Religions Project Research Paper 8*, University of Leeds.

Knott, Kim (1986a) *Hinduism in Leeds: A Study of Religious Practice in the Indian Hindu Community and in Hindu-Related Groups*, Monograph Series, Community Religions Project, University of Leeds.

Knott, Kim (1986b) 'Religion and Identity and the Study of Ethnic Minority Religions in Britain', in Hayes, V. (ed) *Identity Issues and World Religions: Proceedings of the XVth Congress of the International Association for the History of Religions*, South Australia, Australian Association for the Study of Religions.

Knott, Kim (1986c) *My Sweet Lord: the Hare Krishna Movement*, Wellingborough, Aquarian Press.

Knott, Kim (1986d) 'Hinduism in Britain', *World Religions in Education*, Journal of the Shap Working Party, pp 10-12.

Knott, Kim (1987) 'Hindu Temple Rituals in Britain: the Reinterpretation of Tradition', in Burghart, R (ed), *Hinduism in Great Britain: the Perpetuation of Religion in an Alien Cultural Milieu*, London, Tavistock, pp157-179.

Knott, Kim (1991) 'Bound to Change? The Religions of South Asians in Britain' in Vertovec, S. (ed) *Oxford University Papers on India*, Vol. 2, No. 2: *The Modern Western Diaspora*, Delhi, Oxford University Press, pp 86-111.

Kripamoya dasa, (ed) (1987) *Rathayatra '87 Souvenir Magazine*, Watford, Nama Hatta Services.

Kurtz, Stanley (1984) 'The Goddesses' Dispute in Jai Santoshi Ma: A Mythological Film in its Cultic Context', unpublished paper, American Academy of Religion, Chicago.

Lannoy, R. (1971) *The Speaking Tree*, Oxford, Oxford University Press.

Larson, Heldi (1988a) 'Photography that Listens', *Visual Anthropology*, 3, 4, pp 415-432.

Larson, Heidi (1988b) 'Culture Exchange: The Religious Life of Children in Southall', unpublished paper, University of London, School of Oriental and African Studies.

Lewis, Oscar (1959) *Five Families: Mexican Case Studies in the Culture of Poverty*, New York, Basic Books Inc.

Liebkind,K (ed)(1989) *New Identities in Europe*, London, Sage.

Logan, Penny (1988a), 'Practising Religion: British Hindu Children and the Navaratri Festival', *British Journal of Religious Education*, Summer, 10, 3, pp 160-169.

Logan, Penny, (1988b), 'The Heart of Hinduism: Hindu Women and the Home', *World Religions in Education*, pp 29-31.

Logan, Penny (1989a) *Practising Hinduism: The Experience of Gujarati Adults and Children*, unpublished paper, Thomas Coram Research Unit, Institute of Education, University of London.

Logan, Penny (1989b) 'Mother-tongue Teaching: A Case Study', *New Community*, 15, 2, pp 241-252.

Lord Mayor's Committee for Racial Harmony (1982) *Coventry: a Multiracial City*, Coventry.

Macauliffe, M.A. (1978) *The Sikh Religion*, New Delhi, S. Chand, Vol. VI.

McDonald, Merryle (1987) 'Rituals of Motherhood among Gujarati Women in East London' in Burghart, R. (ed) *Hinduism in Great Britain: The Perpetuation of Religion in an Alien Cultural Milieu*, London, Tavistock.

McLeod, H. (1989) *Who is a Sikh? The Problem of Sikh Identity*, Oxford, Oxford University Press.

Mahadevan, T.M.P. (1977) *Outlines of Hinduism*, Bombay, Chetana.

Majmudar, M.R. (1965) *Cultural History of Gujarat*, Bombay, Popular Prakashan.

Marriott, McKim (1968) 'The Feast of Love' in Singer, M. (ed) *Krishna: Myths, Rites and Attitudes*, Chicago, University of Chicago Press, pp 200-212.

Marriott, McKim (nd) 'Changing Channels of Cultural Transmission in Indian Civilistion' in Vidyarthi, L.P. (ed) *Aspects of Religion in Indian Society*, Meerut, Kedar Nath.

Martin, Bernice and Pluck, Ronald (1977) *Young People's Beliefs*, London, General Synod Board of Education.

Michaelson, Maureen (1984) 'Religious and Devotional Diversity in a Gujarati Caste', unpublished paper based on *Caste, Kinship and Marriage: A Study of Two Gujarati Trading Castes in England*, unpublished PhD thesis, University of London, 1983.

Michaelson, Maureen (1987) 'Domestic Hinduism in a Gujarati Trading Caste' in Burghart, R. (ed) *Hinduism in Great Britain: The Perpetuation of Religion in an Alien Cultural Milieu*, London, Tavistock.

Minority Group Support Service (nd) *Divali*, Coventry, City of Coventry Education Authority.

Minority Group Support Service (nd) *How a Hindu Prays,* City of Coventry Education Authority.

Mol, Hans (1979) 'Theory and Data on the Religious Behaviour of Migrants, *Social Compass,* 26, 1, pp31-39.

Monks of the Ramakrishna Order (1974) *Meditation,* London, Ramakrishna Vedanta Centre, (2nd edn).

Murphet, H. (1971) *Sai Baba: Man of Miracles,* London.

Nagra, J.S. (1981/2) 'Asian Supplementary Schools: A Case Study of Coventry', *New Community,* 9, 3, pp 431-436.

Nesbitt, Eleanor M. (1980) *Aspects of Sikh Tradition in Nottingham,* unpublished MPhil thesis, University of Nottingham.

Nesbitt, Eleanor M. (1981) 'A Note on Bhatra Sikhs', *New Community,* 9, 1, pp 70-72.

Nesbitt, Eleanor M. (1990a) 'Religion and Identity: The Valmiki Community in Coventry', *New Community,* 16,2, January, pp 261-274.

Nesbitt, Eleanor M. (1990b) 'Pitfalls in Religious Taxonomy: Hindus, Sikhs, Ravidasis and Valmikis', *Religion Today,* 6, 1, October, pp 9-12.

Nesbitt, Eleanor M. (1991) *My Dad's Hindu, My Mum's Side are Sikhs': Issues in Religious Identity, Arts, Culture, Education Research and Curriculum Papers,* Coventry, National Foundation for Arts Education.

Nesbitt, Eleanor M (1993) 'Gender and Religious Tradition: the Role-learning of British Hindu Children', *Gender and Education,* vol 5, no 1, pp.81-91.

Nesbitt, Eleanor M. (forthcoming) 'Valmikis in Coventry: The Revival and Reconstruction of a Community' in Ballard, R. (ed) *Desh Pardesh:The South Asian Presence in Britain,* C. Hurst and Co.

Nye, Malory (1992) *'A Place for Our Gods': The Construction of a Hindu Temple Community in Edinburgh,* unpublished PhD thesis, University of Edinburgh.

O'Keeffe, Bernadette (1980) *Hindu Family Life in East London,* unpublished PhD thesis, University of London, London School of Economics.

Orans, M. (1965) *The Santal,* Detroit, Wayne State University Press.

Pfleiderer, B. and Lutze, L. (eds) (1985) *The Hindi Film: Agent and Reagent of Social Change,* New Delhi.

Planalp, J. (1956) *Religious Life and Values in a North Indian Village,* Parts I and II, Ann Arbor, University Microfilms International.

Pocock, David (1972) *Mind, Body and Wealth,* Oxford, Blackwell.

Pocock, David (1976) 'Preservation of the Religious Life: Hindu Immigrants in England', *Contributions to Indian Sociology,* 10, 2, pp 341-365.

Powney, J. and Watts, M. (1987) *Interviewing in Educational Research,* London, Routledge.

Prabhupada, A.C. Bhaktivedanta Swami (1972) *Bhagavad-gita As It Is,* London, Collier Macmillan.

Rex, J. (1991) *Ethnic Identity and Ethnic Mobilization in Britain,* Coventry, Centre for Research in Ethnic Relations, University of Warwick.

Robinson, Vaughan and Flintoff, Ian (1982) 'Asian Retailing in Coventry', *New Community,* 10, 8, Winter pp 251-258.

Rodway, H. (nd) *The Psychic Directory: The Comprehensive Guide to Practising Psychics in the UK,* London, Futura.

Rorty, R. (1980) *Philosophy and the Mirror of Nature,* Oxford, Blackwell.

Rushdie, Salman (1989) *The Satanic Verses,* London, Viking.

Rutledge, P. (1982) *The Role of Religion in Ethnic Self-identity: The Vietnamese in Oklahoma City. 1975-1982,* PhD dissertation, University of Oklahoma, Ann Arbor, University Microfilms International.

Rutledge, P. (1985) *The Role of Religion in Ethnic Self-identity: a Vietnamese Community,* New York, University Press of America.

Sahukar, M. (1983) *Sai Baba the Saint of Shirdi,* Bombay, Somaiya Publications, (3rd edn).

Said, Edward (1978) *Orientalism,* London, Routledge.

Saifullah Khan, V (1982) 'The Dynamics of Ethnic Relations', in Avtar Brah et al, *Minority Experience,* Milton Keynes, Open University Press.

Sandhu, R.S. (1978) 'Ravidasian te Balmikian de maran sanskar', *Samajak Vigian Pattar,* 9 February, Patiala, Panjabi University, pp 83-99.

Sastri, R.S. Ramaswami (1963) 'The Influence of the Epics on Traditional Cultural Life in India Today' in *Bulletin of the Institute of Traditional Cultures,* pp 17-27.

Sharma, N. (1983) *The Impact and Effects of Video in Asian Households,* unpublished MA thesis, Polytechnic of North London.

Sharma, Ursula (1971) *Rampal and His Family,* London, Collins.

Sharma, Ursula (1976) 'The Immortal Cowherd and the Saintly Carrier: An Essay in the Study of Cults', *Sociology Bulletin,* 19, September, pp 137-152.

Sharpe, E. (1975) *Comparative Religion: A History,* London, Duckworth.

Shepherd, Frances and Sahai, Sharda (1992) Play Tabla, Stoke-on-Trent, Trentham Books.

Shri Saraswatie Basisschool (nd) *Schoolwerkplan,* Rotterdam, Shri Saraswatie Basisschool.

Shri Saraswatie Basisschool (1990) *Informatie-boekje 1990-1991,* Rotterdam, Shri Saraswatie Hindoeschool voorhet Basisonderwijs.

Sims, R (1981) 'Spatial Separation Between Asian Religious Minorities: an aid to Explanation or Obfuscation?' in Jackson, P. and Smith, S.J. (eds), *Social Interaction and Ethnic Segregation,* London, Academic Press, pp 123-135.

Singh, Ramindar (1986) 'Development of Punjabi Culture and Identity in Britain', *Punjab Research Group Discussion Paper* No. 15.

Smith, Wilfred Cantwell (1978) *The Meaning and End of Religion,* London, SPCK.

Smith, Wilfred Cantwell (1981) *Towards a World Theology,* London, Macmillan.

Sohal, Balbir Kaur (1989) *Gender Role Changes among South Asian Women in Coventry,* M. A. dissertation, University of Warwick.

Spradley, James P. (1980) *Participant Observation,* New York, Holt, Rinehart and Winston.

Srinivas, M. (1967) *Social Change in Modern India,* Berkeley, University of California Press.

Stevenson, M.S. (1971) *The Rites of the Twice-born,* Delhi, Manoharlal, (2nd edn).

Swallow, D. (1982) 'Ashes and Powers: Myth, Site and Miracle in an Indian Godman's Cult', *Modern Asian Studies,* 16, 1, pp 123-158.

Tajfel, H (1974) 'Social Identity and Intergroup Behaviour', *Social Science Information,* 13, 2 pp.65-93.

Tajfel, H (1978a) *Differentiation Between Social Groups* London, Academic Press.

Tajfel, H (1978b) *The Social Psychology of Minorities,* London, Minority Rights Group.

Tajfel, H (1981) *Human Groups and Social Categories* Cambridge University Press.

Tambs Lyche, H. (1980a) 'Gujarati Communities in Norway and Britain: Some Comparative Notes', *New Community,* 8, pp 288-294.

Tambs Lyche, H. (1980b) *London Patidars: A Case Study in Urban Ethnicity,* London, Routledge.

Taylor, Donald (1984) 'The Sai Baba Movement and Multi-Ethnic Education in Britain', *Religion Today,* October, pp 13-15.

Taylor, Donald (1987) 'Charismatic Authority in the Sathya Sai Baba Movement' in Burghart, R. (ed) *Hinduism in Great Britain,* London, Tavistock, pp 119-133.

Taylor, J.H. (1976) *The Halfway Generation: A Study of Asian Youths in Newcastle upon Tyne.* Slough, NFER.

Vaidya, C.L. (1966) *Shri Vallabhacharya and His Teachings,* Baroda, Shri Vallabha Publications.

Van der Burg, Corstiaan (1991) 'The Structural Conditioning of Identity Formation: Surinamese Hindus and Religious Policy in the Netherlands' in Shahid, W.A.R. and Van Koningsveld, P.S. (eds) *The Integration of Islam and Hinduism in Western Europe,* Kampen, Kok Pharos.

Vertovec, Steven (1987) *Hinduism and Social Change in Village Trinidad,* unpublished DPhil thesis, University of Oxford.

Vertovec, Steven (1988) 'Hinduism in Diaspora: The Transformation of Tradition in Trinidad' in Sontheimer, G.D. and Kulke, H. (eds) *Hinduism Reconsidered,* New Delhi, Manohar, pp 152-179.

Vertovec, Steven (1989) 'Differential Trends in London Hindu Temples - Some Implications for the Study of Hinduism in Diaspora', *Punjab Research Group Discussion* Paper No. 25.

Vertovec, Steven (1992a) *Hindu Trinidad: Religion, Ethnicity and Socio-Economic Change,* London, Macmillan.

Vertovec, S. (1992b) 'On the Reproduction and Representation of 'Hinduism' in Britain', unpublished paper, Conference on 'Culture, Identity and Politics: Ethnic Minorities in Britain', St. Antony's College, Oxford, May.

Vertovec, S. (1992c) 'Community and Congregation in London Hindu Temples: Divergent Trends', *New Community*, 18, 2, pp 251-264.

Vidya Vihar (1987) *Gopal Krishna Souvenir Diary*, Harrow, The Academy of Vedic Heritage.

Vitsaxis, V.G. (1977) *Hindu Epics, Myths and Legends in Popular Illustrations*, Delhi, Oxford University Press.

Waardenburg, J. (1973) *Classical Approaches to the Study of Religion*, The Hague, Mouton (2 vols).

Weinreich, Peter (1986) *Manual for Identity Exploration Using Personal Constructs*, Research Papers in Ethnic Relations no 1, University of Warwick, Centre for Research in Ethnic Relations.

Weinreich, Peter (1989) 'Variations in Ethnic Identity: Identity Structure Analysis' in Liebkind, K, (ed) *New Identities in Europe: Immigrant Ancestry and the Ethnic Identity of Youth*, London, Gower, pp41-75.

White, C. (1972) 'The Sai Baba Movement: Approaches to the Study of Indian Saints', *Journal of Asian Studies*, 31, August, pp 863-878.

Williams, Raymond (1984) *A New Face of Hinduism: The Swaminarayan Religion*, Cambridge, Cambridge University Press.

Williams, Raymond (1988) *Religions of Immigrants from India and Pakistan: New Threads in the American Tapestry*, Cambridge, Cambridge University Press.

Winchester, S.W.C. (1975) *Spatial Structure and Social Activity: A Social Geography of Coventry*, unpublished DPhil thesis, University of Oxford.

Wittgenstein, L. (1958) *Philosophical Investigations*, Oxford, Blackwell.

GLOSSARY

☐ Note on Indian Terms

We have used some Sanskrit, Hindi, Urdu, Punjabi and Gujarati words. The alphabets of these languages have more letters than the Roman alphabet and represent phonetically some sounds which are unfamiliar to many English speakers. We have not used diacritical marks to indicate these as readers may be unfamiliar with the scholarly system for transliterating Indian languages. So, for example, we do not differentiate t and ṭ (for which the tongue is rolled against the palate).

In the glossary a macron indicates that a vowel is long. 'A' is pronounced like the vowel in 'punt' (not 'part'): 'ā' like the vowel in 'far': 'i' is pronounced like the 'i' in 'pin' (never as in 'pine'): 'ī' is like the vowel in 'feet': 'u' is the sound in 'pull' and 'ū' resembles the vowel in 'pool'. Where terms have entered English we have used the English form (eg, 'Punjabi' not 'Panjābī').

Many words are used, sometimes in slightly different forms, in more than one language. We have indicated when a word is more or less specific to a particular language.

205

agiāras (Gujarati)	the eleventh day of each half of the lunar month, on which many Hindus fast.
ahimsā	non-violence.
Ahoī Matā	a goddess and the *vrat* in her honour, observed by Punjabi women, four days after Karvā Chauth.
alūna	'no salt'; a *vrat* observed by Gujarati girls.
Ambājī	(Sanskrit *'ambā'* = 'mother') Goddess, depicted with eight arms and riding a roaring tiger.
amrit	'undying'; holy water.
ānand	joy.
Anāvil	a category of Gujarati Brahmin
ār(a)tī	a popular form of worship in which a light and other items are circled in front of a representation of the deity.
Arya Samāj	'Aryan Society'; a Hindu movement begun by the nineteenth century religious reformer, Swāmī Dayānanda Sarasvatī.
Asādh	month of Hindu lunar calendar.
āshrama	a stage of life; according to Hindu texts a man's life consists of four *āshramas*.
atham	eighth day of a lunar fortnight.
ātma(n)	self, soul.
avatār	'a descent' ie to earth; an incarnation of the divine, usually referring to Vishnu's appearance in a succession of forms, including the heroes Rama and Krishna.
bā (Gujarati)	paternal grandmother (original meaning is mother).
bābā	term of affectionate respect used for some religious leaders.
bābājī	a more respectful form of 'bābā'.
bāiā	left; the metal drum played with a *tablā*.
bāl	child, infant.
Bāl Vikās	'child development'; classes run by followers of Sathya Sai Bābā.
Bālaknāth	a saint, revered by many Punjabis. He is depicted as a blue youth.
bandhan	'tying'. See Raksha Bandhan.

barat	Punjabi form of '*vrat*'.
Basant	a spring festival.
ben (Gujarati) bahin (Hindi)	sister, term used of girls and women of one's own age.
betī	daughter.
bhābhī	brother's wife.
Bhādrapad	a month of the Hindu lunar calendar
Bhagavad Gītā	'Song of Krishna'; Krishna's sermon to Arjuna on the battle field, exhorting him to carry out his duty. For many Hindus this is the holiest scripture.
bhāī	brother, term used of one's male contemporaries.
Bhāī Bīj (Gujarati)	day shortly after Dīvālī when married women cook for their brothers.
bhaiyā (Hindi)	brother.
Bhaiyā Dūj (Punjabi)	day shortly after Dīvālī when girls mark their brother's brow with saffron.
bhajan	devotional song
bhakti	devotion to God.
bhangrā (Punjabi)	Punjabi folk dance and music or a westernised adaptation of this which flourishes among youth of South Asian origin in Britain.
Bhārat	India.
bharat nātyam	a classical South Indian dance.
Bhartrhari	a celebrated Sanskrit poet, an aristocrat turned saint, popularly associated with Bālaknāth.
Bhātrā	endogamous community who pioneered Sikh settlement in Britain.
bhent (Punjabi)	devotional song addressed to the goddess.
bhojan	food.
Bhūvaneshvarī Mā	a goddess particularly associated with Gondal in Gujarat.
biriānī	fried rice dish.
Brahmā	God as creator, represented with four heads or faces.

Brahmakumārī	member of a twentieth century movement stressing celibacy.
Brahma Samāj	the community organisation of Gujarati Brahmins in Britain.
brahmasambandh(a)	'connection with God'; initiation as a follower of a *guru* eg as a Pushtimārgī.
Brahmin	(more correctly 'Brahman'). Member of the hereditary priestly class, ritually the most pure.
buā	father's sister.
buddhi	intellect, wisdom.
bustee (Hindi: bastī)	slum
caste	(from Portuguese '*casta*' meaning 'breed'). Used in this book to mean *jati*, endogamous group associated with an occupation. Hindus often use the term more loosely.
chāchī (Hindī)	father's younger brother's wife, aunty.
Chaitanya	Bengali saint, especially honoured by ISKCON.
Chamār	'leather worker'; in Punjab a *jati* long regarded as ritually impure.
chanā (Hindi)	gram, chickpea.
chaniyo (Gujarati)	long, decorative skirt worn by Gujarati girls on festive occasions.
chauth	fourth day of lunar fortnight.
chhath	sixth day of lunar fortnight.
chokhā (Gujarati)	rice
cholī	short, tight fitting blouse worn with sari or *chaniyo*.
chor	thief. See *makkhan*.
chunnī (Punjabi)	shoulder drape used by women for a headcovering as a sign of respect.
chunrī (Gujarati)	length of diaphanous cloth worn over a *chaniyo* and *choli*.
chūriān	bangles.
dandiyān (Gujarati)	sticks, in particular those used for festive circle dances.
darshan	glimpse, the experience of being blessed by a deity's or *guru's* gaze.

208

darzī	member of the *jati* whose traditional job was tailoring.
Dasehrā	the autumn festival immediately preceded by Navarātri. On Dasehrā day many Hindus recall Rāma's defeat of Rāvana.
dashmī	tenth day of lunar fortnight.
Desai	a Gujarati Brahmin name.
Devanāgarī	Script in which Sanskrit and Hindi are written.
devī	goddess.
devrānī	husband's younger brother's wife.
Dhannā	a poor man whose devotion to Krishna is legendary.
Dharam rājā	title meaning Lord of Righteousness, used for the god of death.
dharma (Sanskrit)	a behavioural code appropriate to one's gender, seniority and status. Often translated as 'religion', see *sanātana*.
dholak, dholkī	a convex sided wooden drum, held horizontally and beaten with the fingers at both ends.
dhotī	male attire consisting of a length of cloth wrapped to form loose trousers.
Dhro Atham.	eighth day of the lunar month Bhādrap named after a type of grass which is used in worship. Some Gujaratis observe a *vrat*.
dīdī	affectionate term for elder sister.
dīvā	oil light (the size of a night light) consisting of a lipped earthenware bowl in which a wick of twisted raw cotton is put.
Dīvālī	popular, all-India, annual festival of light in late October or early November.
Divāso	a *vrat* day and vigil observed by young married Gujarati women shortly after Jaya Pārvatī.
Durgā	a goddess; name of Shiva's wife, Pārvatī.
Durgā Pūjā	festival, especially popular in Bengal, which falls in late September or early October.
Easwarammā Day	Day of celebration in memory of the mother of Sathya Sai Bābā.

ekādasī	the eleventh day of the lunar fortnight, *agiāras*.
ethu (Gujarati)	*jūthā*.
Eshwarambā	see Easwarammā.
Evrat Jivrat	a *vrat* day during the lunar month of Asādh on the same day as Dīvāso. This is observed by married women who have children. The *pūjā* focuses on a picture of a child's swinging cradle.
Ganapati	the elephant-headed God who removes obstacles, Ganesha.
Gangā	the river Ganges.
gar(a)bā (Gujarati)	plural of '*garbo*', an earthen pot with holes in it, used as a lamp; usually means dancing in the goddess's honour, particularly on the nights of Navarātrī.
gar(a)bī (Gujarati)	polygonal shrine round which Gujarati dances take place at Navarātrī.
Gāyatrī mantra	ancient Sanskrit prayer for enlightenment.
ghāghrā pulkā (Gujarati)	another term for *chaniyo* and *cholī*.
ghānthiā (Gujarati)	a crisp, savoury snack.
ghī (Hindi)	clarified butter.
Gītā	see *Bhagavad Gītā*.
gopī	usually refers to the cowherds' wives who sported with Lord Krishna in Vrindāvan.
got (Punjabi)	see *gotra*.
gotra (Hindi)	lineage, exogamous group with common ancestor.
Govardhan(a)	the name of a hill which Krishna lifted, so showing his divine power.
Govinda	a title for Krishna.
goyanī, goranī (Gujarati)	term for a female who plays a key role in an act of worship of the goddess. Provided she is not menstruating any girl or married woman (whose husband is alive) can be a *goyanī*.
Gujarātī	A person whose family originated from the area covered by the present Gujarāt state of India. The language of this area of India. Adjective referring to its culture.

210

guna	quality.
gur	brown, unprocessed sugar, sold in compressed cakes.
gurdwārā	'gateway of the Gurū'; Sikh place of worship.
Gurmukhī	the script of the Sikh scriptures. It is now the officially recognised script for Punjabi.
guru (Hindi) gurū (Punjabi)	teacher, spiritual guide.
Gurū Granth Sāhib	the volume of scripture, regarded by Sikhs as the living Gurū.
Gurū Nānak	the first of the Sikhs' ten Gurūs (1469-1539).
gurukula	a traditional Hindu school.
hari	Lord, God.
havan	fire-sacrifice, ritual centred on a fire which is fed with aromatic substances.
Hindī	India's official and most widely spoken language.
Holī	Spring festival. In India merrymakers drench each other in coloured water.
Holikā	evil sister of Hiranyakashipu and aunt of Prahlāda. At Holī her destruction is celebrated.
Indirā Betījī	a living woman *guru* of the Pushtimārgī movement.
ISKCON	International Society for Krishna Consciousness, the Hare Krishna Movement.
izzat (Urdu)	family honour.
Jagannāth	'Lord of the universe', deity worshipped at Rathayātra.
jāgaran	vigil.
Jain	(from 'jina' ie 'belonging to the conquerors') a religion, rooted in Hinduism, and strongest among Gujaratis of merchant castes.
jal	water.
Jalarām Bāpā	Gujarati saint (1799-1881).
Jamunā	main tributary of the Gangā.
Janmāshtami	birthday of Lord Krishna.

211

janeū	sacred thread with which male Hindus are invested in the *upanayana* ceremony.
japa	repetition.
Jat	the largest caste in Sikh society, a *jati* associated with land ownership and farming.
jati (Hindi)	endogamous group with a hereditary occupation (seldom followed in Britain). Each *jati* is ascribed a place on the scale of social classes (*varna*).
jawār	millet
jay, jai	greeting to the Gods.
Jayā Pārvatī	a *vrat* kept by female Gujaratis.
Jayanti	anniversary of a deity or hero.
jethānī	husband's elder brother's wife.
jholā	bag (for rosary)
jī	suffix indicating respect.
jīva	soul
Jivantīkā Mā	goddess honoured by Gujarati women, some of whom observe a *vrat* on a Friday.
jūthā (Hindi)	food which is to be avoided because contact (even indirect) with another's saliva has made it impure.
Kālī	'black'; a goddess. She is depicted as black and garlanded with skulls.
kamīz	approximately knee-length top worn over a *salvār.*
kanjak (Punjabi, plural kanjakān)	young girl.
kanku (Gujarati)	red powder which is used in worship and for marking the face, called *kumkum* in Hindi.
kanthī	rosary worn tightly around the neck.
karāh (Punjabi)	mixture of sugar, wheatflour and clarified butter, given as *prashād* by Punjabis.
karma	cosmic law of cause and effect ensuring that one reaps the result of good and bad deeds.
kartāl	a tambourine-like percussion instrument.
Kartik	a Hindu lunar month.
Karvā Chauth	a *vrat* observed by Punjabi women and girls about eleven days before Dīvālī.
kathā	religious discourse, story.

katthak	a classical dance.
Kāthiawār	central Gujarat.
kendra	centre.
khandā (Punjabi)	double edged sword, symbol of the Sikh faith.
Khatrī (Punjabi)	(cogn. Kshatriya) Punjabi caste with an urban tradition.
khichrī	rice and lentils boiled together, kedgeree.
khīr	sweet, creamy rice pudding.
Khodiyār Mā	a form of the Goddess represented with a crocodile.
kīrtan	corporate hymn singing.
Krishna	incarnation of Vishnu. He is worshipped as a mischievous boy and as the preacher of the *Bhagavad Gītā*.
Krishnamurti, Jiddu	Philosopher and spiritual leader (1895-1986).
Kshatriya (Sanskrit)	member of the *varna* of warriors although this has no bearing on present day occupations of Kshatriya Hindus.
kuldev	divine patron of a lineage.
Kumbhār (Gujarati)	potter, the *jati* traditionally engaged in this work.
kurtā	shirt, loose top worn over *pajāmā*.
Kurukshetra	town in Haryāna, India where the battle celebrated in the *Mahābhārata* was fought.
Lakshmana	Rāma's younger brother who voluntarily shared his exile.
Lakshmī	goddess of prosperity, wife of Vishnu.
linga(m) (Sanskrit)	aniconic representation of Shiva.
Lohānā	endogamous Gujarati *jati*, traditionally involved in business.
Lohrī	Punjabi celebration on January 13th of particular importance for those with sons born in the previous year.
lotī (Gujarati)	small pot (about 3" high).
loto (Gujarati)	small pot (about 6" high). During worship a coconut is often stood in a *loto*.

213

lūnūtārvī (Gujarati)	refers to custom of girl (*lūnārī*) from the bridegroom's family patting the bridal couple's back with a small pot filled with moong beans and covered with a green cloth.
Mā	mother, title for the goddess.
mag (Gujarati)	moong beans.
Māgha	month of Hindu lunar calendar.
Mahābhārat(a)	ancient epic recounting a great battle.
Mahashivarātrī	'great night of Shiva', an annual festival in honour of Shiva.
Mahārāj	'great king'; honorific for a respected person.
mahārishi	'great sage'.
Mahesh	another name for Shiva.
Mahishāsur	a demon buffalo, slain by the goddess Durgā.
makkhan	butter.
makkhan chor	butter thief, name for Krishna who as a boy stole butter from his foster mother and neighbours.
mālā	a rosary, usually of 108 beads. These are often made from wood or seeds.
Māl Bāpā (Gujarati)	snake deity. A sweet mixture of sesame seeds is offered in his honour, especially by some Sonī families from Kāthiawār whose *kuldev* he is.
māmā	mother's brother, maternal uncle.
māmī	mother's brother's wife.
mandal	circle, group.
mandir	temple, shrine.
mangalsutra	necklace of black beads and gold which a bride receives on her wedding day.
manjīrā	Indian bells, small cymbals used to accompany singing.
mantra	sacred syllable, word or phrase.
maryādā	discipline.
māsī	mother's sister, aunt.
mātā	mother; term used for the goddess and for pock diseases which are traditionally believed to show her presence.

Matiya	section of Patel community.
māyā	illusion.
mehndī	henna. A paste made from the powdered leaves is applied in delicate patterns to a girl's palms and, less often, feet, particularly for her wedding. A reddish stain remains for several days.
mishrī	sugar crystals.
Mistrī (Mistry)	carpenter.
Morāri Bāpū	a preacher and singer, popular with Gujaratis worldwide for his rendering and interpretation of the *Rāmāyana*.
mridang	a large, convex-sided Indian drum beaten with the hands.
mukat	crown.
mundan (Hindi)	head-shaving.
murti	image of deity.
naivedya	food offered to the deity.
nāmakaran	naming ceremony.
Nāmdhārī	follower of the living Gurū of a movement which began in the nineteenth century as a Sikh reformist movement.
nanad	husband's sister.
Narsinghadev(a)	Vishnu's incarnation, half-man, half-lion. In this form he destroyed Prahlada's evil father, Hiranyakashipu.
Navarātrī (Sanskrit)	'nine nights'; autumn festival honouring the Goddess.
nirguna	without qualities, beyond attributes; an epithet for God.
nishān sāhib (Punjabi)	the orange pennant, emblazoned with a black circle bisected by a sword and cupped by two more. This flies outside public places of Sikh worship.
Nortā (Gujarati)	Navarātrī.
om (Sanskrit)	sacred syllable, used in prayer and meditation.
pajāmā	light-weight trousers worn with *kurtā*.
panchamī	the fifth day of a lunar fortnight. See *rishi*.
pandit	a Brahmin.

215

panj pyāre (Punjabi)	'five beloved', the first five Sikhs to be initiated in 1699.
Patel	a surname used by Gujaratis of several communities.
Patidar	a Gujarati *jati*
Phālguna	a month of the lunar calendar (February/March).
pharārī (Gujarati)	foods such as nuts, homemade potato crisps and root vegetables or plantain (cooked with no spice except green chilli and black pepper) which Gujarati women eat when observing a *vrat*.
phūmtu (Gujarati)	a tassel.
Pongal	festival celebrated in Tamil Nadu at the winter solstice.
Prahlāda	a prince whose devotion to Vishnu was vindicated. The story is associated with Holi.
Prajāpati	honorific title for Gujaratis of traditionally artisan castes.
prashād (Hindi)	'grace'; fruit, nuts, sweets etc. which are distributed after worship as a sign of divine grace.
prashādam (Sanskrit)	ISKCON devotees use this term for the blessed vegetarian food which they distribute.
pratishthā	installation of images in a temple.
pūjā	the most widespread form of Hindu worship, often performed at home. It involves making offerings to the deity.
pūjārī	Brahmin who conducts *pūjā*, usually guiding a family through a special act of worship.
Punjābī (Panjābī)	belonging to Punjab; the language of Punjab (the 'land of five rivers').
punya	merit which accrues from performing good deeds.
purānic	relating to the *Purānas*, collections of mythological stories.
Purī	town in Orissa, North East India, famed for temple of Jagannāth.

Pushtimārg	(literally 'way of grace') a Gujarati *sampradaya* emphasising devotion to the infant Krishna.
Pushtimārgī	a follower of Pushtimārg.
Rādhāsoāmī	an international movement, led by North Indian spiritual masters. Followers practise meditation and are strictly vegetarian.
rājas (Sanskrit)	passion, one of the three *gunas*.
Rājpūt	name for a Punjabi endogamous community which some equate with Kshatriyas.
rakh (Punjabi)	protection.
rākhī (Hindi), rakhrī (Punjabi)	an ornamental thread tied by a sister on her brother's wrist at Rakshā Bandhan.
Rakshā Bandhan(a)	full moon day of lunar month of Shrāvan. Sisters honour their brothers (whose role is to protect them).
Rāmāyan(a)	ancient epic whose hero, Rāma, endures unjust exile before returning to his kingdom.
Rāmazān	the Muslims' annual month of fasting.
Rāndal Mā	one of the two wives of Sūrya Nārāyan, the sun god. Her worship involves honouring *goyanīs*.
rās	a Gujarati circle dance associated with Krishna.
rāsgarbā	Gujarati circle dance.
rath	a large vehicle for conveying the gods in a procession.
Rathayātra	a festival involving a procession headed by a chariot bearing an image of Jagannāth. An annual event in London.
Ravidāsī	a follower of the medieval saint, Ravidās. Followers are from his *zāt*, the traditional leather-workers' community.
rishi	a sage.
Rishi Panchamī	fifth day of a lunar fortnight in Bhādrapad; also known in Gujarati as Rakh Pancham and Sambo Pancham.
rotī (Hindi)	*chapātī*, circular unleavened bread, the staple of Punjabi diet.
rotlo (Gujarati)	*chapātī* made out of millet flour.

217

sahabālā, sarbālā (Punjabi)	boy escort of bridegroom.
Sahajānanda	a religious teacher (1781-1830). See Swaminarāyan.
Sai	part of Sathya Sai Baba's name, used as an adjective for his devotees.
salvār	trousers worn below a *kamīz*.
Sāma Veda	one of the four Vedas.
samādhi	merger with the divine. Term used for the physical death of the spiritually enlightened.
samagri	aromatic substances which are sprinkled on a holy fire.
samāj	'society'; a religious or caste organisation.
samosā	a deep-fried, savoury, triangular pastry, usually stuffed with a spicy potato mixture.
sampradaya (Sanskrit)	'a handing on'; a Guru-led movement such as Pushtimārg or ISKCON.
samskāra (Sanskrit)	'process'; a life cycle rite.
sanātan(a)	ageless, unchanging.
sanātan(a) dharma	'ageless religion'; term used by Hindus for Hinduism.
sandhya	twilight, early evening.
sannyāsī	a renunciant.
sant	a Punjabi religious leader.
Santoshī Mā(tā)	a goddess to whom many Hindu women pray in a succession of Friday fasts. Nothing sour may be eaten on these days.
saptvār	the seven days of the week.
Saraswatī	Brahmā's consort, the goddess of learning and music.
sarbālā (Punjabi)	see *sahabālā*.
sargī (Punjabi)	sweet food eaten before dawn on Karvā Chauth.
sārī	women's dress, consisting of about five and a half metres of light-weight cloth worn over a blouse and ankle length petticoat.
Sarvan	in mythology a devoted son who carried his infirm parents in panniers on a pilgrimage and was accidentally killed by Lord Rāma's father.

satam	seventh day of lunar month.
Sathya Sai Bābā	a god-man from South India, b. 1926.
sathiyo (Gujarati)	swastika
satsang	'true gathering'; a religious gathering.
sattva	the quality of purity.
sattvik	refers to food such as fruit and milk which is conducive to a pure life.
sevā	loving service.
sevādār	someone giving service as a volunteer at a religious function.
Shakti	Shiva's consort; creative energy.
shagun	a propitious gift usually of money, given for a newborn baby or at certain stages in a marriage, or on someone's departure on a long journey.
Shankar	Shiva
shānti	peace
sharāb	alcoholic drinks
Sharad Pūnam	the day of the full moon preceding Dīvālī.
Sherānwālī Mā (Punjabi)	Ambājī, the goddess seated on a tiger.
Shikshapatri	a book of Swāmīnāryan's teaching.
Shirdi	town in South West India.
Shītalā	smallpox, worshipped as a goddess.
Shiva	name of major god.
Shiva-Shakti	God as male and female, Shiva and Shakti together
Shivling	a lingam, symbol of Shiva.
Shravan	Hindu lunar month.
Shrī, Shree, Srī	title of respect for males. A name for the goddess Lakshmī.
Shudra	the lowest (in terms of ritual purity) of the four *varnas*.
shukravār	Friday.
sindur (Hindi)	red powder.
Sītā	the virtuous wife of Rāma.
sitār	classical stringed instrument.
slok(a)	Sanskrit verse.

Sonī	Gujarati caste, many of whose members still work as goldsmiths or in related businesses.
Srīnathjī	a form of Krishna, iconographically represented as a black, stylised figure with one hand above his head.
suhāgan	items signifying that a woman's husband is still alive.
supārī	betel nut.
suprabhātam	morning prayer
Sūrā Pūrā Bāpā	holy man revered by some Gujaratis, eg Sonī families from Kathiâwār, at certain times of the year.
Swāmī (Svāmī)	Lord, a title for a holy man.
Swāmi Satyamitrānanda Giri	a North Indian spiritual leader, widely respected among British Hindus.
swarg	heaven
swastika (Sanskrit)	'health-bringing'; ancient auspicious sign.
Swāmīnārāyàn	'lord God'; title for a religious movement with many Gujarati adherents and for its founder, Sahajānanda, worshipped as an incarnation of God.
Swayam Sevak Sangh	a Hindu cultural organisation.
tablā	wooden drum played with the fingers of the right hand.
tāī	father's elder brother's wife.
tāl	rhythm
tamas (Sanskrit)	dullness, one of the three *gunas*.
tamasik	dull. *Tamasik* substances, such as meat and alcohol, are believed to have a dulling effect on the consumer.
tandoori (tandūrī)	food cooked in a traditional clay oven.
thālī	round metal tray, usually stainless steel. In Britain this is seldom used at mealtime but is still used in worship.
Theosophy	the philosophy of the Theosophical Society, founded 1875. Its principal members were admirers of Hindu tradition.
tīkā (Hindi)	a dot eg a red mark on the brow.
toran (Gujarati)	a hanging which decorates a shrine.

Tuljā Bhavānī	goddess depicted standing in front of a lion and holding a sword. She is worshipped in Kathiāwār and South India.
tul(a)sī	a variety of basil (*Occimum Sanctum*), a herb of which leaves are offered in worship of Vishnu.
Umā	the goddess Pārvatī, consort of Shiva.
Upanis(h)ad	'sitting near'; Sanskrit texts in which God, the self and the universe are discussed.
upāvas	fast — abstinence from all food except fruit and milk.
ut(a)sav	festival
Vaikunth(a)	Vishnu's home, heaven.
Vaishno Devī	a goddess; temple of goddess situated in Jammu.
Vaishnav	worshipper of Vishnu; a vegetarian.
Vaishya	the *varna* consisting of families traditionally involved in business.
Vallabhācharya	sage venerated especially by Pushtimārgīs.
Vālmīkī Jayanti	annual celebration of Vālmīk(ī)'s birth.
Vālmīkī	member of the lowest caste of Punjabi society, a worshipper of Vālmīk(ī), the composer of the *Rāmāyana*.
varna (Sanskrit)	'colour'; term for the four classes into which Hindu society is classically divided.
veda	'knowledge'; the oldest Sanskrit texts.
vibhutī	the powdery ash which is distributed as *prashād* and eaten after worship of Sathya Sai Bābā.
vidya	knowledge.
vihār	academy.
Vijay Dashmī	see Dasehrā.
vikās	development.
vīnā	a classical stringed musical instrument resembling a sitār.
Vishnu	God as maintainer of creation. Rāma and Krishna are two of his incarnations.
vishva	universal
Vivekānanda	Hindu revivalist and reformer (1862-1902).

vrat	religious vow involving abstention from certain foods. Days observed with specific types of fast and prayer.
yagna (Sanskrit)	literally sacrifice, a fire-centred ceremony.
yagnopavīta (Sanskrit)	the sacred thread, *janeu*.
yajmān	person hosting and, under the priest's guidance, performing a *pūjā*.
Yamunā	the Jamunā river in north India. The goddess associated in pictures with Vallabhācharya and Srīnāthjī.
zāt barādarī (Punjabi)	people of one caste who interact socially.

About the authors

Robert Jackson is Reader in Arts Education at the University of Warwick and Director of the Religious Education and Community Project. His publications include *Approaches to Hinduism* (John Murray) and *Moral Issues in the Hindu Tradition* (Trentham Books), both co-written with Dermot Killingley.

Eleanor Nesbitt worked as a teacher in India and Coventry and is Senior Research Fellow at the University of Warwick on the Religious Education and Community Project. Her publications on South Asian communities in Britain include *'My Dad's Hindu, My Mum's Side are Sikhs': Issues in Religious Identity* (National Foundation for Arts Education).

Index

225